HIDDEN HISTORY *of* MONROE COUNTY MICHIGAN

HIDDEN HISTORY *of* MONROE COUNTY MICHIGAN

Shawna Lynn Mazur

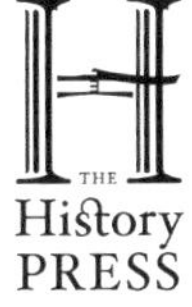

Published by The History Press
Charleston, SC
www.historypress.com

Cover photos courtesy of the Monroe County Library System.

Images are from the author's collection unless otherwise specified.

First published 2022

Manufactured in the United States

ISBN 9781467147347

Library of Congress Control Number: 2022943533

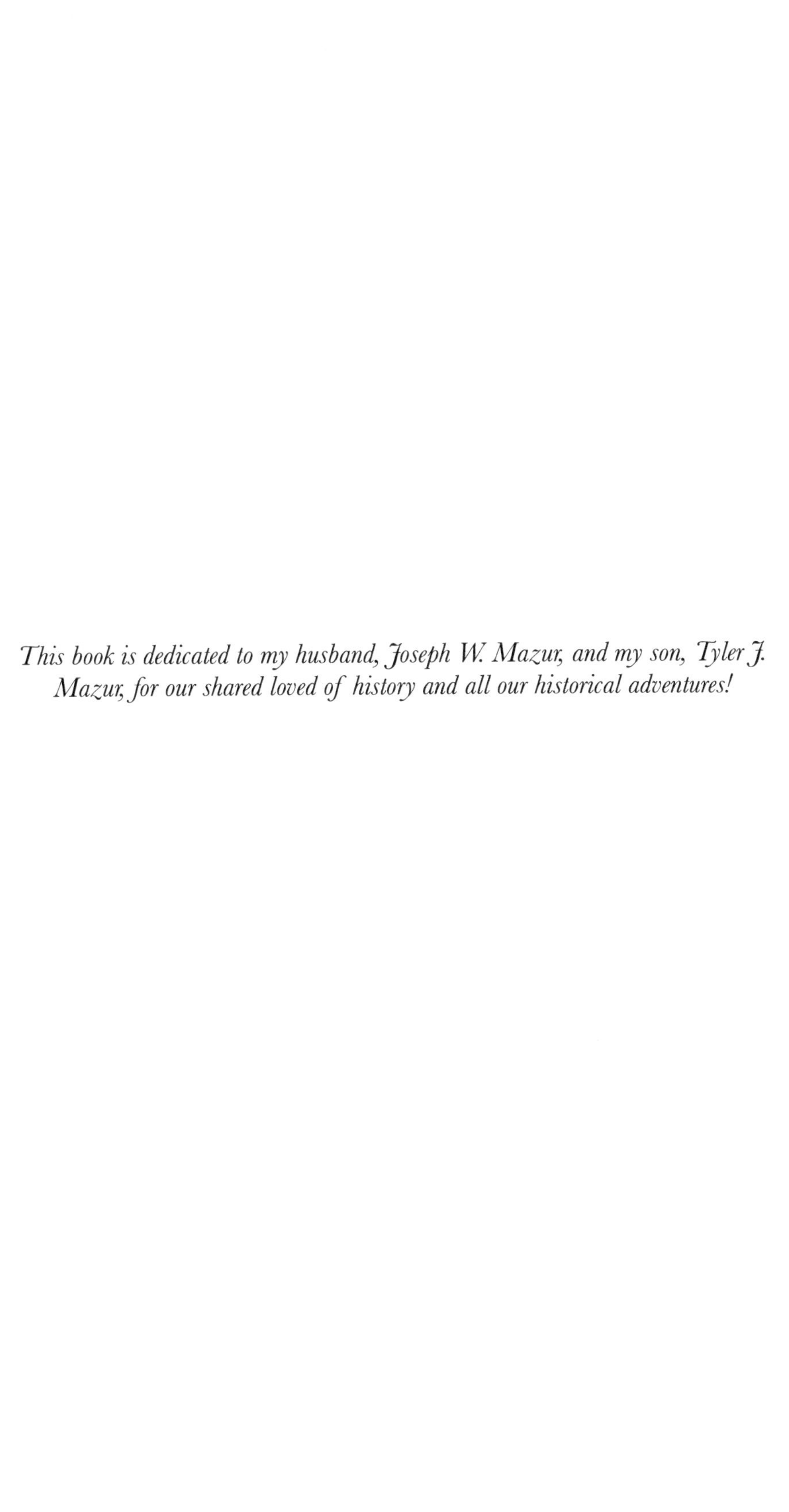

This book is dedicated to my husband, Joseph W. Mazur, and my son, Tyler J. Mazur, for our shared loved of history and all our historical adventures!

Contents

Preface

I am privileged to be able to say I have spent my whole life in Monroe. I was born and grew up in the city of Monroe. Now, I live in the county. Like most people who have lived in Monroe their whole lives, I know it is a true historical gem. Yet, there are so few books about Monroe. We have two definitive history books compiled at the turn of the twentieth century that are very valuable if you wish to learn more about the area and its people. You will see the two authors mentioned throughout my narrative: they are John Bulkley and Talcott Wing, who each wrote a definitive history of Monroe County. But my purpose in writing this book was to highlight the interesting and often forgotten or unknown history of the community in the light of today.

We tend to take for granted the historical area all around us. Monroe has always been a charming, quaint, moderately small community where everyone knows everyone or their families. In fact, many of the families who live here can trace their ancestors all the way back to the founding of the settlement.

I wanted to write a book that would give a glimpse into life in early Monroe as well as some key aspects of its community and historical significance. We have the advantage of looking back over 240 years. In writing the book, I quickly realized that even though my purpose was not to write about the core history, there was so much to write about that I barely skimmed the surface. Volumes upon volumes could be written about Monroe.

I hope that this narrative will inspire others to appreciate the history of this fascinating city and county and discover more gems themselves. I hope they will learn more about those who lived here, those who struggled here and all those who made sacrifices for us to be here today.

I spent three years preparing this book, and I am indebted to many individuals in writing it, as well as many historical sources and institutions. I would like to thank the Monroe County Library System (MCLS), the Monroe County Museum System, the Labor History Museum, the *Monroe News* and the River Raisin National Battlefield Park.

I want to express my gratitude to the following individuals:

John Rodrigue, acquisitions editor, The History Press
Zoe Ames, copy editor, The History Press
Joseph Mazur
Tyler Mazur
David Grosse
Russell Davis, author and historian
Ralph Naveaux, author and historian
William Saul, Monroe County Historical Society president
Daniel Harrison, maritime archaeologist
Charmaine Wawrzyniec, Monroe County Library System, Ellis Reference and Information Center reference technician
Regina Manning, Monroe County Library System, Ellis Reference and Information Center reference librarian
David Ingall, author and historian
Bruce Vanisacker, artillery expert

INTRODUCTION

Officially, Monroe County was carved out of the southernmost area of Wayne County in 1817. Michigan was not a state yet and was part of the Old Northwest Territory. Detroit was the only city with a population of over one thousand. When Monroe County was set off, so was the city of Monroe, which was called Frenchtown at the time. Monroe was named after then President James Monroe.

Monroe County is situated in the southeasterly corner of Michigan, covers an area of about 542 square miles and has fifteen counties. The city of Monroe is the largest city in the county. The county has the lowest elevation in the state, and much of it was marsh in 1817. The River Raisin cuts a swath for 139 miles from Hillsdale County through the entire County of Monroe until it dumps into Lake Erie. Lake Erie, the shallowest of the Great Lakes, runs adjacent to the eastern border of the county. The River Raisin and Lake Erie are the features that drew settlers to the area. Today, people are still drawn to Monroe's scenic river views, sandy beaches and eclectic mix of urban and rural areas. In 2022, Monroe County's population was 151,478.

Monroe is not your typical quaint, small-town community; it is steeped in history. We will travel back in time to when the Native Americans roamed the area and see how the French Canadians decided this was also a good place to call home. How well did that bode with the Native people? Is that where some of the earliest reservations come in? Or maybe that's why a pivotal international battle was fought on the doorsteps of the settlers. Where does

Shawnee warrior Tecumseh fit into all this? And what of George Armstrong Custer? He was not even born yet…

What about plagues and the Michigan rash; did it devastate the settlers, or did they have cures for these maladies? Be warned; the cure can be worse than the ailment. For the settlers, traveling by horse and buggy was an adventure in and of itself, especially when taverns lined the entire route. But how did crime fit into that niche—crimes such as stagecoach robberies, bank robberies and even grave robberies?

Why were there werewolves running around in the dark woods and ghost orbs floating in the trees or goblins stealing horses? Not to mention all the issues with the witches.

What about the Underground Railroad? Not much of it was in Monroe—or was it? And what of Prohibition? Temperance township's namesake means Monroe was essentially dry, right? Thus, Prohibition was not really a problem here; then why was the main highway called "Avenue de Booze"?

How in the world could Monroe ever rival beach communities such as Miami Beach, Daytona Beach, etc.? Yet, it became a huge destination for the beachgoers—what? Sandy beaches, swimming, islands, regattas, fancy hotels, carnivals and even a casino in Monroe?

One thing's for sure; Monroe has always been steeped in military pride and has always answered the call. Monroe saw its men in the front lines at places like Gettysburg, Fredericksburg, Antietam and more. After the war was over, a few of its men even rode home on the famed steamship *Sultana*. In later wars across the ocean, Monroe men amassed countless acts of heroism, and one was even at Auschwitz.

Like other communities, Monroe has remnants of such things in the form of monuments. Right smack in the town square is one such monument, a cannon from the battle here—or is it really? There are other different kinds of remnants, too, such as lost villages and lost villages of the dead.

Monroe, like most places, has had its share of natural disasters—but other disasters, too, such as fires, plane crashes, train crashes and shipwrecks with sunken treasure.

Even overlooked, quaint Monroe, tucked between giants like Detroit and Toledo, has garnered its share of the world stage more than once. Industrial giants known the world over, such as La-Z-Boy and Monroe Shocks, call Monroe their home. All eyes were on Monroe when it was known as Frenchtown, during the War of 1812. Then came the Toledo War, where Monroe County was reconfigured and lost Toledo but gained something far more valuable. There was also the powder keg of the Newton Steel labor strike. If that was not enough, Monroe had the world holding its breath when it was brought to the brink of a nuclear disaster.

And just think: this is still only scraping the surface of the history of a small town and county called Monroe.

Chapter 1

La Rivière aux Raisins

For the earliest accounts of Monroe, we can turn to the early Jesuit explorers. Father Hennepin wrote about the beautiful River Raisin valley in 1701, describing it thus:

> *The borders are so many vast prairies and grand forests and charming streams, the freshness of whose waters keeps the banks always green. Long and broad rows of fruit trees are seen, which have never felt the careful hand of the vigilant gardener. Everywhere along these broad natural avenues under the trees are seen assembled by hundreds the timid deer and fawn; also the squirrel bounding in eagerness to gather the plums and nuts with which the ground is almost literally covered. Here the cautious turkey calls and collects her numerous brood and conducts them to gather the grapes and berries which abound most luxuriantly—and here, too, come the mates to gorge themselves on the abundance of good things. Pheasants, quail, partridge, woodcock and multitudes of pigeons beyond the power to count them, swarm in clouds in the woods and cover the country which is dotted with thickets and forests of majestic trees of very great height and size, forming a charming perspective, which sweetens the sad loneliness of the solitude. The fish are here nourished and bathed by living waters of crystal clearness and delicious purity, and this great abundance renders them none the less appetizing. Swans are so numerous, that at times, one would take them for lilies among the reeds in which they are crowded together. The gabbling geese, the duck, the widgeon are so abundant.*[1]

Monroe, like most lands of the United States, was first occupied by Native nations, mostly Potawatomi. After the Revolutionary War, Great Britain ceded the lands northwest of the Ohio River, and the United States referred to these areas as the Northwest Territory, out of which Monroe was born.

The Native nations utilized the rich soils and plentiful waters of the River Raisin and Lake Erie to sustain their settlements. They called the River Raisin the "River of Sturgeon" (Nummaseppe) because of all the sturgeon that resided in its waters. Many Native villages were spread throughout the area.

The first Europeans to settle in the region were primarily French Canadians. Many traveled south from Canada to Detroit. They first came to the area of Monroe in the 1780s or so. The first settler is thought to have been Colonel Francis Navarre, who migrated from Detroit, as did most of the French Canadian settlers. They hoped to carve out their own niche in an area they heard had rich soil for their farms, plenty of wildlife for sustenance and fur trading, and ample waterways and marshes teaming with fish.

The French Canadians traded with the Native nations in Detroit and had a good relationship based on the fur trade commerce. In fact, Francis Navarre received a deed to his land from the Potawatomis. The translated deed read:

> *We the principal chiefs of the village of the Potawatomi's, know. Askiby, Mongi-a-gon, Oua-Ouri-Attenne, Sac-Co-Nibbinne that both in our names, as well as with the consent of our village, we declare that of our own good will, we have granted to Francis Navarre, surnamed Schigoy, and to James, his brother, both our allies, the whole extent of land which belongs to us on the side west of the River Raisin, otherwise called by us, NametCyby; this comprises about twenty arpents in breadth...that they themselves and their representatives may enjoy the while in full ownership and perpetuity. We have in faith and testimony of this made the ordinary marks of our signatures at Detroit, on the third day of June, 1785.*[2]

The settlement soon saw an influx of French Canadians who named it "La Rivière aux Raisins" due to the wild grape clusters hanging from the trees over the graceful waters of the river. They built their homes in the French style and within feet of the river, in proximity to each other. Even today, Monroe is unique because of its French layout; the French ribbon lot farms, which were unlike grid patterns, can still be seen. The farms were called "long ribbon lots" due to the narrow but deep yards they had. In

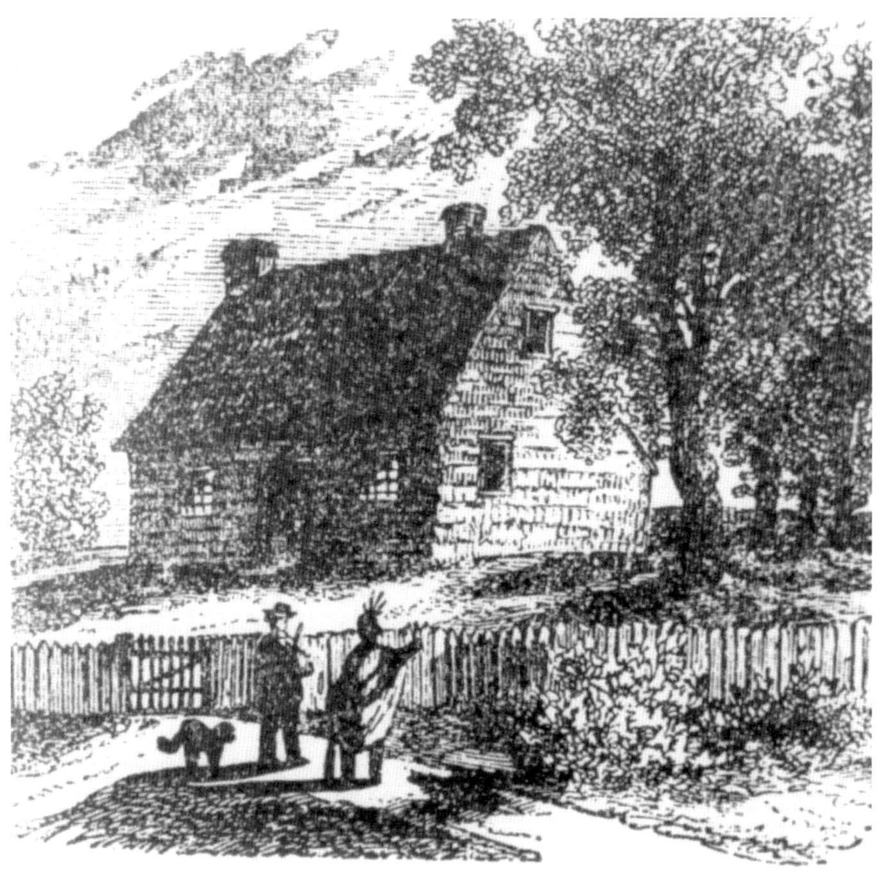

Cabin of Colonel Francis Navarre, founder of the River Raisin settlement. *Monroe County Library System.*

their lots, the settlers cultivated gardens and orchards. They usually marked their area off with a puncheon fence (much like a picket fence). With all the French Canadians making the River Raisin their home, the area became known as "Frenchtown."

There were also a few settlers who were not French Canadian but "Yankees," as the French called them. The settlement grew rapidly, and the relationship between the Native Americans and the settlers grew into a large métis (mixed) society. The area became so populated that homes extended

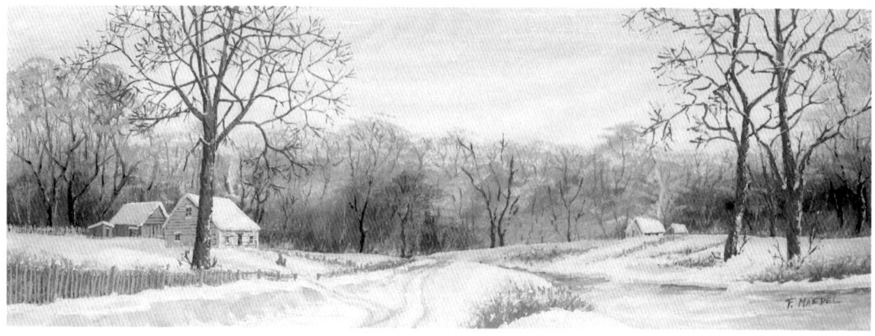

Ribbon Farms by Fran Maedel. *River Raisin National Battlefield Park.*

up and down the river for twelve miles by the time of the War of 1812. It was the second-largest settlement in the territory, and it was thought it would soon rival Detroit.

As more settlers poured into the area, especially non–French Canadians from the west and south, the demand for land grew as well. These land speculators did not wait for a treaty or deed to their land from the Native Americans but simply squatted where they desired. Tensions started to grow.

But everything changed with the Battles of the River Raisin in the War of 1812. The battles devasted the settlement. Many of the settlers fled the area, never to return. Those who did would fail to recognize the area they called home. And those who stayed faced the elements with little to no food, their homes and farms destroyed, their animals gone. The area was just a shadow of its former self. It would never regain its former glory.

Yet, in November 1817, Monroe was given a helping hand when it was thrust into the spotlight by Samuel R. Brown. Brown wrote the *Western Gazetteer*, published in Auburn, New York; in it, he described the Michigan Territory in eighteen pages, including three specifically about Monroe. Brown was a veteran of the War of 1812 and served in General William Henry Harrison's U.S. Army. He was respected by his peers, and his book proved to be very popular and was often quoted in other works.

Regarding Michigan overall, he said, "Hitherto this territory has not enjoyed the character to which its soil, climate, and advantageous situation for trade, justly entitle it." But he also figured "time, and the enterprising emigrants, who are now rapidly increasing in number, will place its reputation in a proper point of view." He described the natural elements as "extensive forests of lofty timber. There is no state or territory in North America so beautifully supplied with fish, aquatic fowle [*sic*], and wild game;

all the rivers…afford an inexhaustible supply of fish, to say nothing of the vast lakes, which wash 600 miles of its frontier."[3]

Focusing on Monroe, he wrote that the River Raisin got its name from "the vast quantities of grapes which are found on its banks" and that "the settlements extend from within two miles of the lake to the mouth of the river Macon, a distance of 15 miles. The inhabitants are mostly French, who raise wheat, corn, and potatoes, more than sufficient for their own consumption. The soil proves to be rich and durable, and the settlements have been blessed with unusual health….There are several grist and saw-mills on the river." Referring to the orchards, he wrote, "cider and peach brandy are made for exportation."[4]

Also in 1817, President James Monroe was set to visit Detroit, and the residents decided to lure him to the River Raisin by officially changing the name of the settlement to Monroe in his honor. Incidentally, he still did not visit the town.

In 1825, there was no shortage of settlers calling Monroe home as a result of the Erie Canal opening. We are given another glimpse into life at the River Raisin a couple years later by Amanda Clarke, wife of a storekeeper, who wrote to her sister in Connecticut in 1827:

> *For several weeks past we have had the most excellent sleighing, either on snow or on the ice, the latter of which is very fashionable, & to us a delightful & novel amusement. The River Raisin is crooked, & interspersed with small islands, its borders adorned with French & English settlements, with grape vines & lofty trees & prairies; the ice being smooth & level, it serves well for running races….Detroit gentry make our village a place of fashionable resort. If snow is denied us, they travel by ice, on Detroit River, and the great folks from Fort Meigs (at the Miami rapids) also come here on the ice by the way of the Miami River & the lake, so that we are very far from being shut out from the gay world.*[5]

Apparently, horse racing on the frozen River Raisin was another popular sport. An ad was placed by Medard Labadie in the local newspaper on January 30, 1828: "River Raisin against North America! The subscriber offers to lay a wager of from $100 to $600, to pace his Horse GASCON, upon the ice, against any horse in North America—a distance from 3 to 6 miles."[6]

Later, in the mid-1800s, Monroe was referred to as the "Floral City" with the establishment of the large Ilgenfritz Nurseries, Greening Nurseries

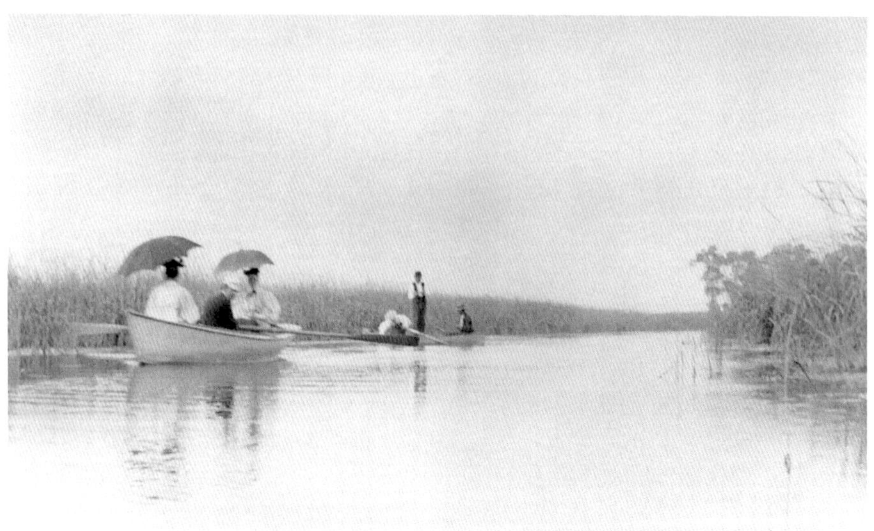

Old Raisin River, near Raisin Point, 1895. *Monroe County Library System.*

and others. In fact, Arbor Day was actually founded by J. Sterling Morton, a Monroe resident, in 1872.[7] The christening of Monroe as the Floral City actually came from a promotion by the Michigan Southern Railroad to launch its new steamship and rail route between Buffalo and Chicago. On a beautiful day in May 1852, a steam train made its way two and a half miles along the shore of Lake Erie, where the passengers were greeted by a blanket of billowing white lotus pedals lying atop large green leaves interspersed with wild rice plants and graceful marsh grasses dancing in the breeze.

The train headed back into the nucleus of town, the courthouse square, where it seemed the whole town was gathered along with a band and fifty young girls dressed in white and adorned with ribbons and flowers waiting for them. The girls handed out flowers to everyone gathered and strewed them all along the tracks. When the train pulled up, the townspeople held up a banner that read, "The Floral City Welcomes You!"[8]

As early as 1834, the first paper products were produced in Monroe, starting an industry that would dominate the landscape. Monroe was transformed by the paper industry; factories littered the area, and many people came to Monroe from the south to work in the paper mills throughout the decades.

During the first half of the twentieth century, Monroe Auto Equipment introduced the world to its shock absorbers, and "Monroe Shocks" was born

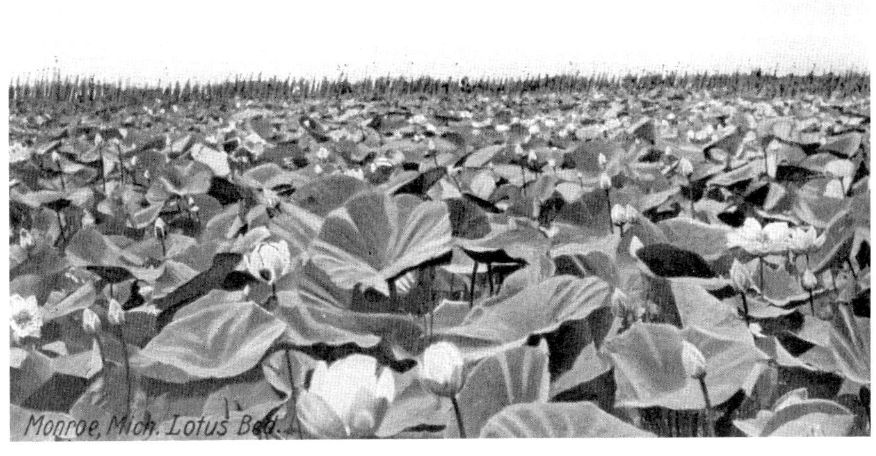

Lotus beds. *Monroe County Library System.*

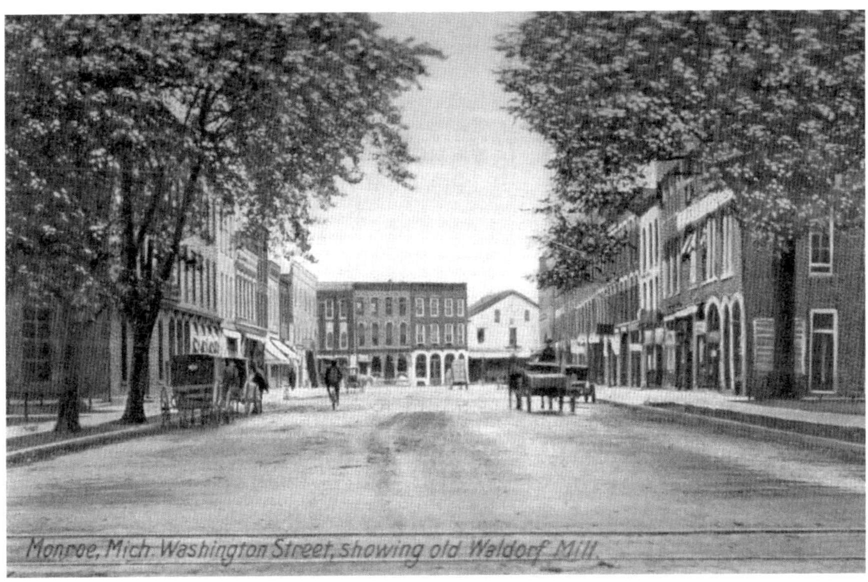

Washington Street downtown, showing Old Waldorf Mill, 1900. *Monroe County Library System.*

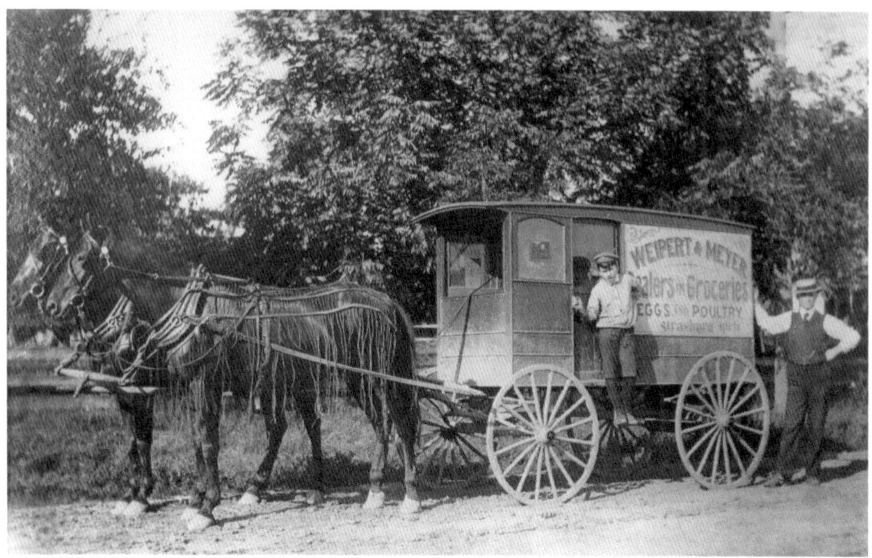

Weipert and Meyer delivery wagon. *Monroe County Library System.*

and became a worldwide commodity. A little-known furniture store opened by two cousins in Monroe evolved into the world headquarters of La-Z-Boy Incorporated, and the La-Z-Boy chair is now synonymous with reclining chairs all over the world.

Numerous other industries helped build Monroe throughout the ages as well. One of the largest is DTE Energy, which also established the first nuclear power plant in Monroe, Enrico Fermi.

Chapter 2

Legends and Lore

Monsters, ghosts, witches, Le Feu Follet, Le Loup-Garou and Les Lutins are all familiar beings we have heard of—or are they? What are Le Feu Follet, Le Loup-Garou and Les Lutins? These are French names for legendary beings that roamed the marshes, rivers, lakes, woods and farmers' fields of the River Raisin settlement, according to the French Canadians that settled here.

Over two hundred years ago, family members and friends gathered on chilly, dark nights around the warm, sparkling fire and told stories of the past. Children listened eagerly for the next word that fell from the lips of the storyteller, all the while cringing, terrified, yet spellbound to know what would be revealed next.

In the 1780s, French Canadians started to make their way south from Detroit to the area of the River Raisin. They wanted to carve out their own little niche in a marshy wilderness that would come to be known as Frenchtown. Along with their families, they brought with them centuries-old French traditions. As they were living isolated in an unknown dark wilderness, these traditions helped to give an explanation to some of the mysterious sights and sounds they encountered. The legends would take on a new life to reflect the local area of the folks who lived there.

Probably the best-known legend is that of Le Loup-Garou. This monster is much like the modern-day werewolf. Le Loup-Garou is most often depicted as a werewolf-like creature but can take on any animal form. The monster will lure its human victim into a trap and suddenly transform it

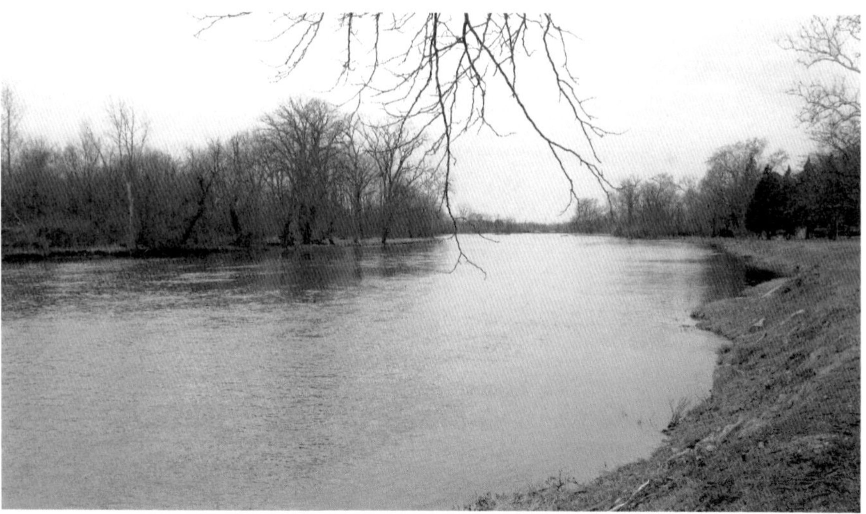

River Raisin.

into an animal, which can be anything from a mouse to a horse. But there is something about the animal that contains an enigmatic quality that reveals it is not an ordinary animal but, instead, a transformed human being.

Some tales talk of this person making a deal with the devil in exchange for money or some kind of favor. There was a time frame attached to the agreement, and when the time was up, Le Loup-Garou would have to figure out a way to bloodlet. Bloodletting was the only way for the victim to become fully human again. If Le Loup-Garou could not achieve this, it would be bound to the devil forever. Thus, many tales tell of the animal having to attack so as to have the victim hit it and make it bleed. On the flip side, however, if the blood got on the unsuspecting victim, they would be transformed into an animal, too.[9]

Jo Hirst of Monroe, who was a child in the 1920s, related a tale her grandfather used to tell her about the Le Loup-Garou: A man traveling down Pointe aux Peaux Road saw a dog he was afraid might be Le Loup-Garou, so he quickly ran away from it. When he told an old friend about it, he was told to hit it and draw blood the next time he ran into it. The old man explained that someone's soul was caught up in the dog, and it was actually a soul stuck in purgatory. So, the next time the man saw the dog, he managed to kick it in the nose, causing it to bleed. The act released the soul and allowed the soul to resume its human form again.[10]

In 1978, historian and author Dennis Au interviewed Edward Labadie, a ninety-eight-year-old Monroe resident. Labadie retold a tale his parents told him about some disturbed people who were driven crazy by a large dog incessantly knocking against their door month after month. They were advised to hit the dog on the head with their keys until they drew blood. So, the next time they heard the dog at their door, they opened it and quickly hit the dog between the eyes as they were told. They were totally shocked when the dog transformed into a human right in front of them; furthermore, it was someone they knew.[11]

Monroe resident Geraldine Robinson, when interviewed in 1976, relayed how when she was young, her uncle Pete would gather the kids around the potbellied stove and tell such outlandish tales. She thought surely, they couldn't possibly be true. He loved to tell wild stories about Le Loup-Garou, as she remembers it:

> *At the full of the moon this creature, who appeared to be a normal man at other times, would turn into this Loup Garou—still in the shape of a man, but quite hairy, claws in place of fingernails, fangs for teeth. And what horrible things he did, we did not know. We assumed, maybe, that he ate up little children and all sorts of horrible things like that. We were so frightened we just let our imaginations run wild.…I think if you carried holy water with you or a cross…and would have shown this creature…he would have vanished.…I suppose it would have been something like the exorcist today.*[12]

Obviously, this version of Le Loup-Garou sounds like our modern-day werewolf.

Robinson was told other tales by her uncle Pete as well, although this particular one wasn't quite as scary as the others. In fact, the tale of Les Lutins was more curious. Les Lutins were little, agile green creatures, much like trolls. They were about the size of a monkey and had whiskers. These little fellows, however, weren't interested in anything but horses. The belief was that Les Lutins were the spirits of dead horsemen doing penance. Geraldine remembers hearing how the River Raisin Lutins were known for being especially mischievous. They would steal the horses away under the cover of darkness and ride them fast and furious through the night. When they had their fill, they returned them to the barn covered in thistles and burrs from mane to tail. A particularly evil Lutin might do this each night until the horse was so exhausted it was useless to the farmer. They were also known to braid horses' tails and then tie them together "so that the framer would have an awful time getting them untied in the morning to do the plowing."[13]

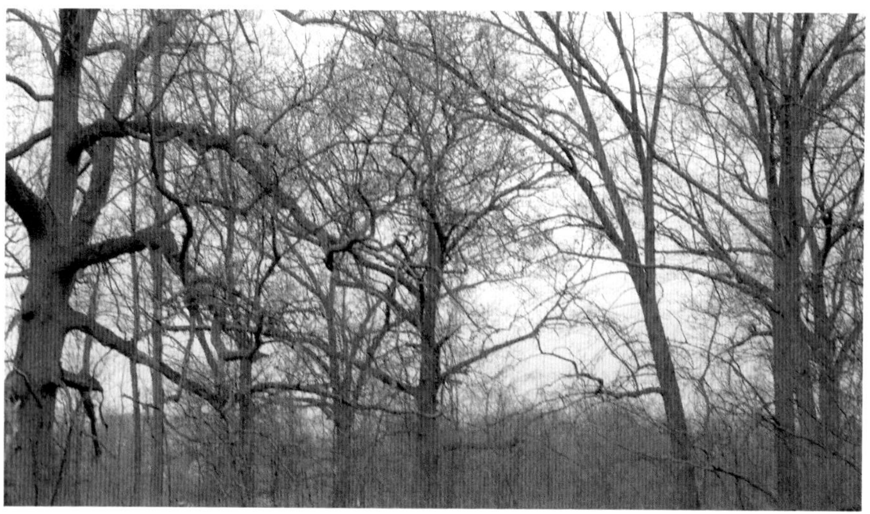

Typical woodsy area in Monroe.

Another tale Robinson remembers her uncle Pete sharing was about Le Feu Follet. Le Feu Follet is a bewitched flash or ball of light that would suddenly appear in the darkness. It was believed to be the soul of a dead sinner, much like people think of orbs or ghostly apparitions today. The belief is that the devil lets the soul transform into this light and bewitch the unsuspecting victim to follow it, usually right into a dangerous situation, such as off a cliff or into a lake.

Robinson's uncle Pete and his family lived on Johnsons Island in the River Raisin (no longer there). When they wanted to come to the mainland, they would have to hop into a rowboat. He told of how one night, they were on the river going home, and suddenly, a "huge ball of fire settled on one end of the boat." Scared to death, they feverishly paddled to get home and away from the light. He felt as if the "devil was chasing them out of Monroe!"[14]

Another tale of Le Feu Follet concerns the founding family of the River Raisin, the Navarres. Monique Navarre was in love with William Macomb Jr., who lived in Grosse Ile. She decided to go visit him and her brother, Robert, went along. When they arrived at his house, however, William was not at home, and the servant said he should have returned by now. With a storm brewing, Monique feared the worst and started getting hysterical. Her brother tried to calm her down.

Suddenly, there was a loud whistling noise, and a flash of light pierced the darkness. Monique screamed that it was Le Feu Follet! Robert was not sure

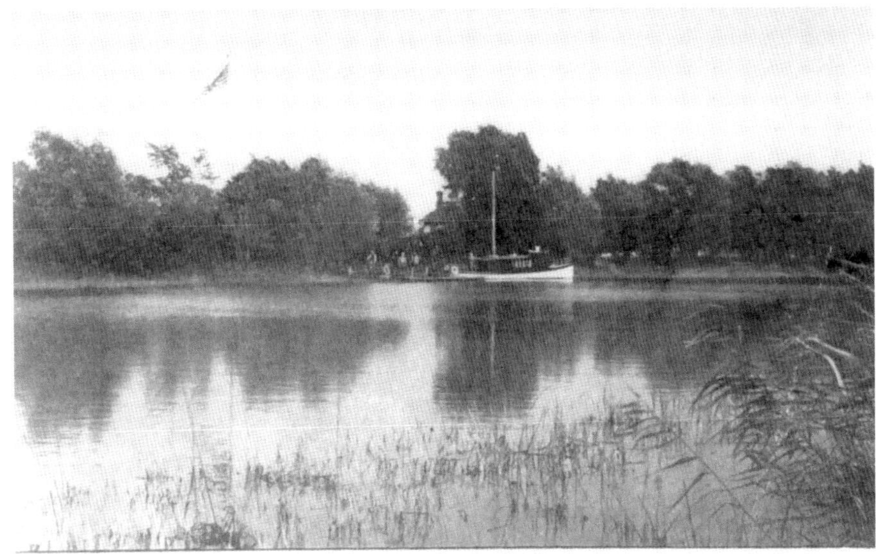

Johnson's Island in the River Raisin. *Monroe County Library System.*

what she was talking about and asked her to explain. She told him how Le Feu Follet can be male or female, and the light is the soul of a sinner who asked the devil to transform them into light. Two lights are not necessarily dangerous, but one light is a very bad omen, and "he who sees it must at once throw himself on the ground covering his face, for so seductive is its fascination that it allures him to deserted bogs and steep ravines, and leaves him to die."[15]

The tale unnerved the servant, and he and Monique grew increasingly upset. Robert decided that the best thing to do was to search for William. They set off through the darkness, yelling loudly as they went, so they could be heard over the roar of the thunder and lightning. But, before they knew it, they were a long way from home. Monique, desperate and exhausted, let out one last cry. Suddenly, the sound of a pistol shot filled the air, and the group followed it to a murky swamp. They were utterly startled to see a body lying in the water; then they realized it was struggling to stay afloat. They joined hands to be able to reach the body, and when they pulled it out, everyone was relieved to see it was William.

Monique was beside herself asking if he was OK and what had happened. William explained that he was on his way home when it got dark and stormy, and he lost his way, until suddenly, a bright light appeared. The light actually seemed to try to lead him, so he followed it, hoping to find the trail. Before he knew it, he fell right into the deep swamp, and when he screamed for help, he heard "the mocking laughter of the goblins!"[16] After treading water for so long, exhausted and no longer able to scream, he accepted his fate. Then, all of a sudden, he heard the desperate voice of his loved one yelling his name. Monique retorted that it was Le Feu Follet who led him astray. At that moment, it seemed everyone wondered if she might indeed be right. A few months later, the two were married in Detroit.[17]

Witches

We have all heard tales about witches. In earlier centuries, the existence of witches was fairly accepted. Usually, the accused were women of advanced age who lived on their own and kept to themselves. Yet, few realize that Monroe has its own witchy tales. In Monroe, it was believed that the witches practiced black magic and often cast spells and hexes by using a book called *The Sixth and Seventh Books of Moses*. They could use the book to practice good or evil.

> *The 6th Street neighborhood had several "witches." They were old ladies—widows—who lived quite to themselves and who were greatly feared by everyone. The children were all warned never to let one of these witches look them straight in the eye for, if they did, a hex would be sure to follow. These witches obtained their power from a book that each one of them owned: it was the Sixth and Seventh Books of Moses, written in German. It gave all the secrets of black magic.*[18]

A young Monroe girl by the name of Anna had a case of ringworm that covered her entire body. The doctor was unable to do any more to help her. So, the desperate family decided to turn to their neighbor, an old witch doctor. Even though they thought the witch doctor, Old Mother Groat, performed a lot of curious spells, they had nowhere else to turn. Old Mother Groat said she would have Anna cured in nine days. She took Anna to her house, placed her on a wooden stool and stood in front of her making three circles in the air while chanting something, then made the sign of the cross on Anna's nose. She sent Anna home, telling her to pray for nine days. The charm worked, and Anna's ringworms disappeared.

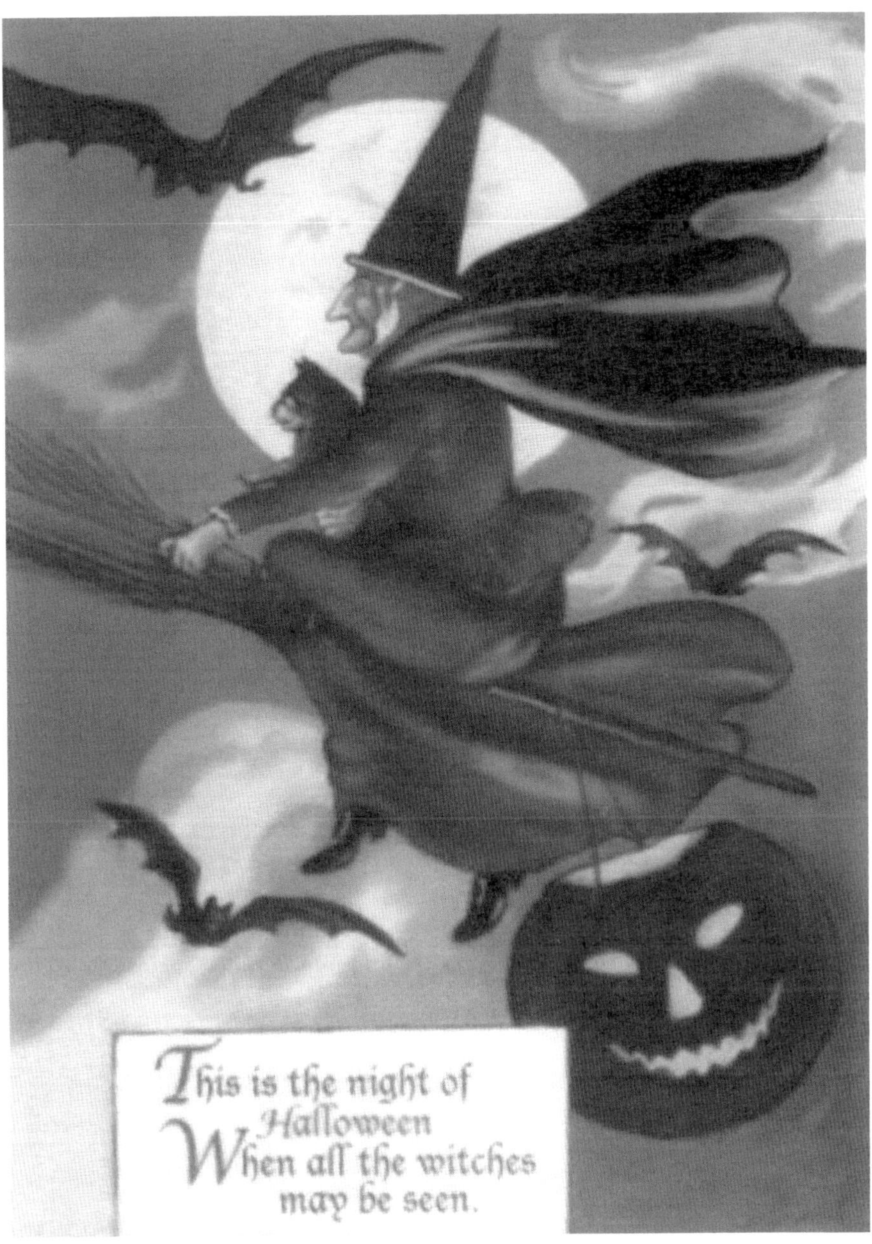

Antique Halloween postcard.

Another time, Anna got a bad cut on her foot, and it was bleeding profusely. The family once again called on their neighbor. Old Mother Groat put spiderwebs on the cut, chewed some tobacco and put the tobacco juice all over the cut. Unbelievably, the bleeding stopped, and the cut quickly healed.[19]

Lulu Sieb of Monroe also related a witch story. She said a Mr. Theilman was the victim of a witch who kept breaking the back window of his house. It got so bad he placed guards to keep an eye on the window. Yet, somehow it kept getting broken, even though no one saw anyone. A friend finally told Theilman to get a piece of the witch's hair, or a piece of her clothing, and burn it. Once he did that, everything would stop. He followed his friend's directions and was surprised when the window breaking did, indeed, cease.[20]

Another Monroe resident, Mrs. Cron, told the story of a neighbor in the 1870s whom everyone in town believed was a witch. She was described as looking like an old hag, and the neighborhood children were deathly afraid of her. At that time, the hag would get milk from her neighbor's cow. But one day, when there wasn't enough milk to go around, she was told she couldn't have any. Everyone believed she must have cursed the cow in her anger because all of a sudden, instead of giving milk, the cow started giving blood! The owners of the cow sought out their priest and told him what happened. The priest asked them to bring in a pail of the blood, which they did. He examined it and after a while tossed it away and told them to return home. After they were home, they got a visit from the witch, and she begged for forgiveness and told them she had cursed the cow but was very sorry and had removed the curse.

Later, it was revealed she had a copy of *The Sixth and Seventh Book of Moses*. When the cow's owner asked the priest if he had ever heard of such a book, the priest replied that he had, but it was not in print anymore because people were abusing it.[21]

Apparently, curses were also the cause of supernatural trouble, at least for the Ambrose LaFountain family around 1908. A thief stole Ambrose's boots, and Ambrose cursed him. Shortly after the incident, he and his wife were awakened by footsteps on their tin roof. This went on for two weeks around midnight each night. Even when they tried to find out who, or what, was making the sound, they could not find anything. The couple got very distraught and finally sought the advice of the local priest. The priest told Ambrose he should never have cursed anyone, and he needed to go to confession and ask forgiveness. Once Ambrose did this, the nightly boot thumping stopped.[22]

On August 29, 1879, an article appeared in the local Monroe newspaper that said LaPlaisance Creek in Lasalle was "infested with witches":

> *A reporter visited the district on LaPlaisance creek last week Saturday, that is infested with witches. From him we gather the following: A German family, living west of Mr. Albain's, claim that a woman living near by is a witch—that she has caused them a great amount of trouble with their horses, cattle, milk and cream, and they themselves have been victims of her wonderful bewitching powers. They have employed witch doctors from Detroit, Cleveland, Toledo, Ypsilanti, Frenchtown and Lasalle, which has cost them not far from $200. They have driven sharp spikes in different parts of the house, nailed old horse-shoes over the doors, and hung a chip of wood in the chimney to dry out, thinking that the witch would die when the moisture of the chip had dried up. All this that they have done was of no avail. They were about to give up in despair when one of the neighbors came to their rescue, and adopted a plan by which the witches have been driven from their stronghold and have sought a more congenial clime* [climate] *farther west. The plan adopted by this good Samaritan neighbor, to exterminate the witches, was as follows: A bull's head, complete except the skin, was raised upon a pole about 10 feet high, with a horse-shoe fastened to the tip of each horn, and a large ear of corn cross-ways in the jaws, a board fastened below the head bearing the inscription "This is a witch killer." It is a fearful looking object, but we understand it has accomplished the work for which it was designed. How strange it is that ignorance and superstition, in these enlightened days, can find fools to operate upon.*[23]

Chapter 3
Keepers of the Fire

The area out of which Monroe County was carved out had a number of tribal nations, but the most prominent were the Potawatomi. It is thought that the Native Americans had nine villages (or camps) and six burial grounds in the area. Most of these followed the River Raisin. According to author W.J. Hinsdale's map of Native American occupation, the townships with villages and burial grounds were:

Monroe and Frenchtown Township: 3 villages, 1 burial ground
Summerfield: 2 villages, 2 burial grounds
Raisinville: 2 villages, 1 burial ground
Dundee: 1 village, 1 burial ground
Whiteford: 1 village
Bedford: 1 burial ground

Villages were often named for chiefs. Two of the villages in Monroe County were Macon, meaning "bear," and Maera, meaning "walk-in-the-water." One burial ground was known as Shimmenecon, meaning "large seed."

Monroe proved to be a good area for the Native Americans because of the river and its proximity to the lake, as well as its length, although it was crooked. It was fairly easy to traverse deep into the area by canoe. The river provided necessary sustenance in the way of numerous fish, especially sturgeon, and the marshes were a great place to collect wild rice. The river was actually called Nummasepee by the Native Americans because of the abundance of sturgeon. Wild grapes growing along its banks and plenty of food-bearing trees and wildlife also made the area attractive. To top it off, a major thoroughfare ran through the area diagonally from the Maumee, Ohio area to Detroit and parts north.

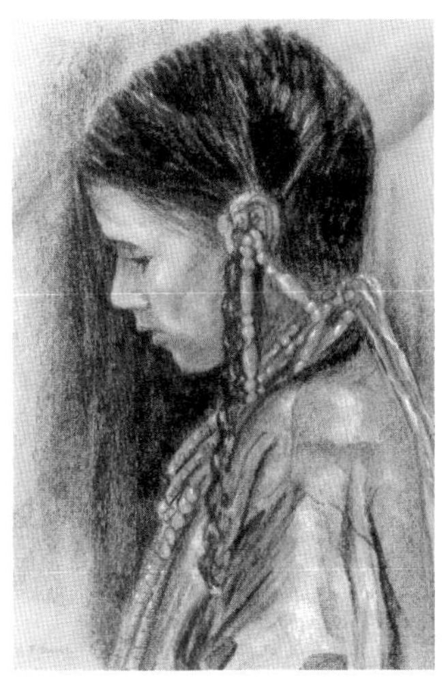

Potawatomi Youth by Fran Maedel. *River Raisin National Battlefield Park.*

Villages were not always permanent but could be seasonal based on weather, availability of food or threats. Once horses and firearms were introduced to the tribes by the whites, tribal habits changed dramatically, making the Native peoples much more mobile.

Villages could vary in size from small to large and were not usually composed of just one family. Many different family units often lived together. The more villages in an area, the more people. If archaeologists have excavated broken pottery, arrowheads, implements, firestones or any accumulation of items within a few acres, then there is a good chance a village existed in the vicinity.

A fairly large village usually had a burial ground next to it. But burial grounds were not always mounds or easily detectable. Most graves were not marked. In Michigan, mound burials were not the norm. "The mounds of Michigan were nearly all low, dome-shaped piles of gravel and sand usually with circular bases."[24] Considering this, burial grounds are usually found by accident. Yet, if one grave is accidently found, there are usually others in proximity to each other and often arranged in a systematic way, although the different tribes in Michigan might have had different customs.[25]

The Monroe-area Native peoples, just as the other Native nations, would find their way of life changed forever with the migration of American settlers to the north and west. On August 20, 1794, General "Mad" Anthony Wayne and the American forces were victorious over the Native Americans and their British allies in the Battle of Fallen Timbers. This was the last battle for control over the Northwest Territory and was fought near present-day Maumee, Ohio. The American victory paved the way for settlement in the wild territory. Monroe (known as River Raisin and Frenchtown) was right in the path of migration. The Native American confederacy met with General Wayne and a U.S. delegation to hash out the details, which would come to be known as the Treaty of Greenville.

Signed on August 3, 1795, the treaty officially opened up the territory to white settlers.

The United States hoped to eradicate the Native Americans from the territory by paying them a sum for their lands and having them move farther west or onto areas of land reserved just for them, called reservations. Governor William Hull negotiated a treaty on November 17, 1807, called the Treaty of Detroit. It was an agreement between the Potawatomi, Wyandot, Ottawa and Chippewa nations. In effect, it created reservations. One was at Macon in Dundee and the other in the Bedford/Erie area, extending into today's Toledo. Thus, some of the earliest reservations were created in Monroe County.[26]

The Treaty of Detroit stated in Article VI: "A tract of four miles square on Miami Bay (now Maumee Bay), including the villages of Meshkeman and Waugau now live."[27] This tract came to be known as the Ottawa Indian Reservation. The area used to be part of Monroe County, Michigan. Today, part of it is in Lucas County, Ohio. It included 10,240 acres. Much of the land was actually under the waters of the Ottawa River and Maumee Bay, however. In 1833, the Ottawa Tribe left the reservation and gave the land back to the United States government.[28] Today, there is no sign of the reservation.

There were also nine sections of land set aside in Dundee Township for the Potawatomi for an area to be known as the Macon Reserve: "Also three miles square on the River Raisin at a place called Macon, and where the

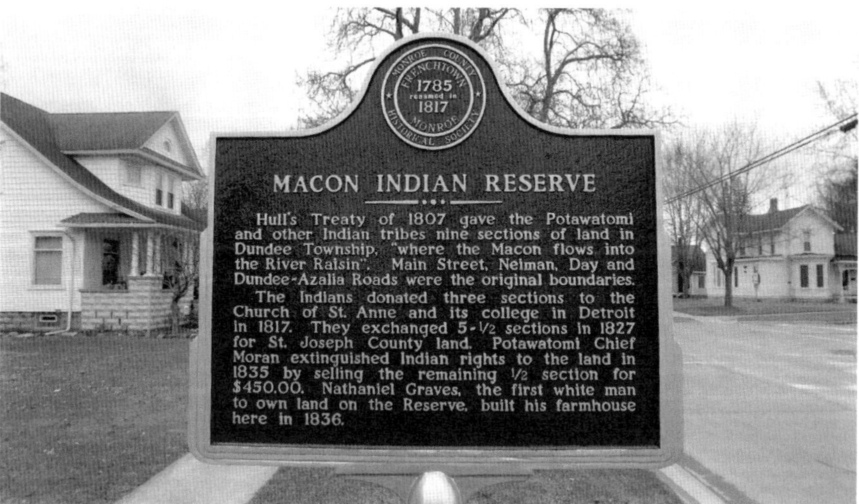

Macon Indian Reserve, Dundee.

River Macon falls into the River Raisin, which place is about fourteen miles from the mouth of said River Raisin." For the lands ceded, the Potawatomi were to receive "one thousand six hundred sixty-six dollars sixty-six cents and six mills…likewise an annuity forever of two thousand four hundred dollars to be paid at Detroit…[and] four hundred dollars to such of the Potawatomies as now reside on the River Huron of Lake Erie, the River Raisin, and in the vicinity of the said Rivers."[29] They were also to retain their hunting and fishing rights on the lands they ceded.

Ten years later, however, a treaty was made that ceded six sections out of the nine to the government. Another ten years later, the rest was ceded except half of a section, which was kept for the Potawatomie chief Moran. In 1832, that portion was ceded as well.[30] Today, you can visit part of the Macon Reservation in West County Park in Dundee, Michigan.

Chapter 4

The Shooting Star

Tecumseh

On March 9, 1768, Tecumseh was born in Piqua, Ohio, to the Shawnee Tribe. His name meant "the shooting star." He believed that all Native nations should join into one powerful confederation to resist the white man's intrusion onto their homelands. Together, they could defend their ancestral lands, their culture, their beliefs and, ultimately, their way of life. Tecumseh's charisma and powerful message resounded with the Native nations, and many chose to join his confederation.

When the United States declared war against Great Britain in 1812, Tecumseh and his confederation cast their lot with the British, since it appeared they would thus have a better chance of achieving their dream of an independent Native nation.

British major general Isaac Brock's aide-de-camp, Captain J. B. Glegg, described Tecumseh as follows:

> *Tecumseh's appearance was very prepossessing: his figure light, and finely proportioned; his age I imagine to be about five-and-thirty* [he was about forty]*: in height, five feet nine or ten inches: his complexion light copper; countenance oval, with bright hazel eyes, bearing cheerfulness, energy, and decision. Three small silver crosses or coronets were suspended from the lower cartilage of his aquiline nose, and a large silver medallion of George the Third…was attached to a mixed-colored wampum string and hung around his neck. His dress consisted of a plain, neat uniform, tanned deer-skin jacket, with long trowsers of the same material, the*

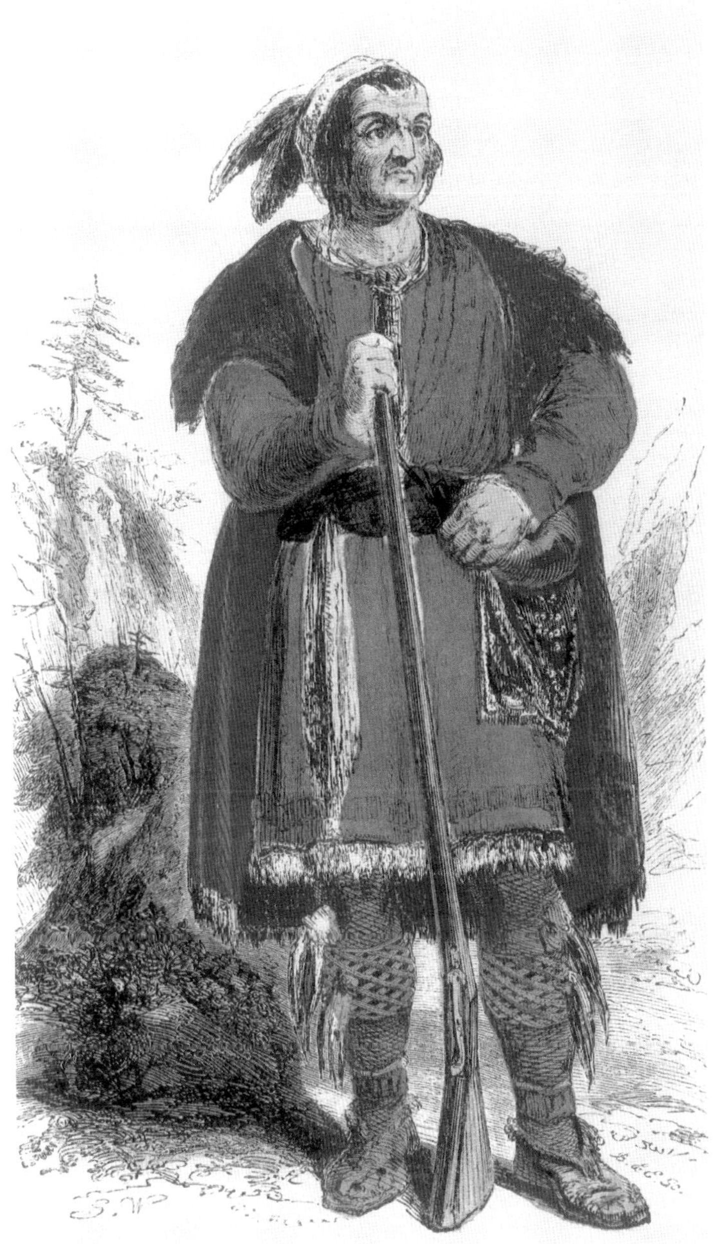

Tecumseh. *Library of Congress.*

> *seams of both being covered with neatly-cut fringe, and he had on his feet leather moccasins, much ornamented with work made from the dyed quills of the porcupine.*[31]

And General Brock wrote of Tecumseh, saying,

> *A more sagacious or a more gallant warrior does not, I believe, exist. He was the admiration of every one who conversed with him. From a life of dissipation he has not only become, in every respect abstemious, but he has likewise prevailed on all his native, and many of the other tribes, to follow his example.*[32]

Shortly after the War of 1812 was declared in July 1812, General William Hull surrendered Detroit, including the settlement of the River Raisin (current-day Monroe). Monroe historian Talcott Wing related an incident in his book *History of Monroe County, Michigan* that exemplifies the character of Tecumseh when he came to the settlement: "The character of Tecumseh was that of a gallant warrior, an honest and honorable man, and his memory was respected by many of our old citizens who personally knew him."[33]

Wing relates an example of Tecumseh's honesty when, after the fall of Detroit in August 1812, Tecumseh was asked by British agent Captain Elliot to go to Frenchtown and pursue American colonel Henry Brush. When Tecumseh arrived, he noticed that the settlement was virtually devoid of meat. Most of the cattle had been driven off by the citizens in order to save them or taken as booty by the Native Americans. Tecumseh was in quite a predicament because his warriors had no food. He was thrilled to spot a yoke of black oxen and explained to the owner, Frenchman Rivard, that he must take the oxen to feed his starving men. Rivard begged him not to take them and explained how he was poor and tending to his ill father, who would surely starve without the oxen.

Tecumseh explained, "We are the conquerors. I must have the oxen, my people must not starve, but I will not rob you of them. I will pay you a $100, which is more than they are worth, but I must have them."[34] Tecumseh had someone write up an order for the reimbursement for Rivard to give to Elliott. But when Rivard presented the order to Elliott, Elliott was very rude to him and refused to pay it. Rivard was downtrodden and returned to Tecumseh and told him about Elliott's refusal. Tecumseh replied, "He won't pay it, will he? Stay all night and to-morrow we will go and see."[35] But the next day, when Tecumseh questioned Elliott about it, he still refused to

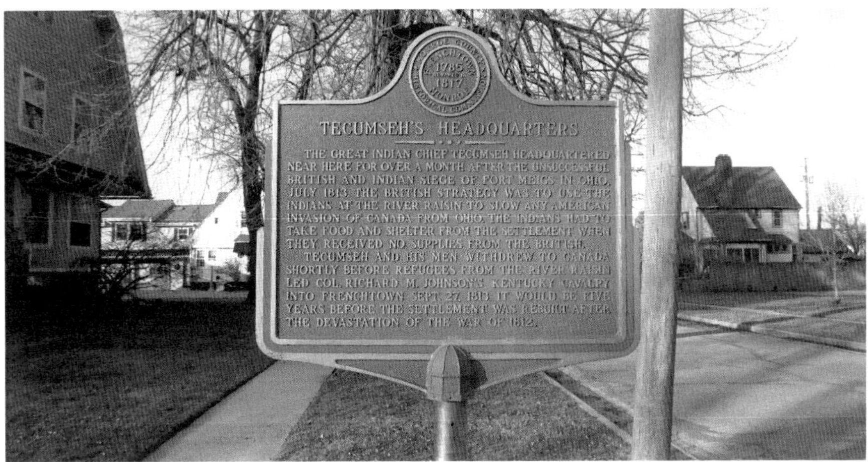

Tecumseh's headquarters, Elm Street.

pay. Tecumseh, feeling insulted replied, "I bought them for my young men, who were very hungry. I promised to pay for them, and they shall be paid for if I have to sell all my own horses to pay for them. I have always heard that the white people went to war with each other and not with peaceable inhabitants; that they did not rob and plunder poor people. I will not."[36]

Elliot still refused, earning him the ire of the Shawnee, who responded, "You can do as you please, but before Tecumseh, the prophet and his Warriors came to fight the battles of the great king, they had enough to eat, for which they had only to thank the Great Spirit and their good rifles. Their hunting grounds supplied them food enough and to them they can return."[37] Tecumseh went on to explain how the man was poor with an ill father and that he should not have to pay for the sins of his own government. Furthermore, if the British were going to act like that, he would pay the debt himself. Then he would gather his warriors and return home and no longer be their ally.

Realizing he had pushed Tecumseh too far, Elliott started to panic and pulled out one hundred dollars in government scrip. Tecumseh told him forget it; he promised Rivard money, not scrip. Elliott, left with no choice, succumbed to Tecumseh's demands and paid Rivard the money and even an extra dollar, at Tecumseh's urging, for all the trouble he put him through.[38]

Tecumseh decided to make the River Raisin area his headquarters. He chose a spot by the river (Elm Avenue today). River Raisin was a good point to launch an attack into Ohio and press the advantage.

The local Potawatomi got along well with the French Canadian settlers, but once war was declared, the tribes in the area had to choose where their allegiance lay. The River Raisin settlers also found themselves caught in the middle. Tecumseh, even though he was in enemy territory, if you will, was respected by the local settlers, and they actually felt more secure when he was around.[39]

Despite promises by the British that the settlers would be protected, the Native warriors started pillaging the area in what was described as "one universal scene of destruction."[40] British captain Thomas McKee and Tecumseh tried to restore order and made every attempt "to put a stop to scenes so shocking and disgusting."[41] Author Sandy Antal writes, "Although Tecumseh deplored maltreatment of captives, many tribesmen clung to ancient traditions that condoned cruelty to prisoners, fully prepared to endure such treatment themselves."[42]

At the River Raisin, Tecumseh asked after his friend local militia captain Hubert Lacroix, and he was told Lacroix had been taken prisoner by the British. The British considered him a Canadian, since he was born in Montreal, and they accused him of treason and took him to Fort Malden as a prisoner. Tecumseh went to Malden and threatened British colonel Henry Procter that if he did not release his friend Lacroix, he would pull his Native confederation out of their alliance. Procter had to bend to the "king of the woods" (his nickname for Tecumseh), knowing that without the Native alliance, they would be in big trouble, since most of their troops were in France fighting Napoleon. So, Procter commanded Lacroix be released.[43]

It is not surprising Tecumseh rescued his friend Lacroix, but he even helped settlers he did not know. One day, while at his headquarters, Tecumseh was holding council with some tribe members and British officers. Unbeknownst to him, about one hundred yards behind him, some Native warriors forced their way into one of the locals' homes and started threatening the family. Genevieve Dusseau Ruland, only twenty-three years old, was alone with her children, since her husband, John, had left to go help in Detroit.

Unaware of what was happening, Tecumseh was still conversing with the officers when he felt a pull on his shirt. Looking down, he was stunned to see a little girl of nine years tugging on his garment. He immediately stopped his speech and listened to her as she explained what happened and that she needed his help; there were some "bad Indians" at her house.[44] Tecumseh, without any hesitation, turned around and walked hurriedly toward the house with the little girl.

When they reached the house, he saw the warrior dragging the family's trunk out the door. A scowl formed on his face, and he angrily grabbed his tomahawk, raising it toward the nearest man. That got the man's attention, stopping him in his tracks. The other warriors came to his rescue but were shocked when Tecumseh loudly and boldly shouted, "Dogs! I am Tecumseh!"[45] They were so stunned and scared at the same time that they quickly ran off into the woods, abandoning their plunder.

Suddenly, some British officers came up, and Tecumseh turned toward them, yelling, "And you are worse than dogs, to break your faith with the prisoners."[46] The officers felt awful and apologized to Ruland, offering to post a guard at her house. But looking at Tecumseh, she replied, "As long as that man is near us, I feel safe."[47]

Tecumseh, and thus the confederation, would not last long, however. The death blow to the confederation was dealt at the Battle of the Thames in September 1813. Monroe historian John Bulkley writes of Tecumseh's character in the battle:

> *Tecumseh the Shawnee and Pontiac the Ottawa stand forth preeminently, as the two greatest Indian chiefs of their time. Differing widely in their personalities as they did in their dispositions and natures, they were much the same in their craftiness, intellectual strength, and magnetic qualities to influence and command large bodies of men, whose nature rebelled against authority of any kind except that exercised by their own chosen leaders—and these two…were, indeed, born leaders and generals, accustomed to be listened to with respect in the councils of their tribes, and to obedience when they chose to exercise the arbitrary right of rulers. Tecumseh's character was perhaps as plainly shown at the battle of the Thames.…The British valued the cooperation of Tecumseh most highly for his sagacity, good judgment, friendly disposition towards them, as well as for his widely extended influence with other tribes besides his own. He was not at the battle of the River Raisin or Frenchtown, being absent on a mission to neighboring tribes in securing the confederation, nor was his brother "the prophet"; had he been there, it is the general belief of those who knew the nature of the great chief, that the massacre of the Kentucky troops and of the French settlers would not have taken place.*[48]

Also, in writing about Tecumseh at the Battle of the Thames, British major John Richardson wrote:

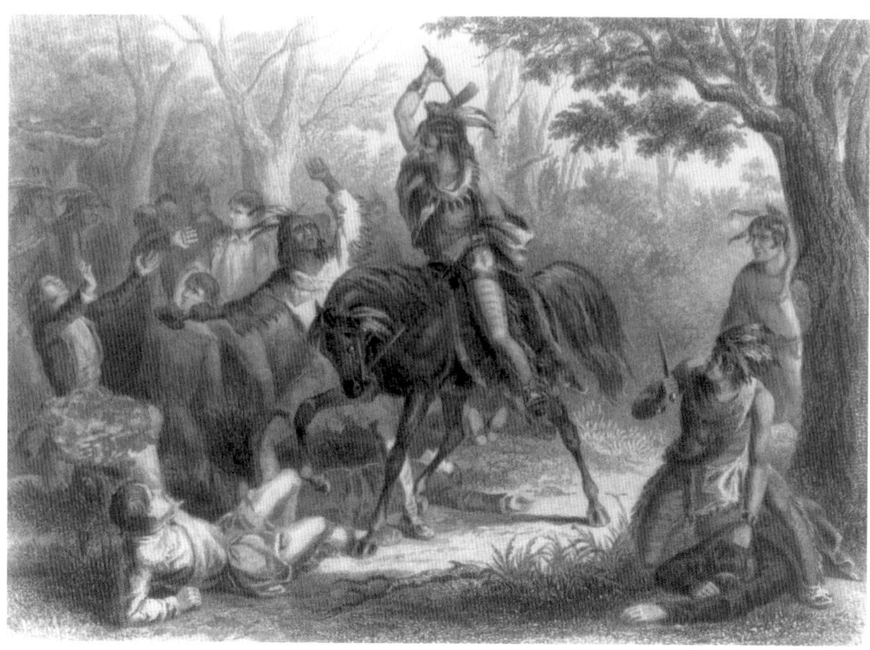

Battle of the Thames. *Library of Congress.*

> *The most serious loss we sustained on this occasion was that of the noble and unfortunate Tecumseh. Only a few minutes before the clang of the American bugles was heard ringing through the forest, and inspiring to action, the haughty chieftain had passed along our line, evidently pleased with the manner in which his left was supported, and seemingly sanguine of success. He was attired very becomingly in his usual deerskin dress, finely ornamented, which admirably displayed his sinewy, athletic figure from which was thrown back a fur mantle which he wore in camp. In his handkerchief, rolled up as a turban over his brow, was placed a handsome white ostrich feather, which had been given him by a near relative of the writer of this narrative and with which he was very fond of decorating himself, either for the council hall or the battlefield. He pressed the hand of each officer as he passed, made some remark in Shawnee, which was sufficiently understood accompanied as it was by the expressive signs of his mobile features, and then passed away forever from view, except as we saw him during the engagement, fighting gallantly, or as he afterwards lay stretched a corpse upon the field.*[49]

Chapter 5
The Civilians Battle

When it comes to battles, we always hear about the soldiers who fought in them, but we rarely hear about the civilians who were involved. At the River Raisin, most of the civilians were still in the settlement when the battle broke out. In fact, many of the local militiamen fought alongside the soldiers in the battles, and the women and children were left protecting their homes.

We will look at a few of the families who lived at the River Raisin and their experiences having a battle being fought on their doorsteps and how heroic stories arose not just from the soldiers but the settlers, too.

The Battles of the River Raisin were fought on January 18 and 22, and the incident termed the River Raisin Massacre by the Americans took place on January 23, 1813. The Battles of the River Raisin were fought in the War of 1812, when the United Sates declared war on Great Britain. The Native American confederation under Shawnee warrior Tecumseh joined the British as allies in the war.

On August 16, 1812, Michigan territorial governor William Hull surrendered Detroit, and the River Raisin settlement was included in that surrender. The settlement was besieged by Canadian militia and Native warriors looking for well-needed supplies. Some Canadian militia also stayed at the settlement as guards. The River Raisin local militia, called LaCroix's Company after Hubert LaCroix, was composed of about one hundred men, and now they found themselves prisoners. Their militia stockade was burned to the ground, and all their weapons and ammunition were seized. Many of

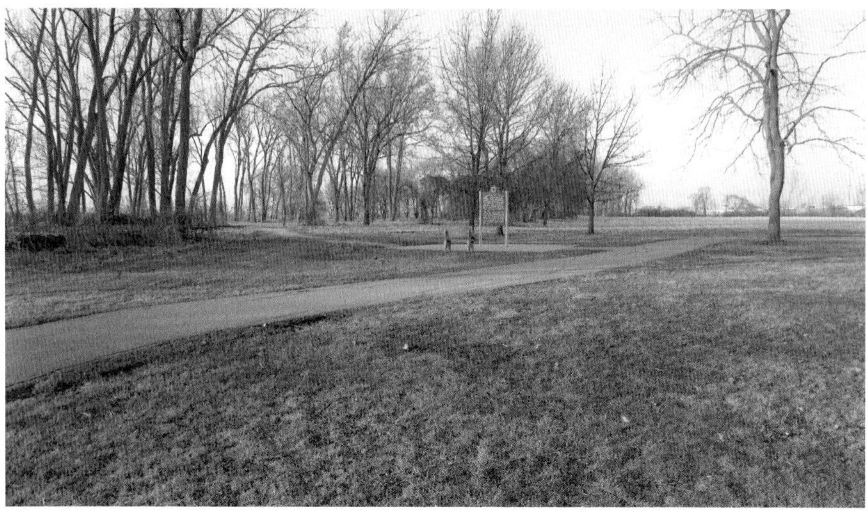

River Raisin National Battlefield Park.

the men had to flee for their lives, leaving behind their families. All citizens were under house arrest and were threatened not to take up arms or lose their lives.

When the settlers heard of a new American army, made up of mostly Kentucky militia, heading their way under General James Winchester, they seized the opportunity to send messengers to their encampment at the Maumee River in Ohio. The messengers brought the army the news of the embattled settlement. Winchester decided to send a detachment of soldiers to rescue it. That was how the first battle on January 18, 1813, got underway.

When the army reached the River Raisin, many of the local militia were waiting to join them in the fight. The first battle of January 18, 1813, was an American victory, liberating the settlement at least temporarily. The citizens were overjoyed and opened up their homes and yards to the soldiers. They fed and clothed them, as well. The officers used the homes for their headquarters, and the yards were turned into encampments for the soldiers. Barns and outbuildings became hospitals and quartermaster supply storage areas. Even the stables were commandeered for the army's horses.

Since the battle was a victory for the Americans, the rest of the army came to the River Raisin to reinforce them for the retaliatory battle they knew would eventually be coming. But everyone was completely taken off guard when only a couple days later, in the predawn hours of January 22, the British and their Native American allies attacked! The battle was an overwhelming victory for the British and Native warriors, with only thirty-

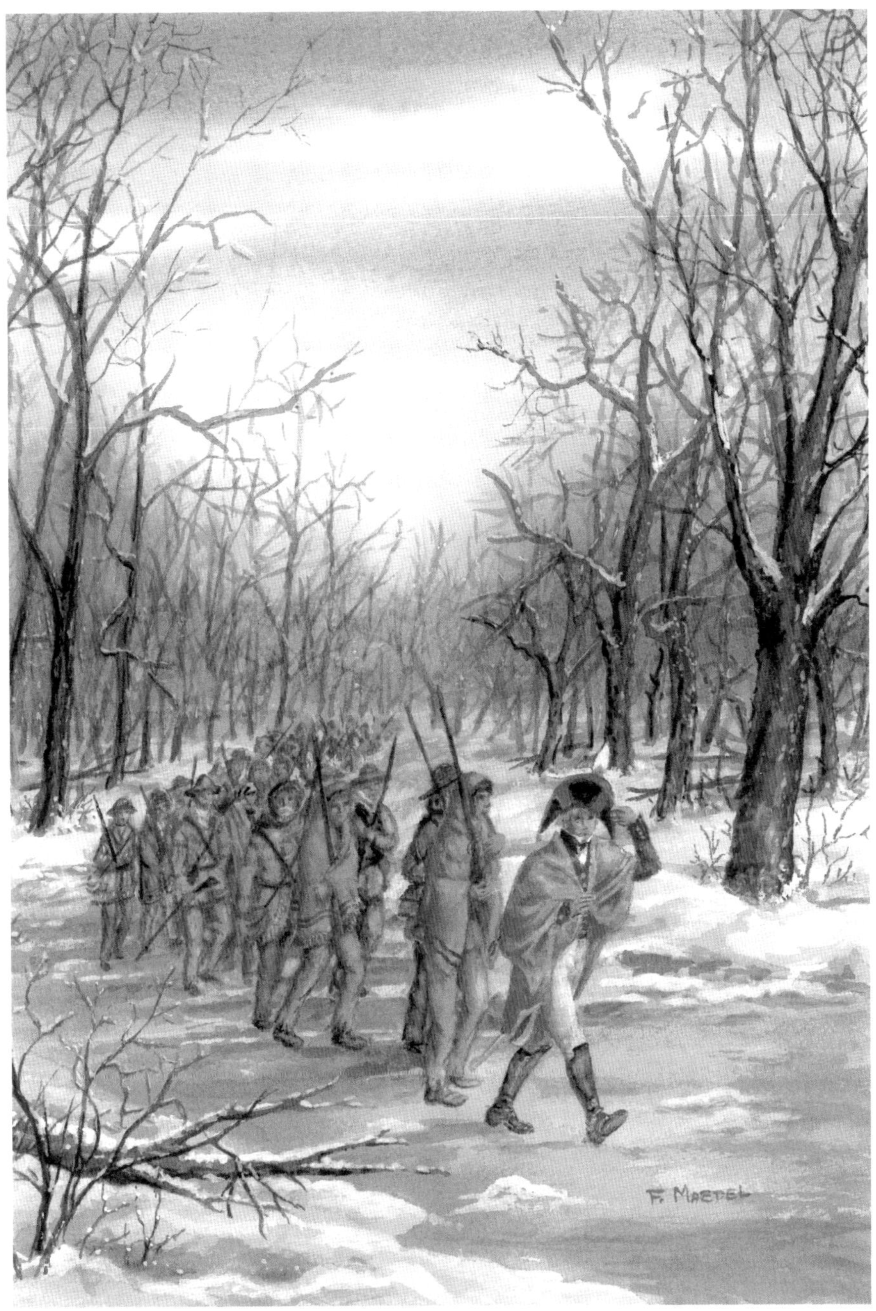

Frenchtown Bound, by Fran Maedel. *River Raisin National Battlefield Park.*

three Americans escaping out of roughly one thousand. It was the worst defeat of the entire war. For the Native American confederation, it was the high tide of the war. On January 23, some of the Native Americans came back and captured or killed the wounded American soldiers convalescing in the homes of the settlers. They also set fire to many of the civilian homes in the settlement. Although some male civilians were killed, no women or children were harmed during the battles.

The River Raisin settlement was a wasteland. So many lost their homes, their belongings, their animals, their crops—everything. Many of the settlers relocated to Ohio and Detroit. Those who stayed faced the rest of the winter starving and with little to no shelter. They were forced to boil hay and eat muskrat to survive. Up to this point, the muskrat was just an animal with valuable fur. The area remained impoverished for five years. Later, the families petitioned the government for reimbursement of all their losses and actually won, yet the money never came.

Jean Baptiste Couture and Medard Couture

Jean Baptiste Couture was a captain in the Second Michigan Territorial Militia Regiment. After the battle on January 18, he opened up his home for the American army officers to set up a headquarters. He sent his wife and young children away to a safer location at Francois Navarre's house. His son Medard stayed with him. On January 21, no fewer than eighteen officers set up in his parlor and enjoyed loaf sugar, whiskey and cider. Three junior officers commandeered the bed. The army set up in his yard, barns and stables.

No one expected a battle the next day except Medard, who heard rumors of the impending attack and tried to warn the army. Unfortunately, no one took him seriously, and they were taken completely off guard the next morning. Jean Baptiste and Medard ended up getting caught up in the melee when the right flank fell within twenty minutes. They were swept away in the retreat across the frozen river and were running through Joseph Robert's farm when, suddenly, they were caught in a crossfire, and Jean Baptiste was struck down. Medard had to keep running, and the last he saw of his father, he was being attacked. Later, when he was finally able to get away, Medard came back to retrieve his father's body. He carried it a half mile back to their property. He quickly hid the body in a stack of straw, hoping to be able to come back that night and bury it.

Medard hoped his mother and family were safe at Navarre's or, better yet, on their way to Detroit. After barely sleeping and being warned to leave while he could, he chose instead to head to Jean Baptiste Jerome's house, where he knew many soldiers were convalescing. He tried to help them as best he could, but the next morning, he found himself in the same danger they were. In the early morning hours of January 23, some Native warriors burst into the house, captured the wounded who could walk and killed those who were seriously wounded.

Medard was taken outside, tied up and stripped, while the warriors set the house on fire. By some stroke of luck, he saw a chief he recognized coming down the road and yelled to him to save him. Ottawa chief Waugon told the warriors that Medard was his son now: "His father lies dead in the yard, and I am now his father."[50] Waugon told the warriors to keep Medard safe. Medard tried to rescue others by offering rewards, and in at least one case, he was successful.[51]

Solo and LeBeau Families

After the American victory on January 18, many of the Native warriors were forced to retreat a few miles to the north. Some Native Americans were passing through Sandy Creek, a settlement of about sixteen farms. Young inhabitant Jean-Baptiste Solo, seeing them, started mocking them, asking if they were running from the "Big Knives" (Kentuckians).

Unfortunately for him, the answer to his question was a bullet that mortally wounded him. He managed to make it to the house of his father-in-law, René LeBeau, yelling that he was shot as he approached the door. René immediately had his two youngest children run upstairs and hide. When he opened the door, Solo fell into his arms and died within minutes.

René had barely laid Solo on the bed when he heard the Native Americans coming up to the house. He ran to the window and peeked out; recognizing some of the Potawatomi, he opened the door. As soon as the door opened, though, the Potawatomi fired, killing René instantly. His adult son, Etienne, immediately ran to the door, pushing it shut on one of the warriors' arms. When the Potawatomi freed his arm, Etienne quickly bolted the door. Surprisingly, the warriors turned around and left the house.

Etienne knew it was time to get out of there. He yelled to his fourteen-year-old sister Genevieve and eight-year-old brother Alexis to come downstairs

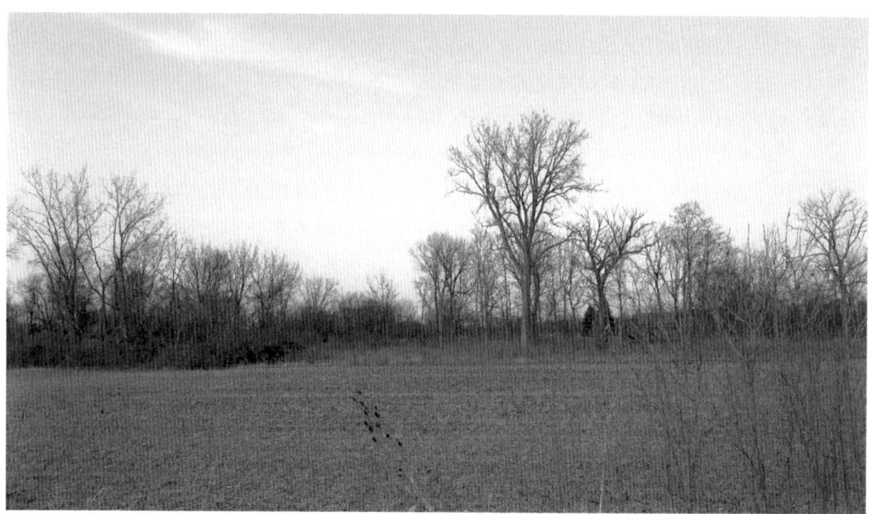

Sandy Creek.

right away. He explained that they would have to escape to the River Raisin. Not even taking the time to grab anything, the children took off running barefoot through the deep snow as fast as they could. They had not gotten far when they heard gunshots being fired at them. In terror, they ran faster through the darkness; the younger ones outran their older brother until they reached the River Raisin at dawn. The citizens could not believe the tale they heard from the lips of the young children, whose feet were raw and bloody from their ordeal.[52]

The Charlan Family

The Charlans were a young couple just starting out. They had set up their first home on the River Raisin and were just beginning to raise a family. Ambrose had joined the local militia and Angelique, only nineteen, had recently given birth to their first baby, Ambrose Junior, just three months before. They had all kinds of hopes and dreams for their future, but on January 22, 1813, their young lives would be changed forever.

When the battle broke out, Ambrose, as well as the other members of the local militia, decided to fight alongside the American army at the River Raisin in order to defend their settlement. Everyone was relieved when the first battle on the eighteenth was won by the Americans and the settlement was secured. Even though it was assumed that the British would counterattack, no one was expecting it so quickly. Ambrose joined in on the fighting on the twenty-second to liberate the settlement once and for all.

Angelique was worried about the fate of her husband. All the River Raisin settlers were technically prisoners since the fall of Detroit. The British said if anyone was caught fighting in the battles, they would be immediately arrested and possibly worse. Ambrose, being a member of the local militia, knew his fate was tenuous if he was caught. Angelique busied herself taking care of the baby and doing housework to keep her mind off the reality of the situation.

Angelique could hear gunfire all around but was startled when she suddenly spotted a man with blood-soaked bandages limping toward her door. On closer inspection however, she discovered it was not her husband. She knew if she was spotted harboring a soldier, it could mean the end for her, just as Ambrose's joining the fighting could mean the end for him. She pushed her fears aside and opened the door to the pitiful man. As he started to enter, he fell down, exclaiming, "The army has been destroyed, all the soldiers are being killed and scalped. There are dead men all over the trail."[53] Her thoughts immediately turned toward Ambrose, but she had no time to think as she spotted Native warriors coming up to her house. She told the soldier to quickly hide in the unused pickling barrel in the corner of the room. The soldier protested, saying he would make a run for it in order not to endanger her and the baby. But thinking about what Ambrose would want her to do, she said to him, "Don't be foolish, our Indian neighbors would never harm a helpless white woman and her children."[54] She then helped him conceal himself in the barrel.

With no time to spare, the warriors burst into the door, demanding "fire water." She wondered if they had seen the soldier coming to her house or if they were actually there for whiskey. She answered them, "No, there's no whiskey in the house."[55] Quick on her feet, though, she offered them some bread she had just made earlier. They accepted it and left. After waiting a little while, she told the soldier it was safe to come out. She couldn't believe her luck but decided it wasn't safe for him to leave until dark; in the meantime, she would fix his bandages.

Just as they thought they were in the clear, they heard scuffling outside and someone coming to the door. Angelique's heart pounded until she could see the person coming in was actually Ambrose. She told him of all that had happened, and he explained how he was captured by the Native Americans and luckily released on parole and told to go to Detroit.

The couple had forged a plan earlier that if the battle was lost, they would load up their sleigh and escape to Detroit. In their compassion for the soldier, however, they decided he should take their horse and flee. At nightfall, he headed off south to Fort Meigs. The next morning, with no horse to pull the sleigh, they grabbed what little they could carry and headed off to Detroit on foot, following the frozen Lake Erie. Barely into their forty-mile journey, they could see their house burning in the distance. Even though they had lost everything, they were grateful they had each other. When they reached Detroit, they searched for friends and families displaced by the battle. Unfortunately for baby Ambrose, however, the exposure to the cold was too much for him, and within eight months, he succumbed to it.[56]

Rachel Sly Knaggs

Rachel Knaggs was eighty years old when the Battles of the River Raisin broke out. She lived alone and ran a trading post. It is not entirely clear what happened to her husband. On January 22, 1813, while the battle was raging, a Kentucky soldier running away from his captors came upon her house. Even though she put herself in danger, she did not hesitate when she heard him rapping on the door. She pulled him inside and hid him in her empty sixty-three-gallon wooden hogshead barrel.

No sooner had she gotten him hidden than she heard a commotion outside, and suddenly, a group of Native Americans burst into her home and started ransacking the place. They had seen the soldier run toward her house, and they were sure he was in there. Rachel cringed and tried to hide her emotion at being found out. She couldn't help thinking about what they might do to her if they found him.

She didn't have long to fear; in the ransacking, they tipped over the barrel, and the Kentuckian came rolling out. They seized him and her belongings, including her warm coat. Then they proceeded to grab her, telling her they were going to take her to British colonel Proctor.

Proctor took no pity on the old woman, accusing her of aiding the Americans; he told her to leave town immediately and go to Detroit. Even though she only had the clothes on her back and was freezing, she managed to root around until she found a sled. She quickly got in and headed to her daughter's house. Her daughter Elizabeth and her grandchildren were relieved to see her. They quickly headed to Detroit in the cold, icy rain.

When the old woman got there, she was reunited with relatives and told them of her ordeal. When they asked her how she made it all the way there in the harsh weather, she said, "My spunk kept me warm!"[57]

Elizabeth Knaggs Anderson

Rachel's daughter, Elizabeth, was a lot like her mother, with a lot of spunk of her own. She was the wife of the colonel of the Second Michigan Regiment, John Anderson. Together, they ran a trading post, which also served as their home. Elizabeth was left alone in the summer of 1812, after General Hull surrendered Detroit. John became a wanted man with a price on his head and had to flee to Ohio.

One day, while Elizabeth was home alone, she saw a band of Native men heading her way. Knowing they were probably looking for whiskey—and how they would behave if they got it—she ran to the cellar with John's axe and broke up the kegs of whiskey they had stowed there. Then, she grabbed her children, putting the youngest one in her lap, and sat on top of a chest that contained all the family's gold. The gold amounted to around $800.

Elizabeth could hear the band rooting around in the house, and it wasn't long before they made their way to the cellar. Suddenly, the door burst open, and they ran in yelling with their tomahawks raised. Elizabeth acted calm, although she was terrified. One man motioned for her to get off the trunk or he would scalp her. She refused to budge, even though he threatened her more. She recognized some of them; they had come into the trading post before. The leader, getting tired of her stubbornness, raised the tomahawk over her head, but she still refused, saying, "No" in Potawatomi. He was shocked at her boldness and replied, "Stand up, or I will scalp you!"[58] But something from deep inside welled up in her, and she tugged open her dress at the neck and said, "If you are such a brave Indian, tomahawk me now!"[59]

The leader was aghast at her bravery and, respecting such a quality, grabbed ahold of her arm and said, "You brave woman, no kill you."[60] He motioned to his companions, and they turned to the door and left. Elizabeth breathed a sigh of relief, but she knew it was definitely time to get out of town.

ELIZABETH ANN GODFROY

Elizabeth Godfroy's story is very similar to the others. During the battle of the twenty-second, she was home alone and did not know the fate of her husband. She was startled by an old métis (half French, half Native) interpreter running toward her house in a panic, all the while watching behind his back. He came to the door and told her that the Native Americans were killing prisoners in her woods and also taking them to her barn. They threatened to burn all the buildings down, and he wanted to warn her. Before she could even react to what he said, he was running off, just as a group of Native men walked up with some prisoners. Elizabeth badly wanted to help them but knew better. She acted preoccupied with her chores and paid little attention to them. Her actions actually angered the men, though, and one threw a tomahawk toward her.

The men proceeded to search the house and imbibe the little whiskey they discovered in the cellar. Since Elizabeth was trapped and not sure just what they would do to her, she quickly thought of an idea. She would give them gifts to pacify them. Her idea worked, and they settled in with their prisoners for the night. All but one, that is; they took him to the yard and started setting up a pyre with the intent to burn him. Just then, Elizabeth noticed the old métis back in the yard. She yelled to him to ascertain if there was something she could do to save the soldier. With the métis's help, it was agreed on that she could adopt the soldier for "ten dollars, a fine black horse, two bundles of dry goods, and 5 gallons of whiskey."[61]

Once she gained the soldier's freedom, Elizabeth hid in the shadows until the men were not paying her any more attention. She quickly and quietly gathered her family, and they slipped out and made their escape. Two days later, they arrived safely in Detroit.[62]

FRANCOIS LASSELLE

On January 18, 1813, Francois Lasselle found the backyard of his home occupied by some Native Americans. He was walking on thin ice during the battles, already being a prisoner and having been told to cooperate. But on January 23, the injured Americans (Kentucky militia) were desperate to escape and find a place to hide. American general Winchester's secretary, Captain Woolfolk, was one of them. He had been captured by the Native

Americans; they had him on a horse, and upon arriving at Lasselle's house, he yelled that "he would give a thousand dollars to anyone that would ransom him." The warriors demanded to know if Lasselle was hiding any American soldiers in his home. He replied from the second-story window that he was not hiding anyone; only women and children were with him. The warriors threatened him that he'd better not hide anyone or let anyone in; otherwise, they would burn the house down with everyone in it.

Francois was telling the truth; he had only Polly Knaggs and her son George, who was only six years old, hidden inside. But he knew that he was taking his life into his own hands, because Polly was the wife of the famous Native American fighter James Knaggs. James was wanted by the British and the Natives, with a bounty on his head. Francois was scared of what the Natives might do if they discovered James Knaggs's family inside. So, he quickly hid George in the fireplace chimney.

Lasselle was in quite the conundrum with Woolfolk and had to think quickly on his feet. Francois yelled back that he was powerless do to anything, but his brother, Jocko Lasselle, could probably help Woolfolk, so they should continue to his place. Luckily for Francois and the Knaggs family, they were not discovered.[63]

Chapter 6
Custer's Connection

A summer day in July found a large group of men strolling the fields in the eastern end of Monroe. But this was no ordinary summer stroll. Some walked with canes; others creaked along, ranging in age from 78 to 102 years, but one, much younger than the others, walked at a brisk pace. He listened to them as they relived those days so long ago, recalling the horror that befell them while others rose up as heroes, making the ultimate sacrifice. The younger man found that he understood them in a way he never could before. At ten years old, when he moved from New Rumley, Ohio, to Monroe to go to Stebbins Boys Academy, he lived with his half-sister Lydia Ann Reed. He was fascinated listening to the veterans tell their stories, but as a young man, he could not comprehend what all those things meant. Now, however, George Armstrong Custer understood them like few others could, being a soldier himself. As they walked through the barren fields on that June day in 1871, his mind was in a perfect chorus with theirs.

Now, his military prowess and reputation were well established in his hometown of Monroe. Perhaps that is why he was invited to be with the veterans on this special day. They had a mutual respect and admiration for each other. No doubt, eighty-eight-year-old veteran Joseph Guyor must have felt that way when he invited George and his father, Emanuel, as his guests of honor for the day. Surprisingly, no reunion or gathering had ever been thought of before, so on June 1, 1871, Joseph Guyor had the following invitation published in the *Monroe Commercial* newspaper: "The Soldiers of 1812 residing in this county are respectfully invited to a free dance and reunion, at my house on House Island (also known as Guyors Island)...on Thursday June 15th."[64]

Roughly one hundred veterans attended, and General Custer, "rusticating in the Floral City" for several weeks, was invited to be the host.[65] The outdoor banquet was enjoyed by all and gave the veterans an opportunity to reminisce about their past deeds of valor. A number of men recounted the horrors of the battles. After dinner, addresses were made by the mayor and many prominent Monroe citizens, "but it remained for General Custer to arouse the most enthusiasm as he rose to greet the men of the past generations, who welcomed him with warmest demonstrations of respect & admiration."[66] The general said "he did not come prepared or expecting to address the assemblage, but could not forbear expressing his pleasure at being permitted to greet these old veterans and take them by the hand."[67] Custer continued his speech by quoting Abraham Lincoln's Gettysburg Address. As Custer echoed these now-famous words, he might have had in mind one of the finest days of his military career, when he defeated Jeb Stuart's cavalry on July 3, 1863, at the Battle of Gettysburg. The general "roused the veterans" so much that it was decided that day to have an official reunion the following year.[68]

After the celebration, the veterans gathered for a picture, in which they also included George and his father, Emanuel Custer.

At the beginning of May 1872, a formal meeting was held at city hall to discuss plans for the next reunion. It was decided that the date would be

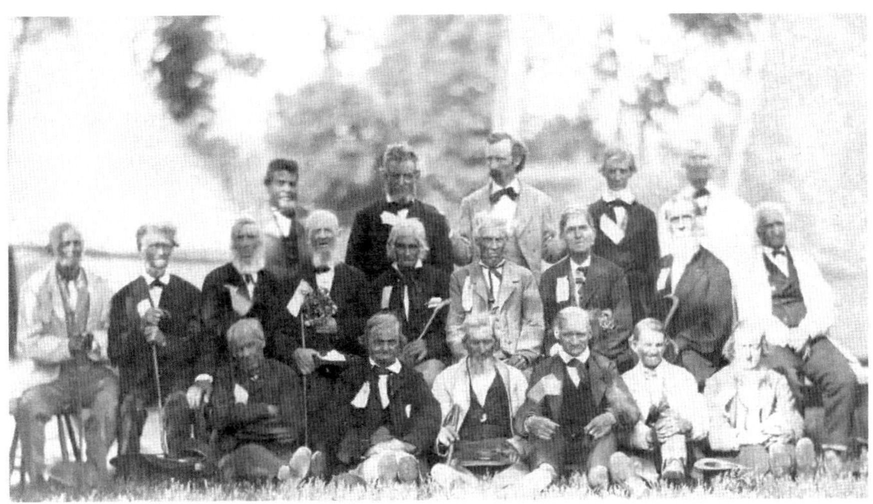

River Raisin War of 1812 veterans' reunion. *River Raisin National Battlefield Park.*

July 4: "It is designed to make the day a memorable one in the history of Monroe." Veteran survivors of the Battles of the River Raisin as well as the War of 1812, plus pioneers of the River Raisin valley, military companies, state officials and Kentucky and Ohio officials were all expected to be invited. "It will be such a celebration as has never been witnessed in the City of Monroe."[69]

In the telegram, Custer said he would be seeing General Leslie Combs and that he would "secure that venerable hero, and a large delegation from Kentucky" to come.[70] Custer and "the Committee of Invitations had extended invitations to nearly every prominent public man in the country."[71]

The reunion proved to be a huge success with some fifteen to twenty thousand people in attendance. Approximately 150 veterans were able to make it.[72] General Custer arrived from the South by train the evening of July 3 with General Combs and the veterans from Kentucky and Ohio. They were greeted by the Monroe Band and many other groups and organizations.[73] A large procession commenced downtown around eleven in the morning and passed the Monroe Street Cemetery (today Memorial Place), which was the burial ground of the Kentuckians who gave their lives in the battles. Interestingly enough, "a dummy monument made of cloth was erected" at the burial site.[74] It was announced that day that a real monument would eventually be constructed to take its place. (It would take another thirty years, however, and unfortunately, Custer would not be alive to join in the festivities, in which he undoubtedly would have been heavily involved.)

In "Noble Grove," a grandstand was made out of the "beams, planks and boards taken from the house of Colonel Francis Navarre,"[75] which, during the battles, General Winchester used as his headquarters. A large number of distinguished dignitaries made eloquent speeches, with many speaking of the unforgotten horrors and sacrifices made over fifty-nine years before. General Custer was the master of ceremonies and did the roll call of the veterans, calling out their names and ages. As he pronounced each one, they stood up to applause. An extravagant banquet followed, with a number of toasts and responses. The evening drew to a close with a grand fireworks display—or at least it was supposed to be, "but owing to an untoward accident the most and the best of them were destroyed. In sending off a revolving rocket, it discharged directly into the box containing the best pieces and these were thereby prematurely discharged and destroyed."[76]

Monroe historian John Bulkley attributes part of the success of the reunion to Custer, in cooperation with Combs, who "were most active in their efforts to secure the large delegation from Kentucky….The endless detail and

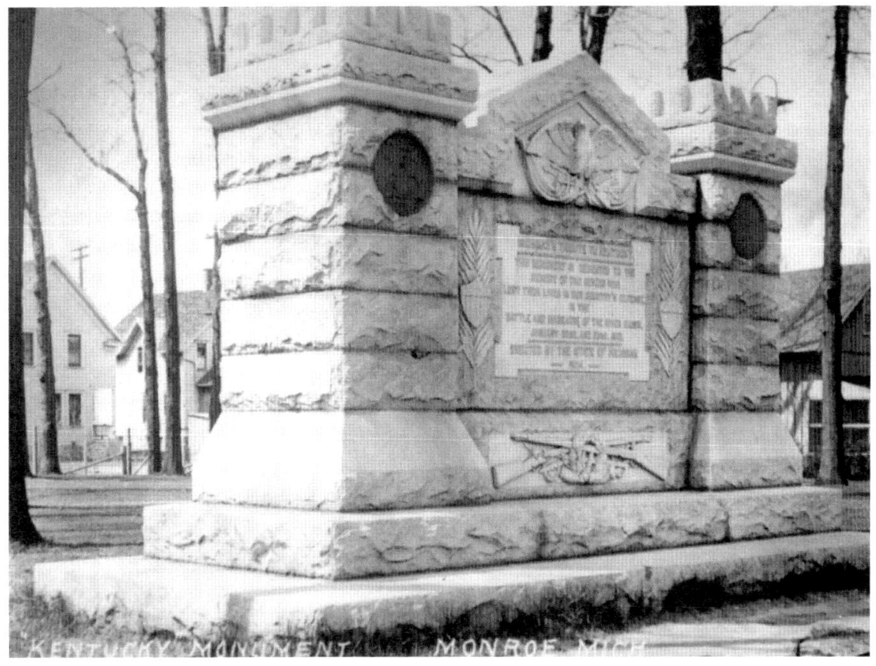

Kentucky Soldiers Memorial Monument. *Monroe County Library System.*

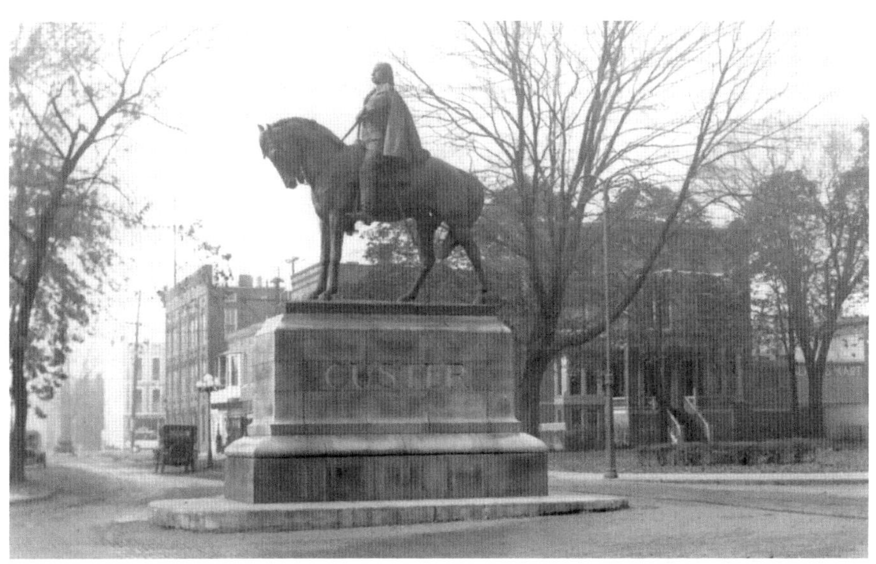

Custer monument on Washington Street. *Monroe County Library System.*

hard work of such an undertaking cannot be realized by anyone who has not had the actual experience. But it was a labor of patriotism successfully accomplished."[77] Obviously, Custer played a prominent role in the reunions of 1871 and 1872. No doubt he would have played just as large a role in future events, but ironically, only four years after the reunion, Custer found himself in much the same situation as those old River Raisin veterans had.

Instead of the dead of winter, it was late June 1876 when Custer and his Seventh Cavalry also found themselves in a wide-open field in Montana, staring right into the faces of the warriors bearing down upon them from all sides. Also, with no protection, Custer ordered most of the horses to be sacrificed to provide at least some kind of primitive barrier. Just as the old veterans of the River Raisin tried to make a last stand and hold on until reinforcements could arrive, Custer and his men desperately tried to fend off wave after wave of the enemy pouring in upon them. A few soldiers fled to the Little Big Horn River, just as some of the old River Raisin vets scrambled across the frozen Raisin River, just to be ambushed later. Custer's men never even made it to the river. Custer joined the soldiers of the Battles of the River Raisin, who gave the ultimate sacrifice for their country—their lives. Monroe would honor its hometown hero, just as it did the soldiers who fell at the River Raisin, with a grand monument, which just happens to be located a mile down the same road that Custer once walked with the old veterans in 1871–72.

Custer in Monroe

Custer was a man about town in Monroe. Wherever he went, he was known for his Civil War exploits. It is no surprise that some of the local residents recounted stories about Custer to Marion Childs when she did interviews in the mid-1900s.

W.C. Sterling commented to Marion Childs that Custer was "a wild sort of chap—nice, though—many girls weren't allowed by their parents to go out with him, because of his wild reputation."[78]

The Nims family knew Custer very well. Katherine Nims told Marion Childs that her grandfather remembered how fond Custer was of croquet. At that time, it was so popular that a smaller tabletop version was created to play inside. Custer came to the house often to play it on their folding card table in the parlor. Katherine talked about the charisma of Custer and said,

"He was the last of the cavaliers," and his heroic death just further enriched his reputation with his peers.[79]

Custer's friend John Bulkley enjoyed retelling the story of Custer sneaking novels into class at Alfred Stebbins Young Man's Academy when he was fourteen years old. He was very clever at not getting caught; he sneakily hid the storybooks behind his textbook. The novels were usually military. Another classmate, Edward Merril, told Childs how the room he and Custer shared at the academy became an after-hours hangout for the boys after the lights went out.[80]

In 1862, while on leave from the army, back in Monroe, Custer met up with some old friends at a bar and indulged too much in spirits. He was so under the influence he could barely walk down the road, but unfortunately for him, when he passed by Judge Bacon's residence, his future wife, Elizabeth (Libbie), was watching him out the window. She later referred to the incident as "that awful day."[81] When Custer's half-sister, whom he was staying with, got ahold of him, she led him into the bedroom, toting a Bible. From that day, on he vowed to never drink again and kept that promise.[82]

Another resident was Charles Verhoeven, who related stories about his father, Bernard, and Custer to Marion Childs in 1958. Charles said his

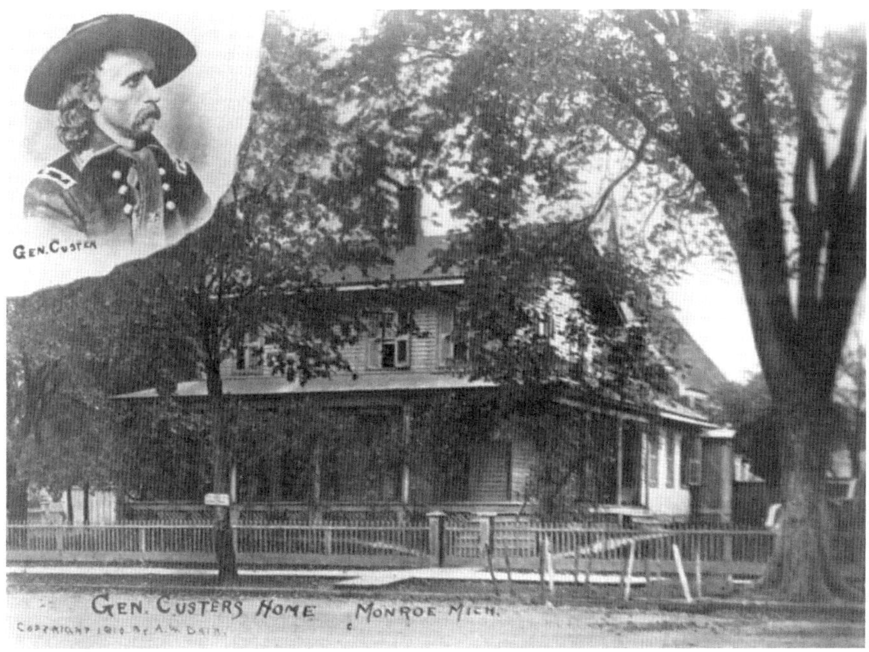

General Custer's home, 1910. *Monroe County Library System.*

family admired Custer, although he admitted that after George graduated West Point, he got a reputation for being wild. But according to Charles, that was due to his outspokenness more than anything. Bernard Verhoeven owned a barbershop on the southeast corner of Monroe and Front Streets. The general was a frequent customer and, in fact, would not let anyone else cut his hair unless he had no choice. He would let it go wild for a few weeks if necessary until he could get home and have it cut. According to Charles, "He wore it longer than anyone else."[83]

The barbershop was not just a place to get your hair cut back then but was also the hangout spot, if you will. Custer tended to hang out there for several hours in the back along with his nephew Autie Reed. The last time both of them were in there was about ten days before they went to the Little Bighorn. Charles said Custer talked about his plans and was excited for the opportunity to prove himself once again to his superior officers after his demotion.

Bernard said he asked Autie, "What are you going to do while your uncle is out fighting the Indians?" Autie replied, "Oh, I'm going along to see the fun."[84] Unfortunately, Custer and Autie would never return to the barbershop again, having perished at the Battle of the Little Bighorn. Custer is buried at West Point, as is his wife, Elizabeth. Autie is in the Custer cemetery plot at Woodland Cemetery in Monroe.

Chapter 7

Monroe's Mysterious Cannon

Monroe, like many hometowns, proudly displays the monuments that are an important part of the history of the city. One such monument sits in the town square, Loranger Square, directly in front of the courthouse. It is iron, weighs almost 1,300 pounds and is six feet long and narrow. It sits atop a sandstone base that has the following words carved on it:

RELIC
OF THE BATTLE OF THE RIVER RAISIN
JANUARY 22d, 1813
PRESENTED TO THE CITY
BY THE COMMITTEE OF ARRANGEMENTS
FOR THE CENTENNIAL CELEBRATION
JULY 4, 1884

This relic is listed as a cannon from the battle. Yet, little is known about this object, and apparently, through the century, it was just accepted at face value. At the bicentennial of the founding of Monroe in 2017, however, this all changed. Experts decided to delve further into the cannon's history and found that everything hitherto believed about the cannon came into question. First and foremost, it became unclear if the cannon was actually a relic of the Battles of the River Raisin at all. Furthermore, there is a possibility that this is no ordinary cannon but has quite the malevolent past.

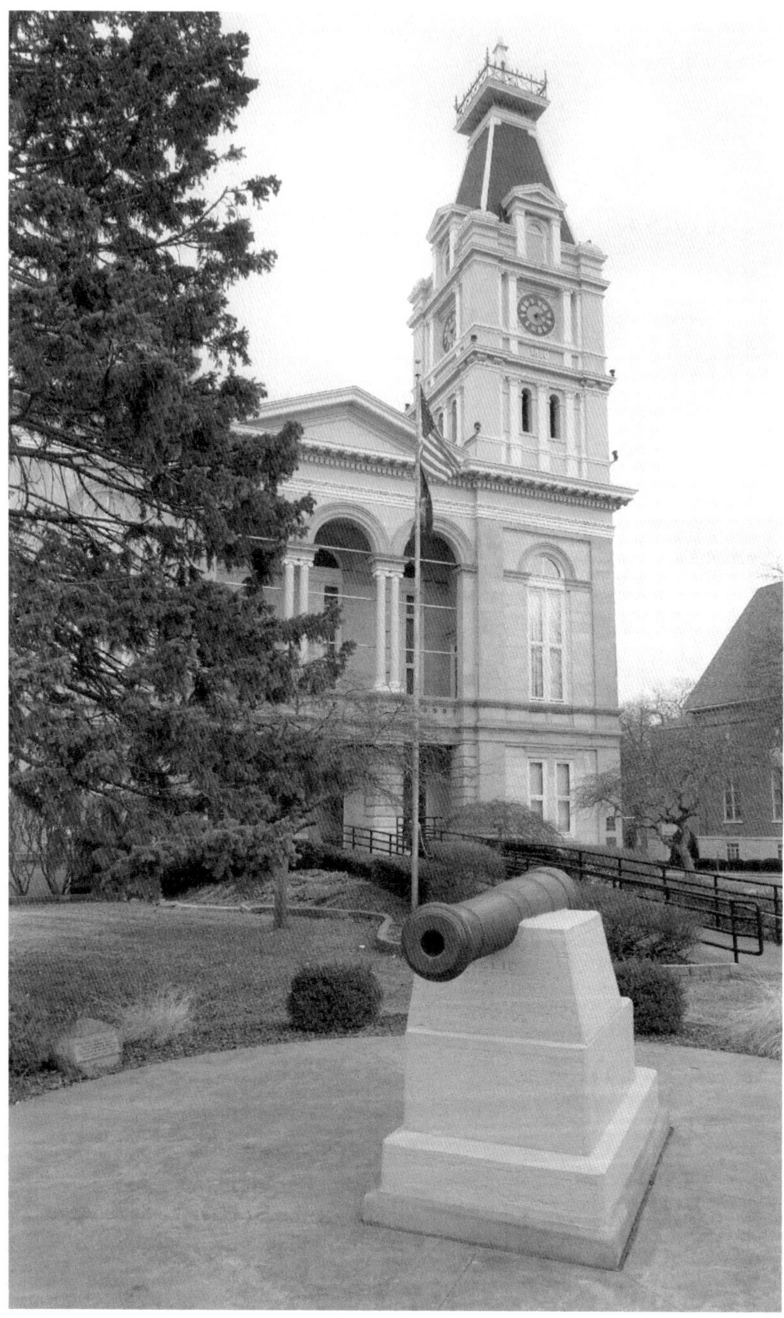

Cannon monument in front of courthouse.

In 1884, on the centennial or one hundredth anniversary of the founding of the settlement by Francois Navarre, the local newspaper printed numerous articles about the cannon. One, on July 31, said the following:

> *The Fourth of July committee has purchased the old British cannon which was presented to the old Cass guards by Gen. Jos. R. Smith about 1846. The old gun has a history, but just what it is previous to its arrival in Monroe from the state arsenal we cannot say. During its active career in Monroe it killed its man and seriously injured several others. It became the property of the Monroe foundry and for a number of years has done duty as a weight. It weighs 1,290 pounds and cost the committee $36. It will be presented to the city and mounted upon a stone foundation upon the public square, probably the southwest corner of the northeast square.*[85]

The following day, more details were given about the cannon and also about its history, even though the day before, the newspaper said it could not say what the cannon's history was prior to its arrival at the arsenal:

> *There is in existence an old cannon, a relic of the war of 1812 and of the battle of the Raisin, which for ten or twelve years past has been owned by the Monroe Foundry. It was decided by the committee to purchase this cannon, properly mount it on stone, and place it on the public square, it being a relic worthy of preservation.*
>
> *The cannon is six feet long, 13 inches in diameter at the butt and 10 inches at the muzzle, weight 1200 lbs, and bears the British crown. It is one of the field pieces used by the British in the war of 1812, and at the battle of the Raisin, was taken from them either during or at the close of the war and was in the territorial—subsequently State—arsenal. About 1846, when several military companies were in existence in Monroe, Fred Waldorf being captain of the Cass Guards, Gen. Joseph R. Smith obtained this cannon from the State arsenal and presented it to the Cass Guards. After they disbanded it was held by the city and was used on all public occasions when "artificial thunder" was deemed necessary. Its breech became badly honeycombed with age and use, and after killing and maiming several men, it was deemed best to get rid of it, and it was therefore sold to the foundry for old iron....It has been painted up and put in good shape.*[86]

A week later, on August 8, the newspaper covered the address given to the city council by Dr. A.I. Sawyer in which more details of the cannon's history were revealed and explained "perhaps" why the cannon was given to the foundry by the city:

> *This old relic was formerly the property of the city, but a former council, for reasons never made very clear, sold it to one of our city foundrymen for old iron. The council at that time may have been actuated by an economical impulse and a desire to replenish the city treasury to that amount, or perhaps they were led to this act by a feeling of indignation or extreme caution, while reflecting over the mischief it had done, and concluded to put a stop to its career in that line by having it melted up and "turned onto plough-shares and pruning hooks"—emblems of peace.*[87]

Let us examine what mischievous acts the cannon was responsible for. It did actually kill a man in 1852. An obituary for Joseph Steiner (1818–1852), son of Johannes and Franziska Steiner, said he was "killed in a freak accident at a celebration in Monroe, a cannon was to be fired by him (he knew how) the cannon backfired and killed him almost instantly. He was the first adult to be buried from St. Michael's."[88]

Another account said Steiner died on October 20, 1851, and was thirty-four years old. He fired the cannon in the public park, and its breech opened and backfired, killing him.[89]

Another victim of that same incident was apparently Christian F. Beck, although he was not killed but maimed. His obituary says he was born August 20, 1820, in Germany and died June 3, 1887, in Monroe.

> *He worked at his trade, blacksmithing, until 1852, when through an accident he lost the thumb of his right hand. This calls up a very sad incident in the history of Monroe. While ratifying the nomination of Franklin Pierce for the presidency* [which was 1852], *the old cannon which stands upon the public square in front of the courthouse was prematurely discharged, killing Joseph Steiner and maiming Mr. Beck. The accident took place at the intersection of Front and First streets near the site of Hurd & Son's elevator.*[90]

Now, let us shift gears and look more into the history, or the supposed history, of this artillery piece. Monroe Historian John McClelland Bulkley, wrote the following "Legend of the Old Cannon":

> *The accurate history of the ancient piece of British ordnance, which stands in the public square in Monroe, cannot be written for the reason*

that none now living can remember the story of its capture or of any person who at any time knew the circumstances of its presence here. The most familiar legend in regard to the old cannon which has become the accepted version of a many times told tale, relates to one of the incidents of the attacks by British and Indians upon the settlement of Frenchtown and the subsequent sanguinary battle between them and the force of Kentucky troops under Winchester which met such a deplorable fate. The old cannon is an iron six-pounder, bearing the British coat-of-arms and the usual marks of the founder who cast the piece. When it was first seen here by any living resident it was mounted on a heavy wooden gun-carriage minus the caisson and front wheels. It is said to have been found at the bottom of the River Raisin, near the site of the battle, which was on the north side of the river, now partly covered by the plant of the River Raisin Paper Company, the theory being that in crossing the ice with their artillery, consisting of six cannon, six-pounders, one of them broke through the ice into the river, which was several feet deep. It was left there, owing to the precipitate haste of the British in getting away from the scene who feared an immediate arrival of the forces of General Harrison from the south which were reported on the march. The old cannon remained in the river undiscovered for many years after the battle. It was finally resurrected and put into condition for use, and its career in the "piping times of peace" when its services were in demand for municipal and political demonstrations, pole raisings, Fourth of July celebrations and the like, constitutes its known history in connection with Monroe.

Another statement upon the same subject, based upon the recollections of an old settler, has it that this cannon one of the number composing the small battery of the invaders, stationed upon the north side of the river when in action, was disabled, or its gunners so repeatedly picked off by the riflemen of the Kentuckians that it was abandoned, and when the troops and Indians left the scene of the surrender by Winchester this cannon was left behind and fell into the hands of the Americans, together with the bodies of five artillerists who successively served the gun and met the common fate. It was put into one of the large barns near the river and lay there neglected for a long time, when it was finally brought out and placed in the hands of the village authorities, eventually becoming city property. So little historic interest did this old relic possess in the minds of one of the mayors and so little sentiment possessed his spirit that a few years ago it was sold to a foundry to be melted up as old iron, to be afterwards redeemed and recovered by a few more patriotic citizens and, with its granite pedestal, placed in its

> *present resting place. The inscription upon this stone base tells this part of the story in the following words: "Relic of the Battle of the River Raisin, January 18–22, 1813.*[91]

In 1935, Margareth Beck, wife of Charles W. Beck (son of C.F. Beck, who was maimed by the cannon), remembered that at the War of 1812 veterans' reunion on July 4, 1872,

> *In front of the speaker's platform was placed an old spiked ship's cannon that had been loaned by the J. and D. McLaren Foundry. It had been brought to the Foundry by a Frenchman who lived south of the city along the lake and he claimed that it had been washed ashore on part of the wreckage of a ship after Perry's Victory. This cannon was returned to the Foundry and some years later in 1884 was mounted and placed in the Court House Square where it stands today.*[92]

In May 1942, the *Observer* interviewed a Mrs. Frederick Kolb, who said that Bulkley's account of the cannon is simply a legend. The newspaper states that she should know, since her father was John McLaren, owner of the foundry and caretaker of the cannon. Kolb, the former Kate McLaren, stated that one day, a citizen, who lived south of town by the lake, brought in a load of scrap, and the load contained an old, rusty cannon. When her father asked about the cannon, he was told that it was dug up by the lakefront some years previously. Her father put it in the moulding room and left it there for years. As a little girl, Kolb would sit on top of it and remembered it well.

In 1872, for the veterans' reunion, Kolb saw it being carried out by two of the foundry's apprentices, Mr. James Grant and Mr. Diffenbaugh. Foundry machinist Mr. Wagner presented it to Mayor Sawyer, and everyone assumed it was a relic from the Battle of the River Raisin—or why would it be there? Kolb remembers that neither her father nor the foundrymen set the record straight on its origins.

The *Observer* article continues:

> *Without much question, the cannon came from some British man-o'-war, doubtless one of the ships that fought Admiral Perry in the battle of Put-in-Bay* [Battle of Lake Erie], *September 13, 1813. It came from originally from somewhere along the shore of Lake Erie, it is a naval weapon, not a piece of land artillery, and it has the British coat of arms*

> *still visible upon its barrel. It is a six-pounder of the type used in the War of 1812. But the inscription on the stone mounting…is slightly inaccurate; it no doubt was fired against the Americans in that war, but not in that battle* [Battles of the River Raisin].[93]

Kolb stated that the cannon was also spiked before it was brought out for public events; therefore, it could not be fired. She said,

> *There was, however, another ancient cannon…which was used on celebrations, and which had an interesting history, though its origin is lost in the dim past. This was a land cannon, mounted on a carriage, and it was used in the Fourth of July celebrations at Noble's Grove for years.… It got so old that people finally became concerned lest it disintegrate, and it was moved up the river, along West Front Street…where it eventually came to a tragic end. One day while it was being loaded and fired in rapid succession it became overheated, and while* [Joseph] *Steiner was ramming home a load of gunpowder it exploded prematurely, fatally injuring him.*[94]

Considering all these histories, we can see that there are many discrepancies. Primarily, it appears the differences focus on where the cannon came from originally. Most concur that it is a British War of 1812 cannon, but that's about it. Let us look at these conclusions again briefly.

Two accounts focus on the cannon being a relic from the Battles of the River Raisin. One says it was abandoned by the British on the battlefield, after the battles, when they quickly left in anticipation of American reinforcements. From there, it was stored in a barn, according to an old settler, until it was finally turned over to the city. Later, it was sold to the local foundry and eventually rescued and mounted in the courthouse square. A second, somewhat similar, account states that the cannon was found at the bottom of the north side of the River Raisin, left there by the British when crossing the ice during or after the battles. Later, after it was found, it was mounted to a heavy wooden gun carriage without a caisson or front wheels and used by the city for ceremonies.

Two other accounts focus on the cannon as being from the Battle of Lake Erie instead. The first says it was a ship's cannon from the Battle of Lake Erie found along the lake. The second contends that it was an old spiked naval cannon found by a Frenchman south of the city along the lake when it washed ashore as part of the wreckage of a ship from the Battle of Lake Erie. The Frenchman brought the old, rusty cannon to the local foundry.

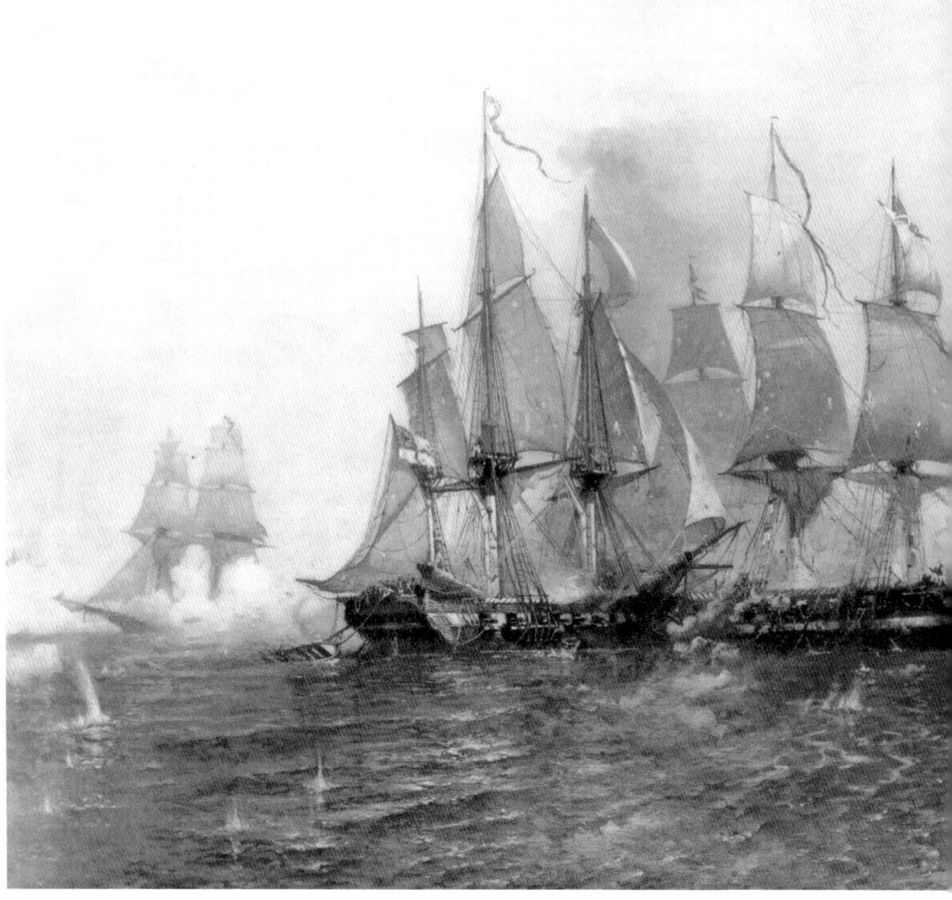

Battle of Lake Erie. *Library of Congress.*

Note that this account is from Margareth Beck (C.F. Beck, who was maimed by a cannon, was her father-in-law). In this interview she mentions nothing at all about the cannon being the one that injured her father-in-law; instead, it seems she is speaking of an entirely different cannon.

Now, let us look at the account of the cannon being from the state arsenal. The claim is that it is from the Battles of the River Raisin, taken during or after the battle, but somehow ended up in the state arsenal and was purchased from there in 1846 for the Cass Guards, then given to the City of Monroe and eventually turned over to the local foundry.

The last account states that there are two different cannons entirely, one being a British spiked naval cannon from the Battle of Lake Erie, dug up

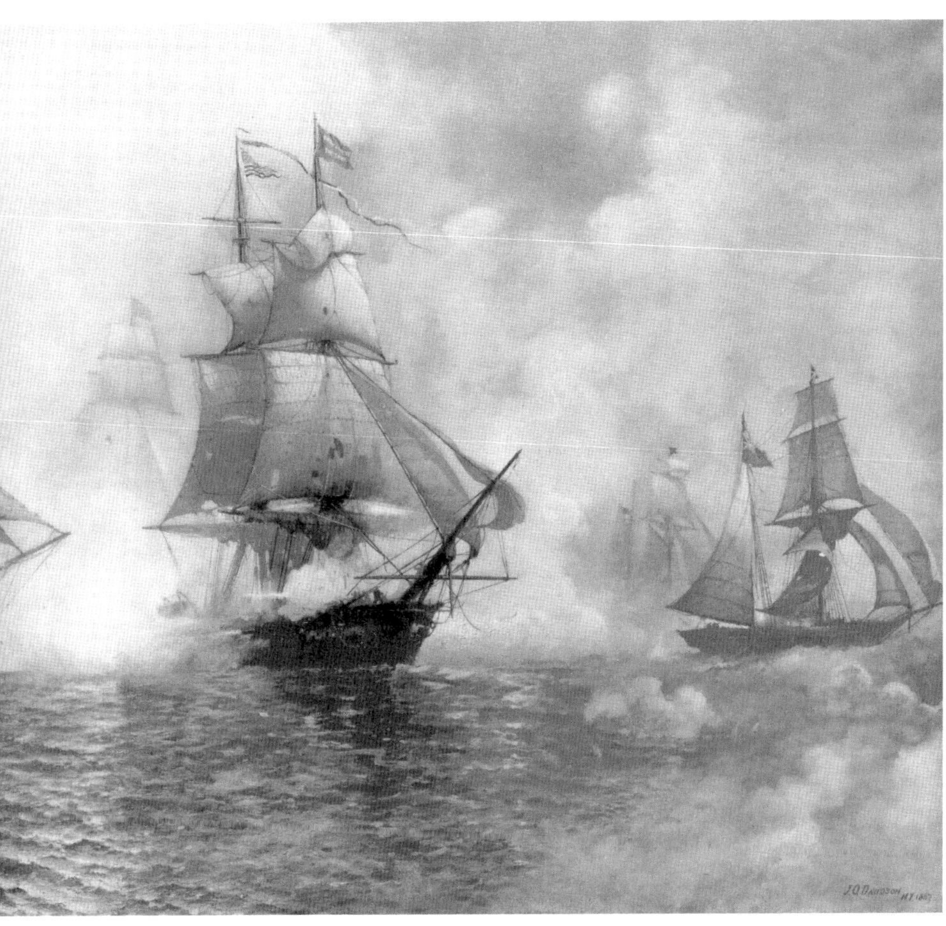

along the lakefront by a settler south of town who brought it in to the local foundry in a scrap heap. That is the cannon mounted in the courthouse square. The other is an ancient land cannon, mounted on a carriage, that was used in celebrations. It disintegrated so much that it was moved up the river to west Front Street and ended up overheating and killing Joseph Steiner. According to Kolb, the cannon also came to a tragic end, although she does not relate how. Interestingly enough, the obituary for Christian F. Beck also stated that "the accident took place at the intersection of Front and First streets near the site of Hurd & Son's elevator."[95]

In a nutshell, the question we have to ask ourselves is: Was this the same cannon all along, or are we dealing with two different cannons?

First, let us look at our Monroe cannon mounted in the courthouse square. Starting in 2012, current local historical society president Bill Saul reached

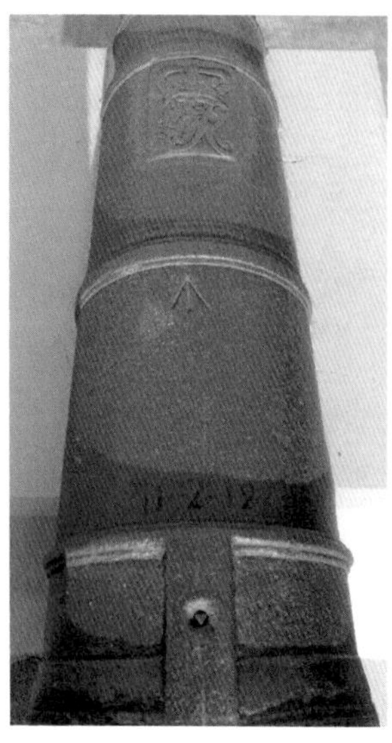

Original cannon markings.

out to Canadian experts to gather information on the cannon in order to identify the piece and its history.

Bob Garcia, historian of the Ontario Service Centre, Parks Canada, calculated the gun's weight at around 1,300 pounds based on the numbers etched on the barrel, 11-2-12, which translates to 11 hundred weights = 1,232 lbs + 2 quarter weights at 28 lbs each = 56 lbs + 12 lbs, for a total of 1,300 pounds. Also, he believes the gun might not be a six pounder at all, but a four pounder. The bore of a four pounder is 3.204 inches, and our cannon is 3.25 inches, whereas a six pounder is 3.668 inches. Over time and use, the bore would have grown slighter larger, as well, as it wore down.[96]

Identifying the cannon as a four pounder gives it a whole new significance. By the War of 1812, four pounders were rarely in use, especially iron ones. Also, the King George III cipher and broad arrow mark mean that the cannon was cast in the reign of King George III (1738–1820) and passed ordnance board inspection. Charles Trollope of the Royal Ordnance Society actually traced the origins of the cannon to Robert Morgan of Carmarthen France, South Wales, who cast it in 1761 or 1763.[97]

Some of the old accounts misread the King George coat of arms as II instead of III, but many of the accounts are close to the cannon's actual weight. Our cannon is a muzzleloader, which fits some of the accounts, yet one account does say it is a breechloader. Furthermore, our cannon does not have a honeycombed barrel; in other words, it's not full of rusty holes, causing it to disintegrate more quickly. It is also not misshapen, as some of the old accounts of the cannon state, nor has it disintegrated to the point of concern that it could hurt someone (which we know happened). In fact, the metal of the courthouse cannon is quite sound.

The clincher is that the cannon is spiked, and the trunnions are missing. When a cannon is spiked, a metal spike is rammed down into the venthole, rendering the cannon unable to be fired. Trunnions are cylindrical protrusions on each side of a cannon, allowing it to be mounted to a carriage. Without trunnions, the cannon cannot be mounted. How or when the trunnions were removed remains a mystery, and we have no way to examine them. That particular area of the cannon is cemented in. But to take the trunnions off a cannon is no easy task. They usually have to be sawn off; knocking them off would take some time. Now, let us consider the fact that the cannon is spiked. The spike fits perfectly in the vent hole and is believed to be a British spike, which would have been made to work in this type of cannon. The British would have wanted to render the cannon useless to the Americans who were capturing it, and this was the quickest and most effective way to do it, thereby rendering the cannon unable to fire.

Considering these facts, there is little doubt there were two cannons. There was a cannon that could be mounted on a wooden carriage, meaning it had trunnions. Also, it could not have been a spiked cannon. A 1,300-pound cannon would not be towed around for artificial thunder; it was too heavy and too bulky for this purpose. So, a land cannon would have fit the bill. A land cannon could have been a muzzleloader or breechloader. In my correspondence with maritime archaeologist Daniel Harrison, he explained that breechloading cannons were not around much at that time, especially at such a large size. Most of them were small swivel cannons that fired a two-pound ball or smaller. These cannons were unstable, crude and could dislodge quite easily, thus being quite deadly.

In Kate Kolb's account, she says the cannon overheated from being repeatedly fired, and Steiner was ramming gunpowder down the barrel when it killed him. This would mean that it is a muzzleloader, not a breechloader. In any case, it would have been a smaller cannon and, according to the reports, was fired so much it ended up with a honeycombed barrel and finally killed and hurt someone. After that, we can surmise it met its fate at the foundry.

Now, let us see if we can make sense of where these cannons possibly came from. The one in the courthouse square says that it is a relic of the Battle of the River Raisin.

We know from one account that the Cass Guards went to the state arsenal in 1846 and got the cannon that they used to fire at celebrations and so on. So, we can surmise that the cannon rolled around on the wooden carriage was indeed from the arsenal, since it was able to be wheeled around and fired. After it killed Steiner, it was sent to the foundry and probably met a grievous end. Even though multiple newspaper accounts claim that this was the same cannon that was mounted in the courthouse square, all such accounts were written in 1884. We do not actually have an article written earlier giving us a description of the cannon from the arsenal. All the 1884 articles refer to the British naval cannon that is, in fact, at the courthouse square. So, somewhere

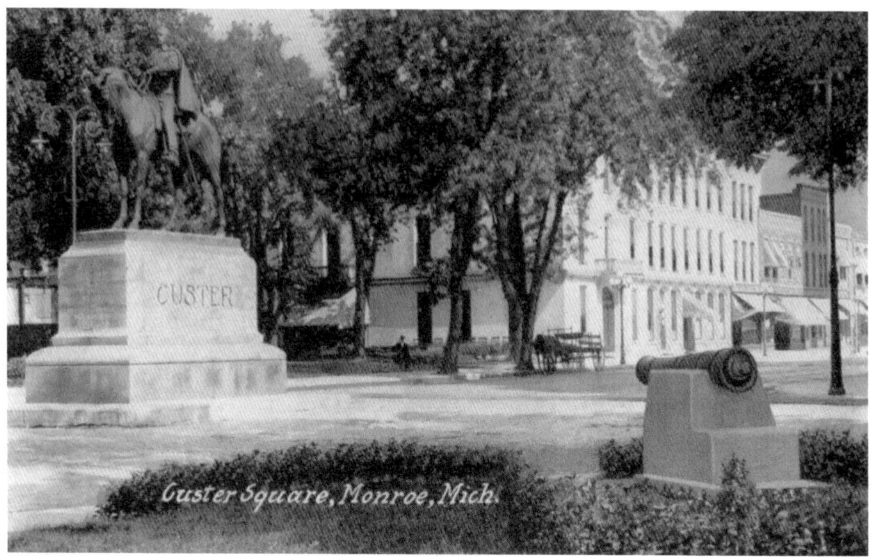

Custer Square, Washington Street.

along the line, the old story of the first arsenal cannon got mixed up with this one. So, did it sit in the foundry until 1872 when it was brought out for the reunion, or was it a different cannon brought out for the reunion?

It would indeed appear that Kate Kolb was correct when she said it was a different cannon brought out for the reunion, because we know that it was spiked, it was described as a naval cannon and it did bear the British coat of arms. At the reunion, everyone assumed it was from the Battles of the River Raisin because it was a reunion of War of 1812 veterans. Kolb said no one set the record straight. But how can we know for sure this cannon was not from the battle? The British did have six cannons at the battle, and they are thought to have been pulled on sleighs by horses and even by the soldiers. There was almost two feet of snow at the time of the battle. Most of the land cannons the British used at that time were two- to eight-hundred-pound brass cannons and howitzers that shot three- and six-pound balls. Thus, the cannons were called three and six pounders. This is a four-pound cannon; it is almost 1,300 pounds and made of iron, with an elongated barrel, and awfully heavy to be a land cannon. There was no cannon lost by the British at the battle, either, so it is highly unlikely this cannon is a relic from the Battles of the River Raisin.

So, where did it come from? Remember, Kate Kolb said that a Frenchman brought in a scrap heap that contained an old, rusty naval cannon found by the lake. "Without much question, the cannon came from some British man-o'-war, doubtless one of the ships that fought Admiral Perry in the battle of Put-in-Bay."[98] But what are the odds that this cannon could be from such a famous naval battle?

In 1984, an iron four-pound cannon was found in the Detroit River; more were discovered in subsequent years, and it turned out that six in total were found in a heap at the bottom of the river. All six were iron four pounders. Five were British, and one was from France. Maritime archaeologist Daniel Harrison examined the Detroit River cannons and Monroe's courthouse cannon and confirmed Monroe's cannon is much like the ones from the Detroit River; two had the same markings and bore wear. He also confirmed there were eight iron four pounders in Fort Amherstburg's inventory of ordnance in 1804. Four were listed as serviceable and the other four listed as unserviceable. One remains there.[99]

HMS *General Hunter*, a British ship in the Battle of Lake Erie on September 10, 1813, was the only brig to have four-pound cannons on it. There were ten such cannon, and it is possible the four serviceable ones came from Fort Amherstburg.[100] Harrison said it is possible that the four serviceable cannons were put on the *General Hunter* nine years later, and the gun crew quickly spiked them as they prepared to surrender to the Americans. These British

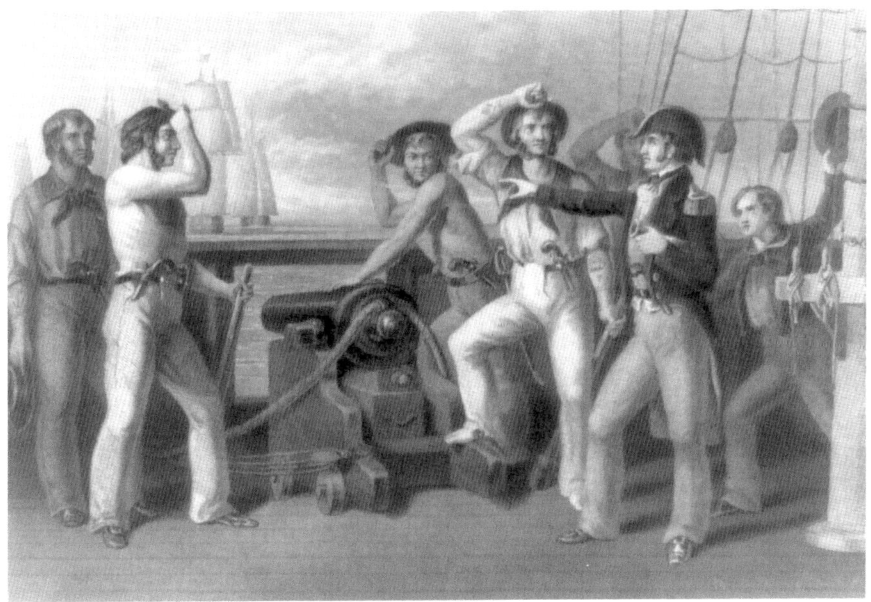

Battle of Lake Erie. *Library of Congress.*

spikes were not something anyone could get their hands on easily, especially in later years. The *General Hunter* was taken back to Detroit, but the lake's water level was low at the time, so it may have run aground near Frenchtown (Monroe), and the crew may have thrown the canon off to lighten the load. There were no shipwrecks from the Battle of Lake Erie either. Years later, at the mouth of the River Raisin, our cannon was found by a French resident and brought to the foundry in a scrap heap.[101]

It appears much of the confusion about these two cannons comes from the fact that they both were at the same local foundry at some point.

Ironically, Kate Kolb and Margareth Beck both said that the cannon was from the Battle of Lake Erie all those years ago. Curiously enough, after the Americans turned the *General Hunter* into a transport vessel, it succumbed to a treacherous gale on August 19, 1816, and crashed on the shore of Southampton Beach in Ontario. In 2002, the hull revealed itself under the sands of the beach and was excavated in 2004. Artifacts from the wreck are on display at the Bruce County Museum and Cultural Centre in Ontario.[102]

We have uncovered much more of the history of this artifact, and we are fortunate to have had experts weigh in and provide us with many essential details. So, can we confidently say we have solved the mystery of this cannon? What do you think?

Chapter 8

Boroughs and Bygone Towns

Not surprisingly, villages often formed where roadways went through. In the early 1800s, these roadways were basically Native American trails or corduroy roads. A corduroy road was built of logs where it forded streams, swamps and the like. The largest was Hull's Road, a military road, which followed a Native American trail that ran south to north. This road was well traversed not only by the army but also by many a traveler, as it ran from Dayton, Ohio, to Detroit. Multiple coaches traversed its length on a daily basis up until the advent of the railroads. In fact, as early as 1836, there was a stagecoach line between Monroe and Ann Arbor that was quite popular.[103]

Like many stops we imagine in those old western towns, Monroe had its share of taverns and saloons in almost every village that popped up along the roadways. Such arduous journeys required a stop to refresh the soul and rest the tired steed. Many taverns of the time advertised home comforts for overnight, as well as good ole home cooking and libations to raise your spirits, just in case music and dancing were not enough.

Later, with the advent of the railroad, settlements knew they needed to be by the railroad route to succeed. Sometimes, they formed in anticipation of the railroad coming through, and if it didn't for some reason, the residents knew it was all over and, in a few cases, they simply moved.

When Monroe County was originally formed, it stretched for sixty miles (ninety-seven kilometers) inland (twice its current size), but the western half was split off to form Lenawee County in 1826.

FIRST ORGANIZED TOWNSHIPS

On February 25, 1825, Congress authorized the governor to organize the territory into townships. Thus, in 1827, five townships were organized in Monroe County. These townships were Monroe, Frenchtown, Raisinville, Erie and Port Lawrence. At that time, since the area was not very populated, the townships encompassed a large amount of territory, much more than today.

MONROE'S BOUNDARY was not changed when the five townships were organized, except all of the City of Monroe was included in it—until 1848, when the city was set off by itself.

FRENCHTOWN included much of the original settlement of the same name. It was the largest.

RAISINVILLE was named after the River Raisin and was very large to start, but later, Ida, London, Summerfield, Milan and Dundee would all be sliced out of it.

ERIE had the distinction of being the first township settled in the county, named after Lake Erie.

PORT LAWRENCE ended up in the disputed territory of the Toledo War and eventually was lost to Ohio, becoming part of Lucas County.

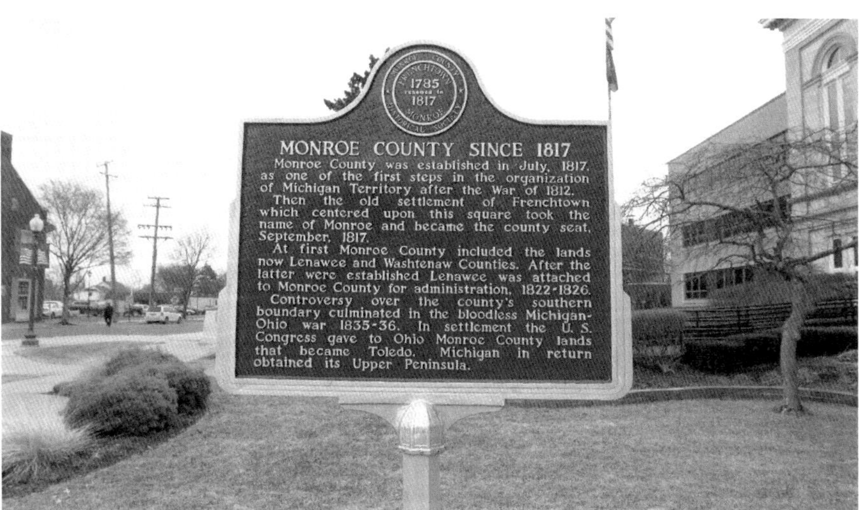

Monroe County since 1817.

Other Townships

ASH was carved out of Frenchtown Township in 1837 and named after Arba Ash.

BEDFORD was originally part of Erie Township and was called West Erie. The town of Bedford was organized in 1836 and named after New York City, where many of the settlers' families came from.

BERLIN was organized in 1867 out of Ash Township and named after Berlin, Germany. In Berlin, South Rockwood and Newport were both founded because of the railroads.

DUNDEE was organized out of Summerfield and Raisinville Townships in 1838. It was named after Dundee of Scotland and was first called Van Nest's Mills.

EXETER was originally part of Raisinville and named after the birthplace of its first supervisor. It was founded in 1836. London was developed out of the township, as was the village of Maybee.

IDA was organized out of Raisinville, Dundee and Summerfield in 1837. It was named after schoolteacher Ida M. Taylor.

LASALLE was one of the earliest settlements, with twenty-two families, in 1794; it was organized into a township in 1830, from part of Erie. LaSalle was named after a Mr. Lasalle, who operated a store there; it was also called the Otter Creek Settlement.

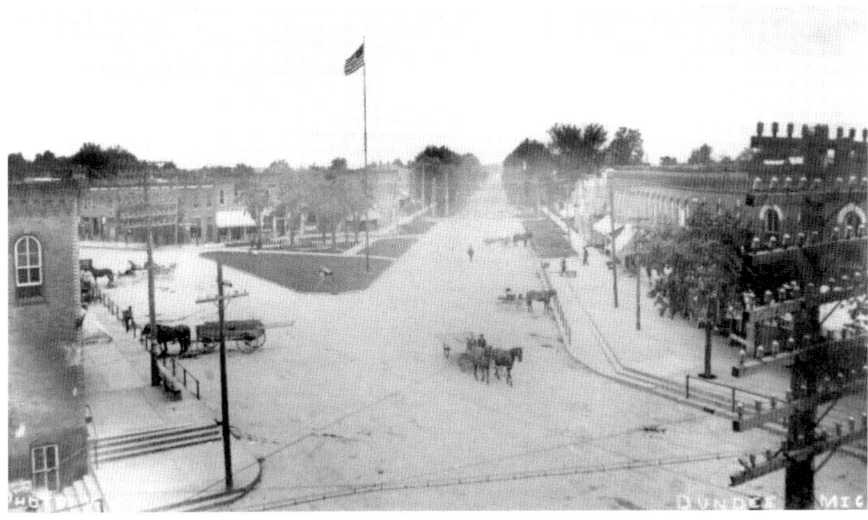

Early Dundee. *Monroe County Library System.*

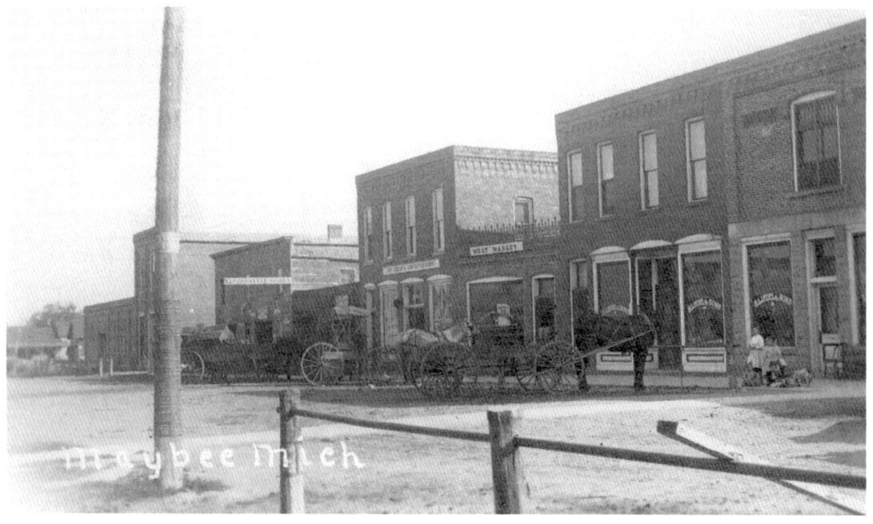

Early Maybee. *Monroe County Library System.*

London was named after London, England, and organized in 1832.

Milan was organized in 1836 by carving out piece of London Township. The township was named by Italian immigrants after Milan, Italy.

Summerfield used to be called Flumen and was actually settled earlier than 1820 but officially founded in 1829. The village of Petersburg was founded out of the land owned by Richard Peters.

Whiteford was in Port Lawrence and Erie and then organized to be its own township in 1834. General David White was first settler to participate in the Toledo War, so Whiteford was named in his honor.

Local Village Namesakes

Azalia and Lulu: Named after Azealia and Lulu Ashley, who were the daughters of a railroad magnate.

Brest: Named after Brest, France.

Carleton: Named after Will Carleton, a famous poet; established in 1872.

Grape: Named after the wild grapes growing along the River Raisin by J.W. Morris.

Lambertville: Named after one Louis Lambert.

Luna Pier: Named after the famous pier that used to run out into Lake Erie.

MAYBEE: Named after Abraham Maybee, whose land became the village.
NEWPORT: Named after the village next to it, called Old Port.
OAKVILLE: Named after all the oak trees in the area.
OTTAWA Lake: Named after the lake nearby.
SAMARIA: Named after Sam and Mary Weeks, who were related to the postmaster.
TEMPERANCE: A dry village before and after Prohibition; in fact liquor sales were prohibited in the local deed for ninety-nine years.[104]

BYGONE TOWNS

Brest

Breast ran from Stoney Creek to Swan Creek in Frenchtown Township. It was located by the water, and a sawmill and a gristmill grew up there, as well as a fishery and a tobacco factory. It even had its own "wildcat bank," owned by H.S. Platt. A wildcat bank actually had no assets to back it up but issued its own money nonetheless. Platt drew up all kinds of plans to lure businesses to the town. Before long, it came to be called the "paper city" because there was nothing to back it up, and when the bank eventually failed, so did the city.[105]

Clark City

In 1854, the Clark family from New York founded Clark City in Ash Township, which was on the way to Flat Rock. The city grew quickly in anticipation of the railroad coming through. At its height, it had two hundred residents, two churches, a hotel, many stores, a school, a library, a jewelry store, a dentist's office, a brickyard and more. But when the railroad opted to bypass the area, the residents knew that the city was doomed. So, they moved away, as would be expected—but they also took their buildings with them. In the winter, they used sleds to pull them across the ice. By 1877, the only remnant of the town was its cemetery.[106]

Cone

In the 1830s, Eratus S. Cone settled in the southwestern part of Milan Township, or West Milan. He moved there from Port Lawrence. His son became the first postmaster in 1869. In 1880, the Wabash Railroad went through the town and called its station Cone. The post office changed its name to Cone in 1882. Today, Cone is south of Milan on Cone Road, but there is little evidence of the community that was once there.[107]

Grape

The village of Grape was located adjacent to the River Raisin on North Custer Road about eight miles west of town. The road was known as the Monroe-Milan Plank Road or the Monroe-Tecumseh Plank Road. A mile outside of the village, the road split; one branch went toward Milan and the other toward Dundee. At the fork was the large Plank Hotel. The road was punctuated with toll gates about every ten miles. The toll was two cents a mile, and the family living nearest the toll booth ran it.

In the late 1860s, Grape had a store, which also included a post office, at North Custer and Doty Roads. There was also a grocery store, a copper

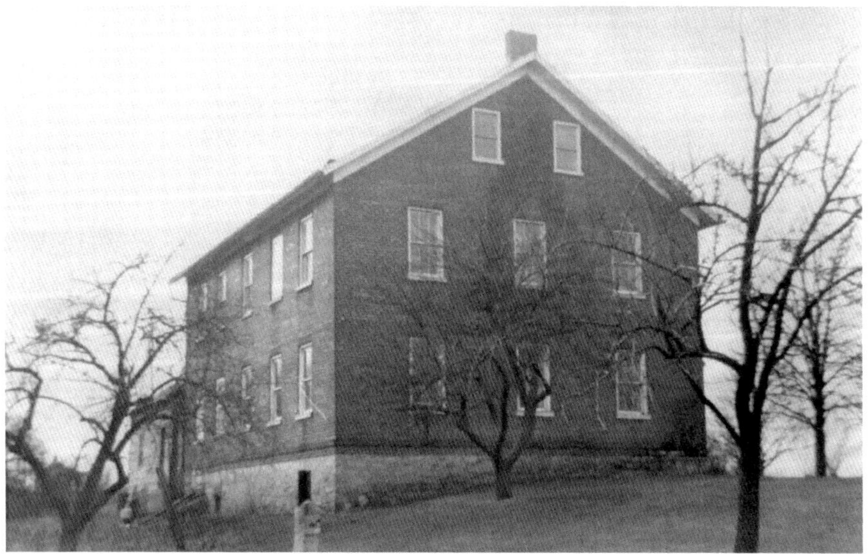

Village of Grape, Soltz Tavern. *Monroe County Library System.*

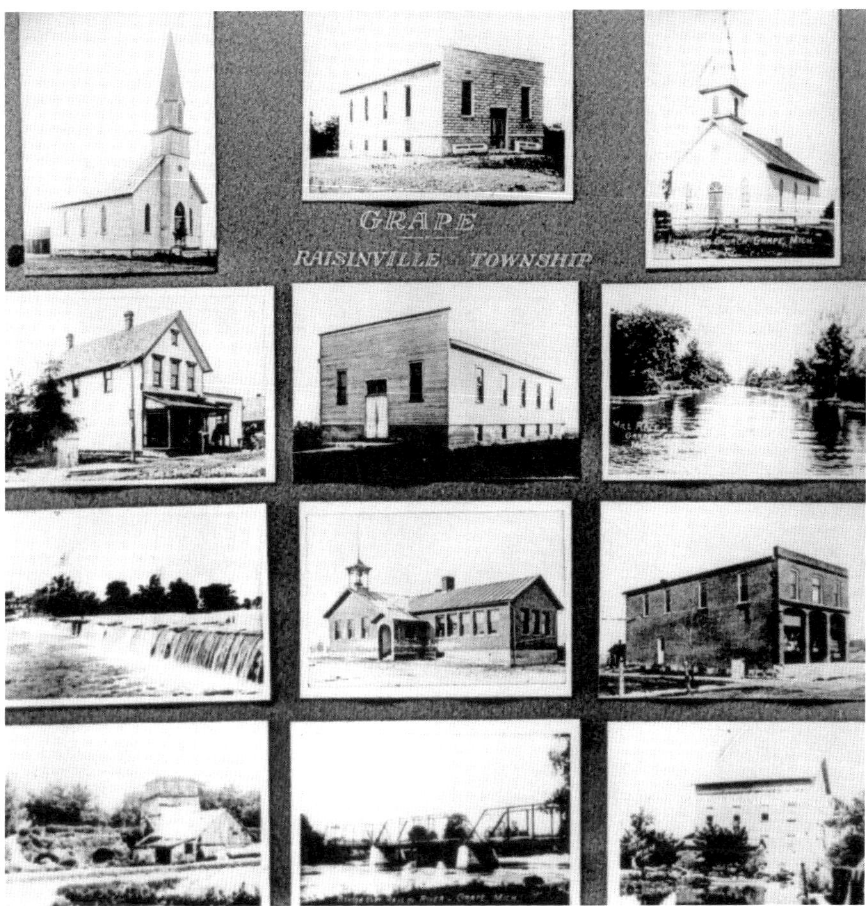

Village of Grape. *Monroe County Library System.*

shop, a blacksmith shop, a wagon factory, a sawmill, a gristmill, a cheese mill and twenty lime kilns.

The sawmill employed an unusual upright saw, and logs would jam up the river for miles. But lime is what Grape was really known for. Grape resident William Cominers remembered, "There were twenty lime kilns in the three mile area between North Raisinville Road and the Doty Road. As a boy I remember seeing teams and wagons lined up, awaiting their turn to load with lime. One poor fellow had come a long distance after a load and he became impatient while waiting for the lime to cool, so started loading and his wagon caught on fire."[108]

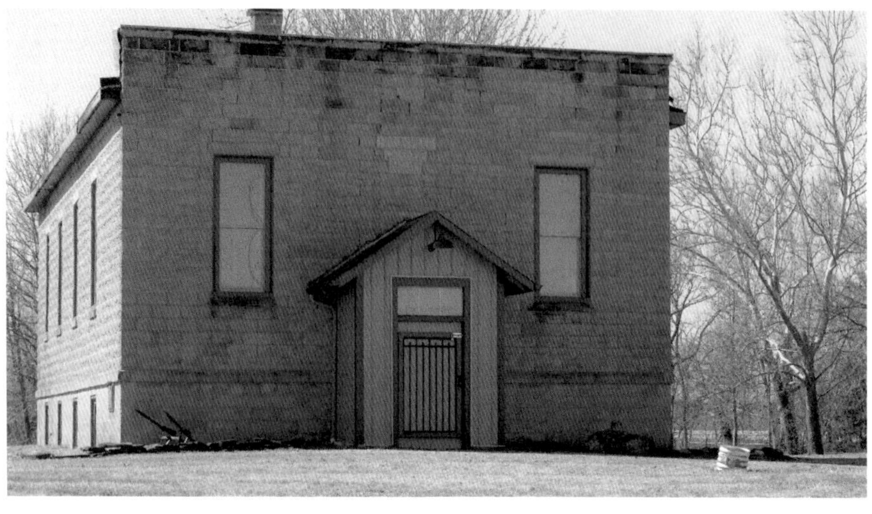

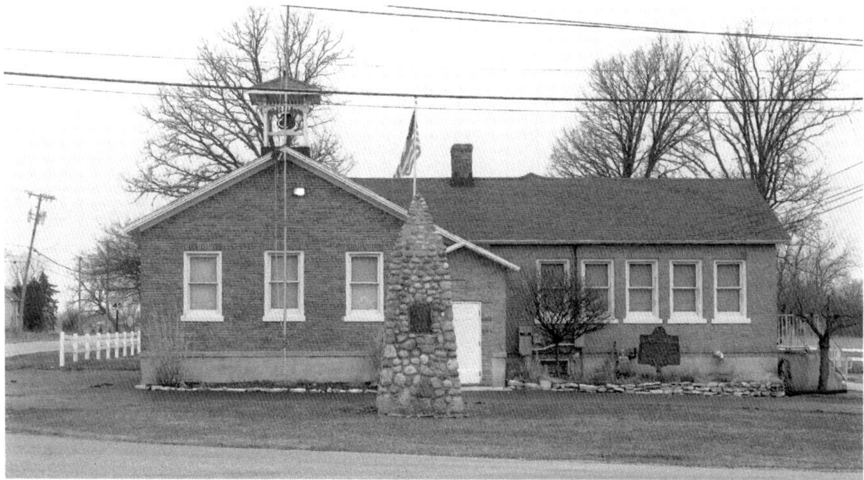

Top: Grape Building today. *Bottom*: Grape School today.

Industry brought in employees who needed a place to stay. John Gold ran a hotel and a tavern. His hotel had only four rooms available but was often fully booked. People employed at Grape's cheese mill or lime quarry stayed there indefinitely. They were given a bargain at seven dollars per week, which included their room, laundry service and ironing. Yet, Gold did have some restrictions, such as closing at ten o'clock and not being open on Sundays or election days.[109] Gold's tavern was known as John Gold's Place and was open for several years.

There were other taverns located at Grape, such as the Soltz Tavern, which was thirty-six by forty-six feet and two and a half stories. The upper floor was a dance hall with a wooden floor and was the only dance hall between Milan and Erie; thus, it was very popular.[110]

In 1899, William J. Seitz opened a saloon he called the Seitz Inn. He also opened a cider mill and a hydroelectric plant. Because of him, the community had electricity until 1914, when Detroit Edison came in. Grape actually was one of the very first villages in the county to have electricity.

Not much remains of Grape. A few buildings and an original house still stand at the corner of Baldwin Road and North Custer Road. The house was built of block by Chris Bruckner, who owned some of the lime kins.[111]

Havre

It was thought in 1836 that Havre, an up-and-coming harbor town, might end up rivaling Monroe. Havre, founded by residents from New York State in 1836, was located at Halfway Creek in Bedford Township, today's Summit Street in Erie Township. The settlers picked the site because of its sheltered area, rich soil and strategic location for a harbor town. But being from New York, they were unfamiliar with Lake Erie's waxing and waning moods and were unaware that, previously, the area was mostly underwater.

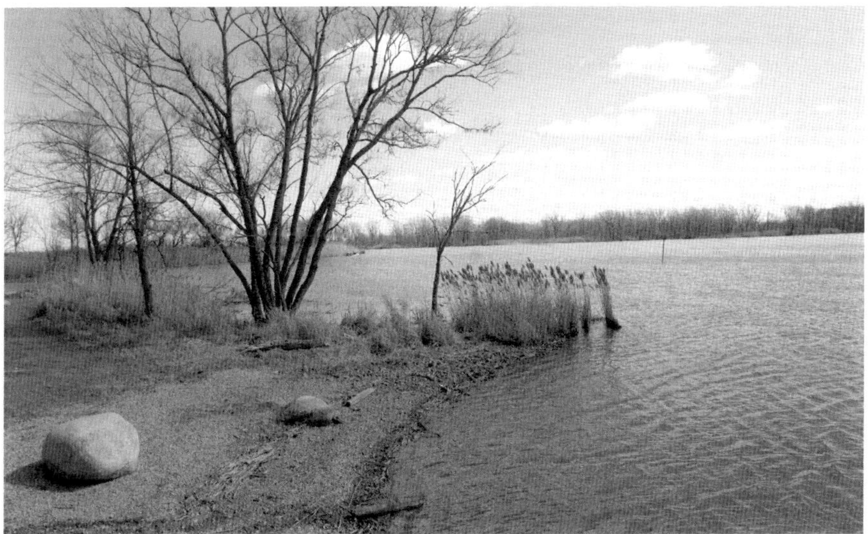

Havre today.

It only was a few feet above lake level, and much of the land surrounding it was marshland.

It was not long before Havre had several homes, warehouses, loading docks, businesses, stores, hotels, taverns, offices and a post office. The Buffalo steamboat *Mazeppa* often stopped at Havre and would stay there in storage during the winter, along with many other steamships. It was thought that Havre was the safest place for the boats to be stored in the winter, away from Lake Erie's rough waters. Havre was on the cusp of achieving the status of a huge commercial harbor town, with the prospect of opening the Havre Branch Railroad, which would connect it to the Erie and Kalamazoo Railroad.

But it was not long before Havre's dreams sank into oblivion, just like the town was destined to do. It only took two years for Lake Erie to show its true colors; it started to rise and did not stop until many of the houses were entirely surrounded by water. In a matter of days, the Halfway Creek swelled into a giant river, and soon the whole town was being engulfed in the cold lake water. Isidore Morin, who sold some of the land to the founders of Havre, wrote about the flooding: "They rowed their pirogues [canoes] right into the tavern and there the barrels were floating all about. Most of the men had all they wanted to drink for nothing."[112]

Ultimately, the water rose to four feet before it decided to stop. The residents quickly tried to rescue their personal belongings and sought shelter on higher ground, hoping to return to their homes when the water receded,

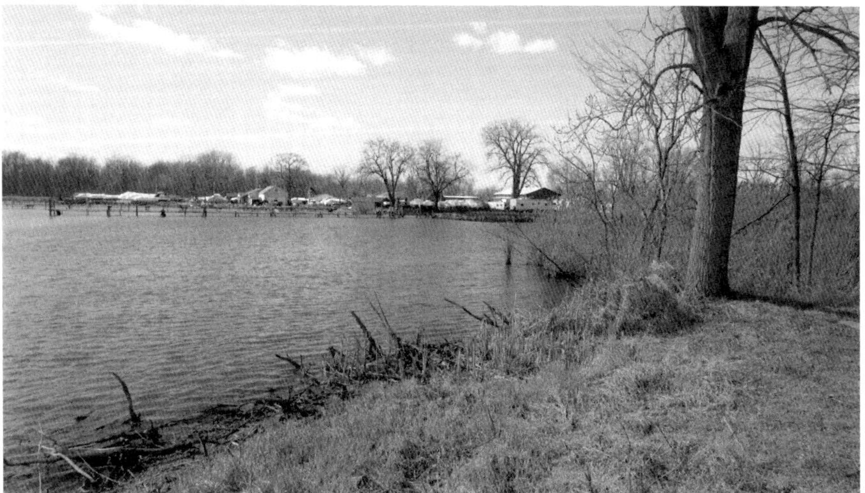

Havre today.

but it never did. Over the winter, when the lake froze, Havre became a busy town again—not for the reason it was created, but for residents to try to salvage as much as possible of the buildings left there.[113]

Marion Childs interviewed Bruce Agnew, whose grandfather talked about an Atlantis-like scenario for the village of Havre. He said that one spring, Havre was "drowned out," and only one building was left standing, a gristmill at the end of Harrison Street. Some buildings were rescued and moved across the ice. After Havre was lost, Bruce's grandfather moved his house from across the ice to Dixie Highway in Erie. Another building was moved and became a Methodist church for a while. Other buildings moved to Erie were Ed Drewyor's saloon at the southeast corner of Dixie and Manhattan and Sam LaPointe's grocery store by a bridge.[114] Today, there are no remnants of the lost city of Havre.

Newport Station

When the railroad came to Swan Creek and Brandon Roads in Berlin Township in 1855, the settlement of Newport Station took hold. The village grew dramatically over a twenty-five-year period, with a lot of saloons, two hotels, a gristmill, hoop-and-stave mills, a cannery, a cheese factory, a creamery, a basket factory and general and hardware stores.[115]

Reeves Corner

In Milan Township, southeast of Milan, is the village of Azalia. Azalia was also known as Reeves Station or Reeves Corners after the Reeves family, who settled there in the center of the community and ran the Star Bending Company. Sayre Reeves, who previously lived in Dexter, got into a fight with a twenty-three-year-old man and shot him in 1845. Evidently, he didn't get into much legal trouble, as he relocated to the southeast corner of Milan. He died in 1877. The same year, the post office there was renamed Azalia.[116]

Steiner

Steiner, founded in 1873 by William Steiner, grew up at the intersection of Steiner and Laduke Roads in Frenchtown Township. It was centered on the railroad depot and ended up having its own post office, a general store, a saloon, a granary, a creamery, a sawmill, a basket factory, a pottery factory and a brick factory. On May 3, 1948, a fire broke out, and the general store and other buildings were destroyed; unfortunately, two people lost their lives, a seventy-year-old and a five-year-old. The sad incident led to the development of the Frenchtown Township Volunteer Fire Department in 1949. Today the only remnants of the town are the basket factory building and a few houses.[117]

Stoney Creek

About four miles north of the town of Monroe was the settlement of Stoney Creek, or Rocky River. It was located four miles upstream from the mouth of the river. A large mill and a couple businesses were operating close to the water, with few people actually residing there. Eventually, about fourteen families moved in on the high and dry banks of the stream.[118] Today, there are no remnants of the Stoney Creek settlement, except perhaps a few houses and the Loranger Gristmill, circa 1832, which is now in the Greenfield Village exhibit at the Henry Ford Museum in Dearborn.

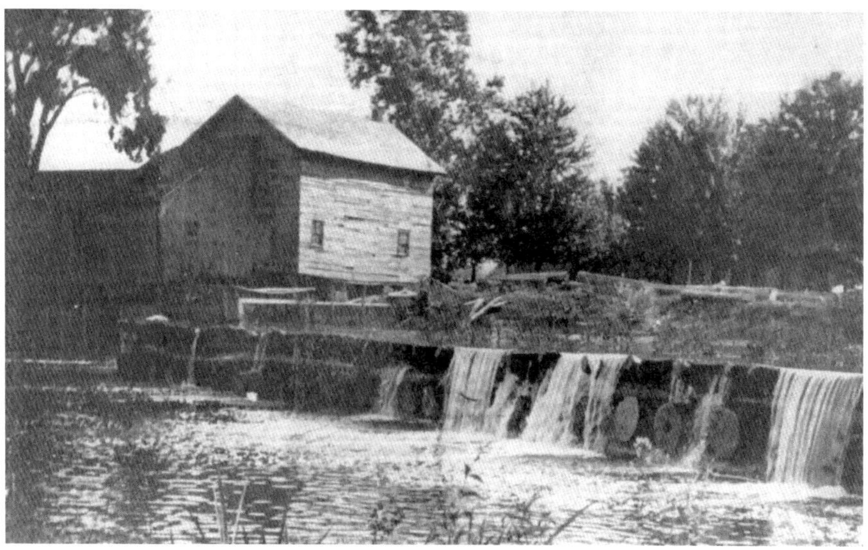

Loranger Mill at Stoney Creek. *Monroe County Library System.*

Vistula

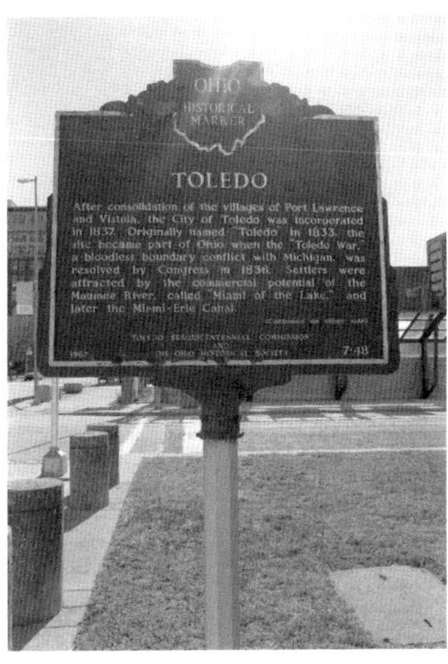

Toledo Marker.

Vistula was a new town created in 1832 in the southern boundary area of Monroe, about twenty miles outside of town. On the rise of a hill, the location offered a beautiful area for a harbor town located by Swan Creek near Lake Erie. Swan Creek had a deep channel, which allowed large vessels to traverse its waters easily. Yet, without apparent reason, the town and development plans were abandoned, and the land was "forfeited to the government." Later, a large iron foundry was established, as well as a gristmill and a steam mill.[119] Today, Vistula and Port Lawrence make up part of Toledo. The area was lost to Ohio during the Toledo War.

Chapter 9

For What Ails You...

Historian Russell Bidlack writes, "In general medical practice in the early nineteenth century seems to have been based on the theory that the more torturous the treatment the more certain the cure. Small wonder that the sick adult often deferred calling a doctor until he was near death, while the greatest terror of childhood was not disease, but the treatment thereof."[120]

In 1826, James J. Godfroy of Monroe wrote a letter saying that most of his friends were "in a bad state of health, the most part of them being… affected by a violent disorder called by physicians influenza."[121] Although this flu was rarely fatal, its victims were struck with a severe headache, high fever and severe body aches. James and his family also fell victim to it.[122]

There was an ailment that the settlers of the area seemed particularly susceptible to; thus, they called it the Michigan Rash. They thought it was caused by the blood being contaminated by something. Families and even surrounding neighborhoods would all suffer from it at the same time. It would break out in a school and pass to every pupil and the teachers. The victims described it as not being choosy but attacking everyone just alike. Of course, the best way to get rid of the rash was to basically peel it off by using a combination of sulfur and lard, applied with a corncob.[123]

Michigan was also known for the "fever ague" or the "shakes." In 1828, Noyes Wadsworth tried to convince his parents to send his younger brother to visit him in Monroe. He half-jokingly said, "I should like to have Wadsworth make me a visit next spring. I can find employment for him until the fever

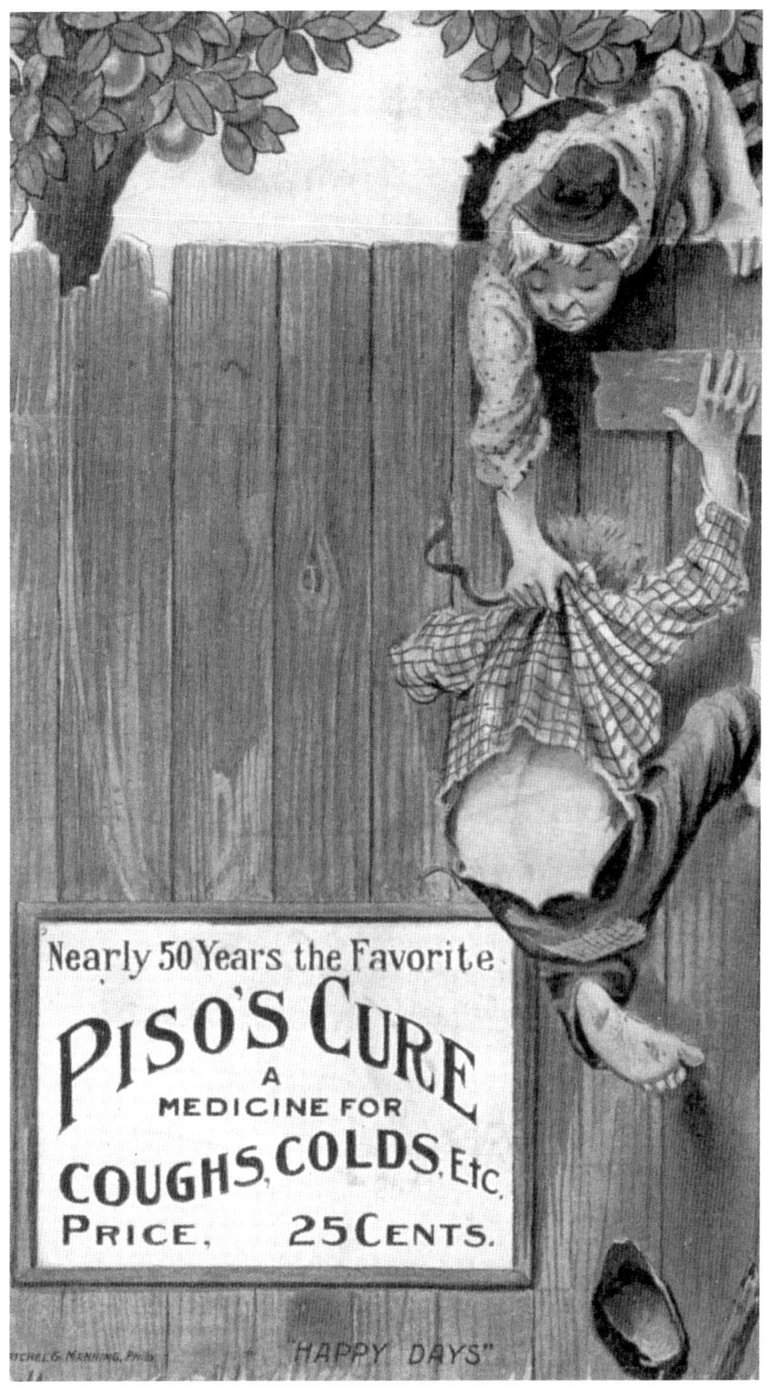

Antique "remedy" postcard.

and ague lays hold of him, then he may lie still and see which can shake the hardest. If he can get along with it as well as I did, I will call him a native of Michigan."[124]

The remedies were all over the map. Some examples included walking barefoot in the fresh dirt; or, at the first sign of a chill, one should run until they simply collapsed from exhaustion. One settler thought they had found the cure for the fever ague: "I was to pare all my finger and toenails, wrap the parings in tissue paper, then bore a hole in a maple tree, put in the nails and plug up the hole."[125]

The fever ague was a common malady until the 1850s, when it seemed to gradually disappear. This was at the same time that the swamps were drained and the settlers had suffered a few abnormally cold winters. But it wasn't until the twentieth century that the true cause was discovered to be malaria carried by mosquitoes.

Monroe also suffered from many of the contagious scourges of the ages: typhus, smallpox, scarlet fever, whooping cough, diphtheria, measles and mumps.

Typhoid fever was particularly bad in late summer when the wells were low. One tragic story from the time was that of the Bulkley's daughter Gracie. When playing with her friends, eleven-year-old Gracie got thirsty and drank from an old, unused well. Turns out the well had a dead cat in it, and Gracie came down with typhoid. Dr. A.I. Sawyer tended to her, but at that time, it was thought the remedy was to prevent the sick person from drinking.[126]

But as bad as these diseases were, the remedies at that time were much worse. Minor illness were often treated with an array of hot tea blends. The most popular blends were composed of catnip, pennyroyal, butterfly weed and sheep dung. Pumpkin seeds were thought to be good for tapeworms, and other worms were treated with scrapings from pewter spoons. Other ingredients such as "sugar, turpentine, alum, Indian turnip root in molasses, gum camphor, lobelia, opium, mercury, and red pepper all had their place, but the favorite of all was calomel [mercury chloride]….Poultices were used commonly, made from such ingredients as fat meat, pepper mint, slippery elm, and syrup of rhubarb with nitro. Even the headache was treated with a poultice of scraped raw potato. A bag of pounded slippery elm bark over the eye of the measles victim would bring out the fever."[127]

For a fever, it was thought that tying the patient down and making them sweat it out was the best remedy. An infection or wound required cauterizing with a hot iron. Bloodletting was one of the most common remedies, usually effected with leeches, a knife and cupping therapy. Once the bloodletting

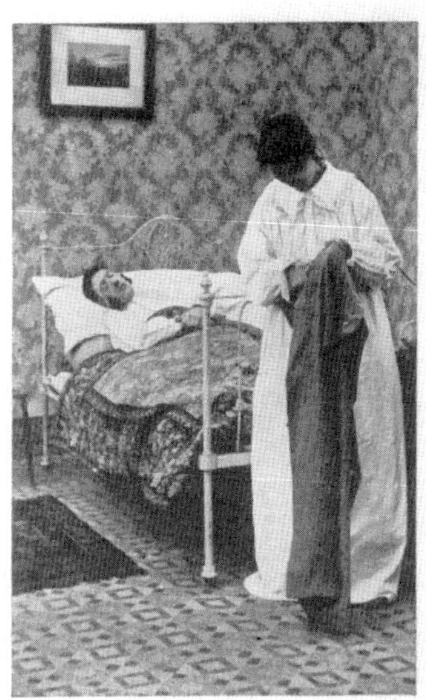

Antique first aid postcard.

began, a horsehair and a piece of wool was often inserted under the skin to cause an infection to draw out the poison that was making the victim sick. Another method was to put the mugwort plant on the skin and have it burn as slowly as possible. It was believed the larger the blister, the better to effect healing.[128]

The Reverend Alfred Brunson, a preacher from Monroe, told of his experience in 1823 when he came down with "a severe attack of inflammation of the lungs and liver: Bleeding was then in vogue, and I was depleted at the rate of a quart at a time, and blistered all across my breast in proportion. I preached with a blister-plaster, ten by eight inches, on my breast, and the exercise, together with perspiration, caused it to rise and fill till it broke and discharged probably half a pint down my chest."[129]

Nick Sieb was treated in his home by a Dr. Southworth for a broken leg. He was tied down to the kitchen table while the doctor administered ether. Once he was out, the doctor sawed the bone off at the knee as the blood dripped into the kitchen kettle. Once the leg was detached, it was put in a box and buried in the backyard. Nick used an artificial leg to get around, but owing to it not healing well, he developed diabetes. He had to undergo the process all over again ten years later when what was left of his leg was amputated at the thigh. His first artificial limb cost $150, but the second one cost $175. One time, Nick complained about a pain in his foot, a phenomenon we know as phantom pain today. When they dug up his leg, it was found to have a root poking between the toes.[130]

Shortly after the turn of the century, Monroe, along with the rest of the world, experienced a flu like none other in the form of the Spanish flu. For almost a year, it wreaked havoc on the world. In Monroe, 1,100 people fell ill, and 136 people succumbed to the virus. The worldwide death toll was 55 million. Along with the flu came an outbreak of 225 tuberculous cases in Monroe. At that time, there were no hospitals in Monroe, but a few years later, in 1922, the city got its first hospital.[131]

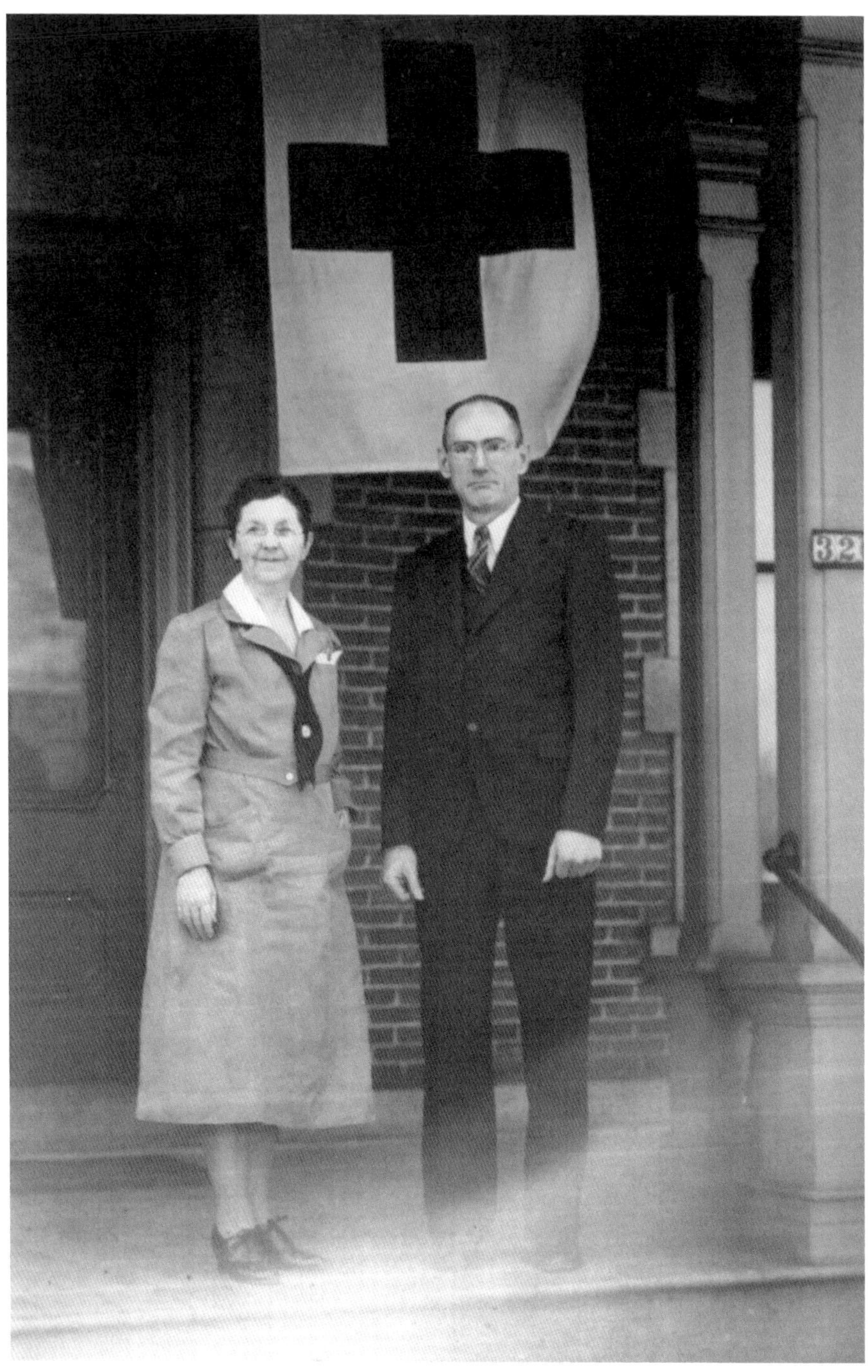

Art Lesow and Lydia Schimeising, 1940s. *Monroe County Library System.*

Mrs. Vincent Barker, when interviewed by Marion Childs in 1959, said her husband, Dr. Barker, was key in the establishment of the Monroe County Health Department. The first task they undertook was to eliminate outdoor privies in the town. They believed a lot of the health hazards the residents faced were due to the unsanitariness of such things. Every year, hundreds of people would flock to the doctor's office with a case of the "bloody flux." Bloody flux, also known as dysentery, was caused by consuming contaminated food or water.[132]

Chapter 10

Monroe's Sordid Past

Back in the day, public chastising and humiliation were a means to punish evildoers. Monroe was no different, having a public whipping post right in the prettiest part of the town, the park area called Loranger Square, right in front the of the courthouse. Peter P. Ferry was the local justice of peace and sentenced many offenders to a lashing. A resident by the name of Thiebault was whipped for committing larceny. No one was exempt from this humiliation, and it only took one person to convict. But the injustices didn't stop there; the poor and the homeless could be sold off to the highest bidder, and convicted criminals could be made part of the ball and chain gang. The practice of public humiliation was finally stopped in 1835.[133]

Horse Thievery

Monroe was also not immune to the problem of horse thieves. Many a farmer would be alarmed when he got up in the morning to find his stables empty, having been cleaned out in the middle of the night. In fact, the problem was so prevalent everywhere in the state of Michigan that societies sprang up to try to combat the problem. There was even a horse thief convention organized, in which lay citizens were ready to take up the cause of justice and help their fellow police officers, even if it was with their own brand of justice. The call issued was thus:

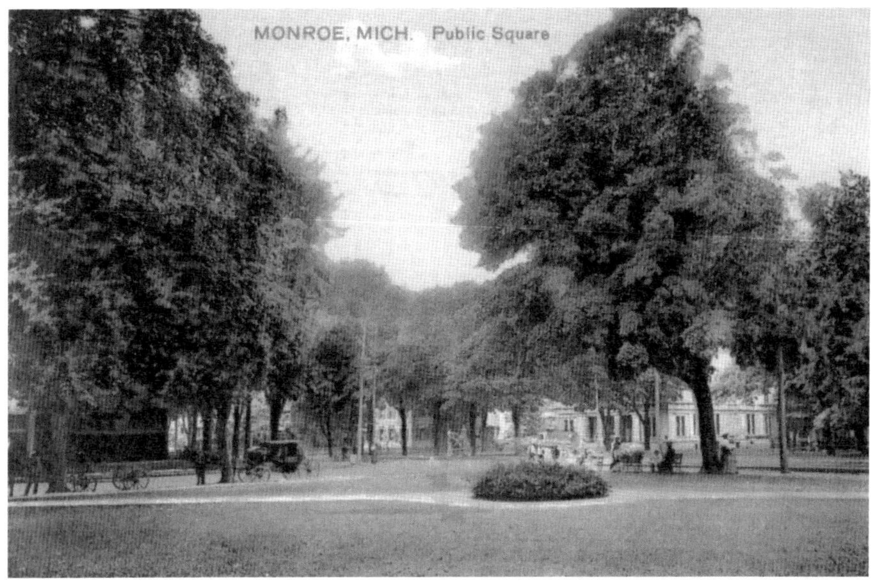

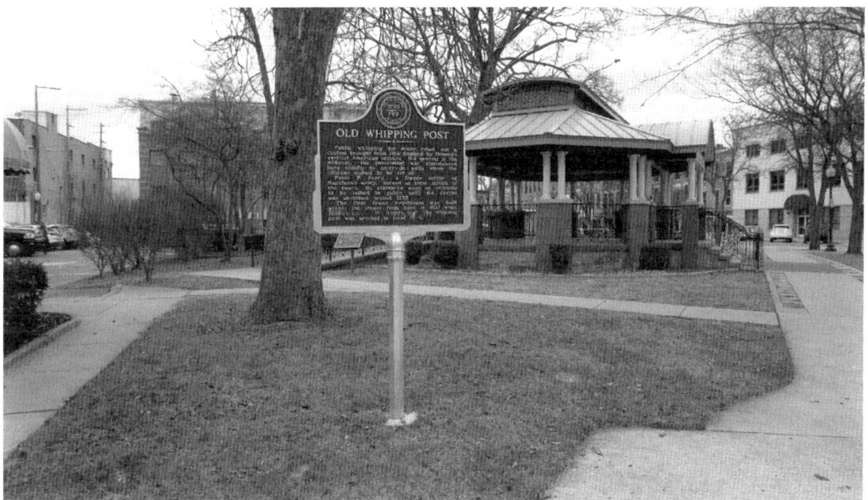

Top: Loranger Square, Washington Street. *Bottom*: Loranger Square today.

> *It is very generally understood that a thoroughly organized band of horse thieves are now operating among us. So well planned and well timed are the numerous thefts of this band that but very few who lose by it ever again see thief or property, notwithstanding large rewards are offered and much money and time fruitlessly spent. We believe that a "State Horse Thief Society" should at once be organized with branches in every county,*

> *that proper men should be selected by the society in each county to be ready at all hours with horses for pursuit, and a change of horses on hand at proper distances, thus obviating the necessity of tracking step by step the course of the thief.*[134]

The societies obtained some success in apprehending suspects. One such suspect was named Sile Doty. Although no proof was ever attributed to Doty, he was brought up on charges and, in fact, imprisoned. He was said to have reformed sometime later.[135]

SALOONS

Monroe County also had its share of taverns, saloons and hotels. Most were a combination. They often lined the stagecoach routes, trails and railroads. Some were also known for their seedier reputations. One particular establishment in Monroe was the United States Hotel. Around the time of the Patriot Wars in the 1830s, the hotel was a haven for highwaymen, also called road agents: men who feigned to help caravans on their journey only to rob them later. It was also a perfect gathering spot for the secret society of the Hunter's Lodges, Patriot War sympathizers. Patrons interested in making a quick buck, wetting their whistles and other activities also frequented the inn. It wasn't until the 1850s, under a new owner, that it managed to clean up its reputation.[136]

Yet, as tavern stops were eagerly looked forward to by passengers, they were just as looked forward to by innkeepers yearning to turn a profit—but maybe in more ways than one, as evidenced by the following incident in 1832–33. A coach traveling from Detroit to Monroe was carrying three boxes of coins that were stored in the rear baggage area, destined for a bank in Monroe. However, when the coach arrived and was being unpacked, it was discovered the bags were missing. Monroe sheriff Levi Humphrey was immediately called. After questioning the driver and learning of the coach's route, he was convinced that a shady tavern keeper at Mongauga (current-day Ecorse) by the name of Bass was the guilty party.[137]

Humphrey theorized that while the travelers dined and the horses were changed, Bass seized on an opportunity that was just too easy to pass up. Humphrey, along with a few backups, decided to pay Mr. Bass a visit at his house. When confronted, Bass characteristically denied he had anything to

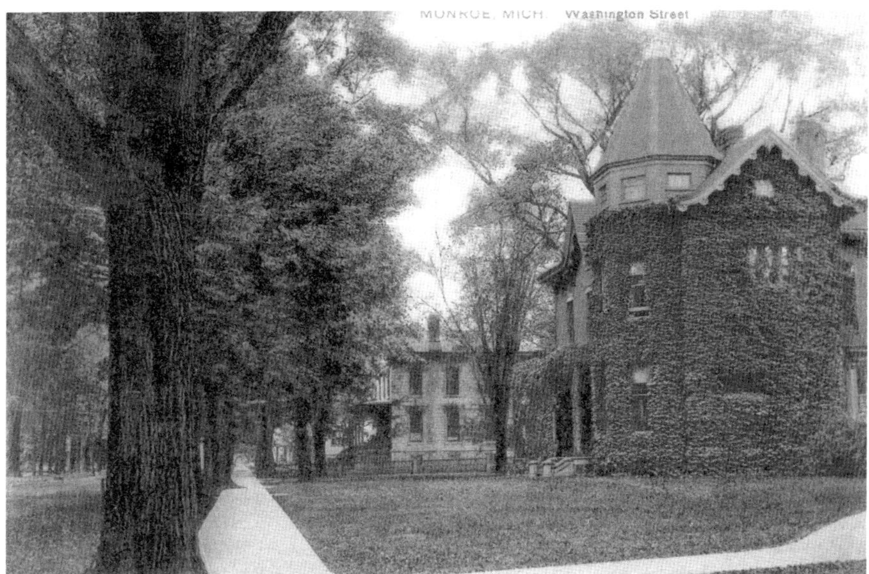

Washington Street.

do with it. The sheriff, along with his posse, decided that Mr. Bass needed a little more encouragement to confess, so they dragged him to the woods across from his house. Finding a good, stout tree, they proceeded to tie him up and coerce him to talk by the way of a switch. Bass didn't own up to the crime easily, which might explain why he wasn't long for this world after the incident. In any case, he finally fessed up and revealed where the bags were hidden. The sheriff returned to Monroe in triumph with all the loot intact.[138]

CRIMES

Even in the early 1800s, Monroe was not immune to counterfeiting schemes. In 1825, Luke Ellison was arrested in Monroe for passing counterfeit five-dollar bills. He was arrested and lodged in the county jail. While he was confined, however, he became ill, "or at least so convinced Jailor Joseph Ferrington, who not only permitted him free access to the family apartments of the Court House, but to the adjoining yard as well."[139] This levity permitted Ellison to make a break for it in a "fashionable dandy white hat, a striped summer roundabout vest and pantaloons."[140] He proceeded to steal a canoe at the mouth of Otter Creek, where he sailed away toward Sandusky, Ohio. A handsome reward was offered, but Ellison was never seen again.[141]

By far one of the most common crimes around 1825 in Monroe was selling liquor to the Native Americans. Lewis Bailey was convicted of such a crime and fined twenty-five dollars. When an article was published in the newspaper about the whiskey laws, arguing that the guilt of many should not ride on one man, the court actually refunded twenty dollars of the fine to Bailey.[142]

Back then, one of the most effective ways to catch a criminal was by putting an ad in the newspaper. One such incident in 1826 shows the value of newspapers and wanted posters. A Raisinville resident read a notice in a newspaper called the *Natchez Gazette* placed by Dr. Francis Fowler of Desdon, Ohio. Fowler offered a reward of fifty dollars for a young man named Rolland Lindsey. The notice claimed that "after having been supported at my expense for eighteen months as a student of medicine, has through fraud…obtained books, medicine and instruments, taken my horse, saddle and bridle at midnight hour, and absconded."[143]

The Raisinville resident was stunned when he realized that the criminal was a new physician who had just opened up an office in Monroe. He immediately turned in the fraudulent Dr. Lindsay to the authorities. Lindsay was arraigned before justice of the peace Peter Ferry and thrown in jail. Yet, he was released only a couple weeks later when his accuser, Dr. Fowler, passed away. "His release was predicated by the notion 'that while living he [Dr. Fowler] was a man of dissipated habits, and much involved in debt that Lindsey, so far from having defrauded Fowler, owes most of his difficulties to having made himself liable for demons against said Fowler.'"[144]

Bank Robberies

Monroe, even though it was a small community in the nineteenth century, had its share of bank robberies and attempted robberies. The following incident reads like some kind of unbelievable fictional story.

In the 1840s, an impressive brick two-story bank with large Corinthian columns flanking its front stood where city hall now stands. The bank, known as the Bank of the River Raisin, was known to keep a lot of cash and coins in its vault.

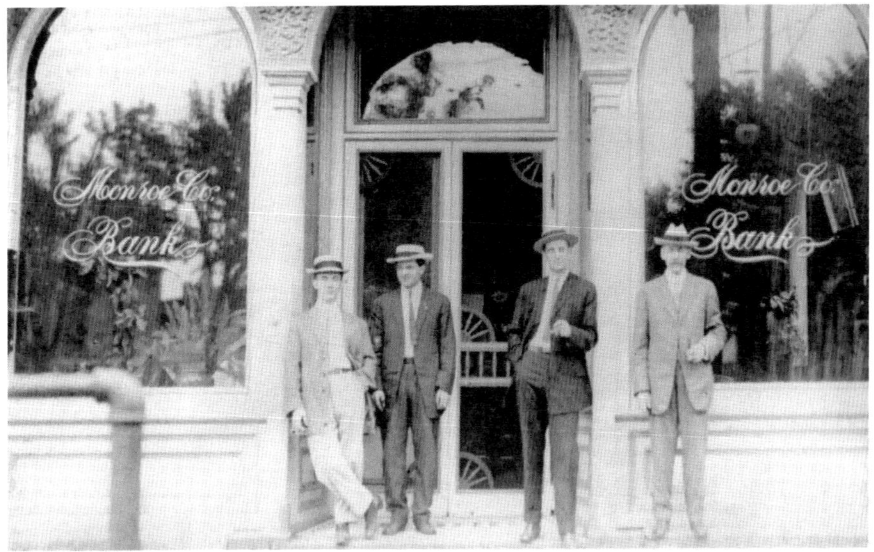

Monroe County Bank. *Monroe County Library System.*

Like in almost every city in the United States, there lived a man in town, Mr. Wells, who was known for trouble; he worked only now and then as a tinner. He did come from a very proper family, however. Wells had a friend in town who was the cashier at the bank, Lewis Hall, although the friendship was one-sided. Hall tried to be a good example to the transient. Many a time did Hall come to his friend's rescue.[145]

Wells hatched an unbelievably cold and calculated scheme to take advantage of his "friend" by telling him that he had a lot of silver coins from Detroit that he planned to deposit in the bank. But due to an unfortunate accident with the stagecoach, he had to hide the silver in the woods just north of town and needed Hall's help to get it to the bank. Hall was determined to help his friend and immediately left with him.[146]

When they arrived in the woods, Hall went ahead into the darkness with a lantern. They were only a few steps into the woods when Hall heard a loud *pop* that startled him; he yelled to Wells, "What was that noise, Wells?" Wells replied, "I stepped on a dry twig and broke it."[147] Then, suddenly, Hall heard a bang followed by a whizzing sound and then felt the bullet graze him. He yelled to Wells,

> *"What in the world are you doing, man; you've shot me!"* [Wells] *explained that he was trying to get his pistol out of his pocket and it was accidentally discharged. Still unsuspicious, Hall said, "Well, you had better be more*

> *careful. I am not hurt much, but I don't want any more accidents." Hardly had he uttered the words than a second shot was heard, and a bullet took effect in Hall's body, and brought him to the ground. "Are you trying to murder me, Wells? What does all this mean? Take me back to town at once. I am badly hurt." Wells helped his victim up and to the wagon, unhitched the team and started back to Monroe, driving rapidly until reaching the river, when, instead of crossing the Macomb street bridge, as he should have done, he drove down a short but steep incline leading to the river.... Hall cried out, "Where are you going, are you crazy, man? Drive me home at once!" The river was crossed, and the wagon driven south on Macomb street, but instead of stopping at Hall's home...he drove past, crossing Second street....Hall, thoroughly alarmed, managed to throw himself from the wagon, and then to painfully crawl to his home.*[148]

Once he was safely in his house, Hall got medical attention and called the authorities to explain what had happened. Wells, who acted like nothing had happened, put the horses in the barn where he got them earlier, proceeded to the Exchange Hotel where he was staying, stopped at the bar and then went to bed.[149]

The story spread like wildfire, and by the next morning, a gang of townsfolk were at the hotel demanding that Wells come out. But as it turned out, he was already arrested and in jail. He claimed that it was an accidental shooting, that the gun went off in his pocket, and he showed the officers the hole. The police didn't buy it and deduced that Wells concocted the whole story about losing his silver in an accident. He maliciously plotted to kill his friend, take the keys to the bank, rob it and make his getaway in the wagon he rented. He was tried and found guilty and sentenced to twenty years of hard labor at the state prison. If Wells had not lost his nerve, it would have been over for Hall. But as it turned out, Hall did recover, although he had to live the remainder of his life with a bullet lodged in his body.[150]

Monroe's seedy past did not stop there, however. On November 24, 1875, another unbelievable bank robbery was attempted at the First National Bank. The story was told in the *Detroit Free Press* the next day:

> *The business portion of Monroe was electrified this morning by the report that the First National Bank had been burglarized at an early hour, and a large sum of money taken. Entrance to the bank was first thought to have been affected through one of the front doors which it had been customary to keep closed and locked. The supposition is that the thieves were in the bank*

during the day previous, and unperceived, unlocked this door....A young man named Durell, watchman...was awakened, he states, by the opening of the front door, and with his revolver in hand, partly rose...while the robbers, three in number, suddenly confronted him with their pistols, and commanded silence, and bound him securely, bandaged his eyes, and carried him into the front office.

A wagon was heard to drive up to the street door, and directly two or three bundles or bags were brought into the bank, and active operations at once began....Valuables were kept in two large safes....In one was a large amount of currency, bonds, and some specie...totaling some $25,000 or $30,000. This safe was at once attacked, the hinges knocked off with sledge hammers, the plates drilled and what must have been a large quantity of powerful explosives, forced into the door.

When all was ready, the operators all retired into the front room, when, almost immediately a terrific explosion took place, shaking the building to its foundation and shattering the safe, woodwork and glass windows. The inner compartments of the safe were opened by the means of crow bars and chisels and access gained to the funds, which were removed, to the last dollar; within a quarter of an hour, the bound watchman said, the entire gang, with their plunder were leaving the place....The scene of the explosion in the bank was one of utter destruction and wreck. The heavy door of the safe was blown against the opposite wall of the room, fifteen feet away, and debris of all kinds filled the space....There were probably fifty people sleeping within a hundred feet of the bank building; but not more than five were sufficiently aroused to realize that something of a startling character was going on, but none of these investigated the cause. It is supposed that the burglars, after leaving the bank scattered in different directions. The wagon heard by Durell, was again heard leaving the bank, where it had evidently remained, during the robbery; this probably conveyed away a part of the gang, while a hand car that was missed in the morning from the railroad station, took the remainder. The horse and wagon had been stolen from a farmer near Monroe, and was left by the thieves about three miles from the city.[151]

The robbers were never caught, and none of the money was ever recovered. It was considered one of the boldest crimes of that nature to occur in Michigan in years.

Yet, only ten years later, another bold robbery rocked the city—literally. The bank of La Fountain & Loranger, located on the southeast corner of

Front and Monroe Streets, was the next victim. In this case, the burglars gained access to the bank's basement. From there, they cut a hole through the floorboards to get inside. Like the First National Bank robbers, they used dynamite to blow open the vault and clear out its contents. Once again, no one was the wiser, and they escaped scot-free and were never found.[152]

Grave Robberies

In 1800s Monroe, bank robberies were not the only kind of robberies going on. A much more sinister crime was taking place. In 1828, surveyors at Kentucky Memorial Place Cemetery made a bloodcurdling discovery when they saw one of the graves had been desecrated. The grave belonged to Nelson Wilcox, who had died nine or so months earlier. "The lid of the coffin had been bored through, ripped up, and the body dislodged from its earthly tonement [entombment]." The poor boy was only seventeen years old when he died and known by everyone as much more mature than his years. The incident sent shock waves throughout the community.[153]

Although grave robbing was a known occurrence in the nineteenth century, it was not known in the Michigan territory and certainly not in Monroe. The motive, however, was virtually certain. It wasn't kids out looking for a spooky adventure or people looking to steal jewelry or valuables; in fact, valuables

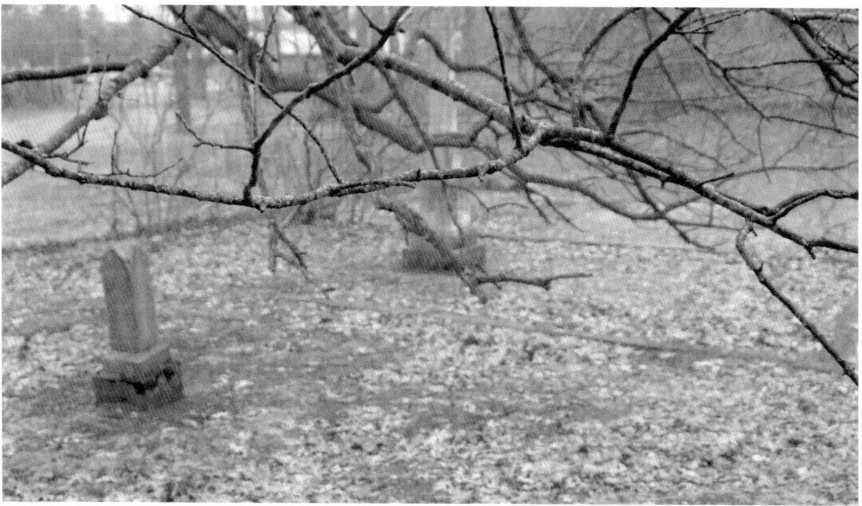

Country cemetery in the northern part of the county.

would often be tossed back in the grave. Unfortunately, in this age, it was for science and the advancement of knowledge. Thus, the poor victim's body was destined to be dissected into many pieces, with all the organs removed. Obviously, cadavers were not easily obtainable, yet many physicians were looking to hone their craft with them. Since disturbing a grave was a serious crime, they would often pay a third party to do the evil deed for them; these parties were known as "resurrection men."[154]

After the desecrated grave of young Wilcox was discovered, all the doctors in town were looked at suspiciously. Since there were only four doctors in Monroe in 1828—Harry Conant, Luther Parker, Robert Clark and Ephraim Adams—it didn't take long for the prosecutors to narrow it down to one suspect. The twenty-nine-year-old Adams was fingered in the crime, mostly because he was a cutting-edge physician looking for new ways to improve on medicine. On December 6, 1828, in a letter to territorial supreme court judge William Woodbridge, Charles J. Lanman wrote: "Doct. Adams is suspected of violating the repose of the grave—the Devil is to pay—and the Doct. Has fled."[155]

Strangely enough, the man they accused was not only a doctor but also a chief justice of the Monroe County court. Dr. Adams returned to Monroe to prove his innocence, but not with the help of a lawyer; instead he relied on young schoolmaster James A. Shedd. The local newspaper, the *Sentinel*, run by Edward D. Ellis, reported: "The examination took place at the court house…in the presence of a numerous concourse of spectators.…After a patient examination of witnesses, and the hearing of counsel on both sides, the opinion of the Court was declared by Squire Choate, in the following words: 'The Court find the testimony insufficient to sustain the charge.'"[156]

Even though the crime was never solved, or even prosecuted, new bylaws were created to make sure it would never happen again.

Yet, this was not the only account of grave robbing in Monroe. There is a cemetery in Ida Township that local resident Tillie Marie Sancraint remembered in an interview with Marion Childs: "On the north side of Todd…there is a small family cemetery belonging to a family thought to be named Bordel or similar to it. The family was well-to-do and it was said that some of them had been buried in the vault with their jewelry. Anyway, the grave robbers did their work there—the caskets were opened, but nobody knows whether anything of value was found."[157]

Woodland Cemetery was also the victim of body snatching, according to a Mr. Munch, when he was interviewed by Marion Childs. Munch said in the 1880s "there was some Body Snatching—the cuff links from a corpse were found on the ground a few days after a friend of Munch's was buried. People often paid watchers to keep vigil over their families' graves for weeks after a funeral. Bodies were said to be worth $10.00 at the U of M. Fingers were pointed at local doctors as fences."[158]

Unfortunately, Munch also related another incident in Monroe history that revealed disrespect to the deceased in the following tale, "A pall bearer tells about the back wheel of a hearse breaking off, hearse door popping open and casket sliding to the road en route to the Petersburg Cemetery. A wagon was hired, blizzard came up. When Cemetery was reached, the grave was on the wrong lot. They just left the casket on the ground and went home."[159]

Chapter 11

The Railroad to Freedom

Many people think the Underground Railroad came into existence in the mid-1800s, but it is thought that it was operating in Monroe County as early as 1818.[160] The Underground Railroad was a route along which people would help escaped African American slaves from the South get to points north in order to ultimately achieve their goal of freedom by crossing over the border into Canada.

Being involved in the Underground Railroad was a dangerous business. If one was caught, there could be fines, penalties and even imprisonment—not to mention what the fugitives would ultimately face. Thus, activities were quite cloak-and-dagger and took place in the darkness. Managers helped with the costs and supplies, while conductors or agents spirited the slaves from one station to the next. Stationmasters were the owners of the places where the station was. Stations were usually homes, barns, churches, etcetera.

In 1850, after the passage of the Fugitive Slave Act, the Underground Railroad became much more dangerous. It was revamped to cover shorter distances and require less time overall. Freedom seekers crossing from the Kentucky region were frequently sent directly north through Ohio to Sandusky and Toledo, or along the Ohio/Indiana border into southern Michigan. Trains from Fort Wayne, Indiana, led to Hillsdale County. At Jonesville, a traveler could transfer to the Sothern Michigan Railroad whose line included a junction at Adrian and terminated at Monroe."[161]

Bear with me, as we are talking about Monroe, but we must first go to Maumee, Ohio, to follow a route to the Underground Railroad in Monroe.

In Ohio, the Underground Railroad was established around 1815–17. Up to and through the Civil War, its activity grew tremendously. According to author S.S. Knabenshue,

> *For fifty years,* [Ohio] *was one of the most traveled of states by the black fugitives....There were eighteen or nineteen organized routes across Ohio. After the enactment of the Fugitive Slave Law in 1850, there were probably twenty main routes with each one having trailing routes crisscrossing the state. The Underground Railroad was to transport the slaves from the south to the north to obtain their freedom ultimately in Canada. So, it makes perfect sense that Monroe the southernmost county next to Canada and bordering Ohio would see traffic across its borders.*[162]

In Maumee, Amasa C. Winslow was a stationmaster and hid the slaves in his barn. The Sylvania stationmaster was David Harroun, who transported the runaway slaves from Maumee to Sylvania. He hid them in two old lumber wagons, with plank bottoms and sides, pulled by horses. The fugitives were covered in hay to disguise their presence. Operators of the Underground Railroad only traveled at night. When the slaves reached Sylvania, they were hidden at Harroun's house in the attic or in the barn loft. Sometimes, they were taken to the house to the west across the fields, the Lanthrop house. There, they were hidden in a secret room in the basement. This room was discovered in 1939, when the home's owners at that time, Mr. and Mrs. Theodore Vogt, were remodeling the house.[163]

From Sylvania, Ohio, the road continued with the purpose of getting the fugitives to freedom in Canada across the border. That is where Monroe comes in. From Sylvania, "Hall Deland, the 'night hawk,' took them to the French settlers along the Detroit river, who ferried them across that stream to Canada."[164] This was if the pursuers were close. If not, the "fugitives were brought either to Toledo, or taken, via Detroit avenue, to Monroe, Michigan, and thence across to Canada."[165]

Hall Deland was sympathetic to the cause and hid the slaves in his large cellar, which had three basements, with the two lowest used to conceal the slaves. From his house, he would take the fugitives by covered wagon through the night to an unknown place closer to Canada.[166]

Hall Deland was born on August 9, 1796, in Massachusetts. He married Laura Goodrich in 1816 at Vernon, Oneida County, New York, and they had three children, Rudolph, Charles and Henry. It appears he came to Monroe, Michigan, in 1850, according to his War of 1812 pension records.

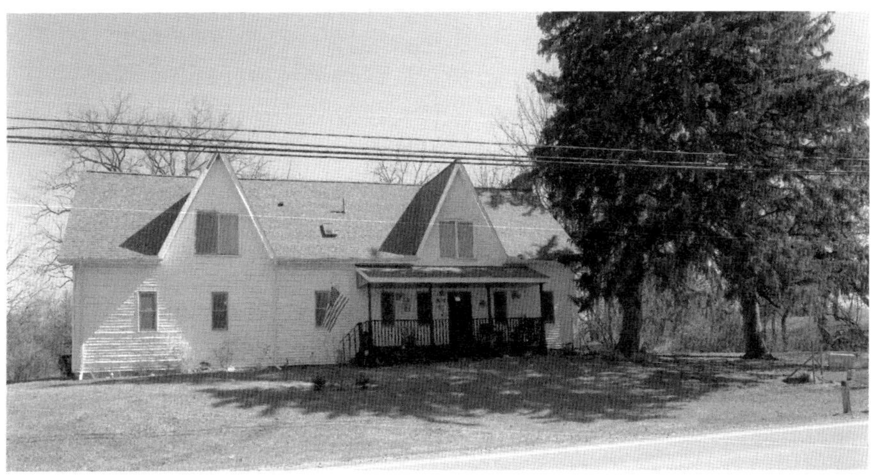

Hall Deland house today.

He lived at the corner of Samaria and Summerfield Roads in Bedford Township and ran a tavern called the Half-Way House, in later years called the Packard House.[167]

Deland was at the veterans' reunions of the War of 1812 and the Battles of the River Raisin in 1871 and 1872, when he was seventy-five and seventy-six years old, respectively.[168] Although he was at the River Raisin reunions, he was not a soldier in those battles. Instead, he enlisted on October 6, 1814, as a private in Captain Reuben Elwood's Twentieth Company, New York State Militia. He was honorably discharged on November 19, 1814, after serving about one and a half months. He died of disease on August 31, 1878, at eighty-two years of age and is buried at the Lambertville Methodist Cemetery. His gravestone does not mention his involvement in the War of 1812 or the Underground Railroad.[169]

Just like Hall Deland, many of the settlers in Monroe were stout abolitionists. When bounties were placed on the heads of slaves who had escaped, settlers ignored them and instead used their homes as safe houses or helped the runaways get to Canada. Thus, many other residents were also "conductors."

The *Sentinel* reported on October 21, 1826: "Twenty-five able bodied Negroes passed through Monroe...on their way to the Quaker settlement in Oakland County....[They] came not as slaves, but in the employ of members of the Society of Friends, who will doubtless reward them well for their labor and pay a scrupulous regard to their moral and intellectual improvement."[170]

WAR OF 1812.

NUMBERS	SOLDIER	BOUNTY LAND
S.O. 15968 rejected	De Land, Hall	
	WIDOW De Land, Laura	13110—40—50
W.O. 33320		55263—120—55
W.C. 21173	SERVICE Pvt. Capt. Elwood's Co. N.Y. mil.	
	ENLISTED Oct. 6, 1814 DISCHARGED Nov. 19, 1814	

RESIDENCE OF SOLDIER 1850 + 1855 + 1871, Bedford Monroe Co. Mich.

RESIDENCE OF WIDOW 1878, Bedford (P.O. Lambertville) Monroe Co. Mich.

MAIDEN NAME OF WIDOW Laura Goodrich

MARRIAGE OF SOLDIER AND WIDOW Nov 27, 1816, Vernon, Oneida Co, N.Y.

DEATH OF SOLDIER Aug. 31, 1878, Bedford, Mich.

DEATH OF WIDOW

REMARKS

Hall Deland's War of 1812 record. *War of 1812 Pension Files.*

In July 1826, a man named Cuffee, a free African American, came to Monroe and found employment with a farmer in the area. Not long after, a Mr. Power from Kentucky, who was a bounty hunter of African Americans, got word of Cuffee's presence and quickly seized him. The residents of the town were not going to allow it and, in no uncertain terms, made Mr. Power aware of their sentiments—so much so that he quickly fled town on his horse back to Kentucky.[171]

Yet, there were a few Monroe citizens who did not oppose slavery and helped a few slave owners capture their slaves. In March 1827, Swan Creek resident Captain Augustus Thorp helped two Virginians, Price and Allen, recapture two of their slaves and haul them off to Fort Meigs. But when they tried to recapture a third slave who was being protected in a settlement known as Waterloo, a mile west of town, those residents "turned out en masse and drove off the depredators."[172] In fact, "when brought before Colonel Peter P. Ferry, Justice of the Peace, the Virginians were prevented from taking their fugitive, but also ordered to jail. Colonel Ferry kept them behind bars for months until the next court session, where they produced "questionable" documents and were sent home, properly dissuaded from setting foot in Monroe in the future."[173]

"Thus," according to historian Russell Bidlack, "although the Civil War was still decades in the future, the code of that irrepressible conflict were being sown, even in such a remote corner of the Union as Monroe County, Michigan Territory."[174]

In 1829, an enslaved family journeyed from Kentucky on the Underground Railroad with Canada in their crosshairs. Saby had just given birth to a baby, Nancy, and she decided along with her husband, Isom, to make the trek to freedom to keep their baby safe. After crossing through Ohio,

> *the Freedom seekers entered the Territory of Michigan at the town of Monroe (Frenchtown), an early French trading post. Prominent men in the village had antislavery convictions, including Colonel Oliver Johnson, judge of the Probate Court. An organizer of the First Presbyterian Church of Monroe (1820), the Rev. John Monteith was known for helping enslaved people escape. Saby and friends encountered no obstacles in Michigan. They reached Detroit, the city called the "Midnight" gateway to Canada. Saby and Ison's journey was one of the first recorded interstate escapes on the Underground Railroad.*[175]

In 1818, the first nondenominational Protestant society was formed in Detroit by the Reverend John Monteith. The following year, the first Presbyterian church was built in Detroit. In Monroe, the Reverend Monteith also helped to develop the first Presbyterian church, "where Saby and Isom passed through."[176] In later years, the Reverend Monteith traveled to New York,

> *where he met Charles Grandison Finney, the evangelist of the Second Great Awakening. Monteith became a serious reformer and moved to Ohio where he joined up with Theodore Weld's band. At first, Monteith helped self-emancipators get to the southern shore of Lake Erie in Ohio, where they boarded boats crossing to Canada. Monteith Hall (1835), his home in Elyria, Ohio, was a station in the Oberlin Underground Railroad network. Monteith returned to Monroe, Michigan, in 1845 as an experienced Underground Railroad operator.*[177]

Later, the Reverend Monteith helped found the University of Michigan.

In Marion Childs' 1960 interview with May Smith, it was revealed that in 1920, a booklet was published by the Presbyterian church in Monroe titled *Centennial Jubilee, 1820–1920*. On page 16, it says: "As abolition sentiment grew…it found a sympathetic chord in this church. The 'Underground Railroad,' by which fleeing slaves were helped to freedom, found stations in the homes of this church."[178] The booklet was written by the Reverend L. B. Bissell, pastor of the church for nine years in the 1890s. May Smith said, "He knew many of the men who were living during pre–Civil War times and undoubtedly had been told of their activities in helping the slaves."[179]

The website for the First Presbyterian Church states: "Located in the heart of Downtown Monroe, across the street from the Monroe County Courthouse and on Loranger Square, our church provided shelter for the Underground Railroad. Dr. John [Monteith], was the founding Pastor and the first President of the University of Michigan. Miss Libbie Bacon and General George Custer were married in our sanctuary. Founded in 1820 our church is older than the State of Michigan."[180]

In the mid-1800s, ministers often found themselves in precarious situations when they believed in abolition but were censored by their congregation. "In Monroe, Michigan a minister stated that there was a strong prejudice against ministers participating in political enterprises to end slavery. While he felt it was the duty of Christians to do anything within their power to overthrow slavery, he would not preach the subject within the church."[181]

Monroe doctor Eduard Dorsch has been rumored throughout the years to have been a conductor on the underground railroad. A native of Germany, he came to Monroe shortly after leaving Germany during the 1848 revolution. He was also a delegate to the first Republican Party convention and practiced medicine in Monroe for thirty-seven years.[182] It is thought that he built his house shortly after coming to Monroe around 1850, according

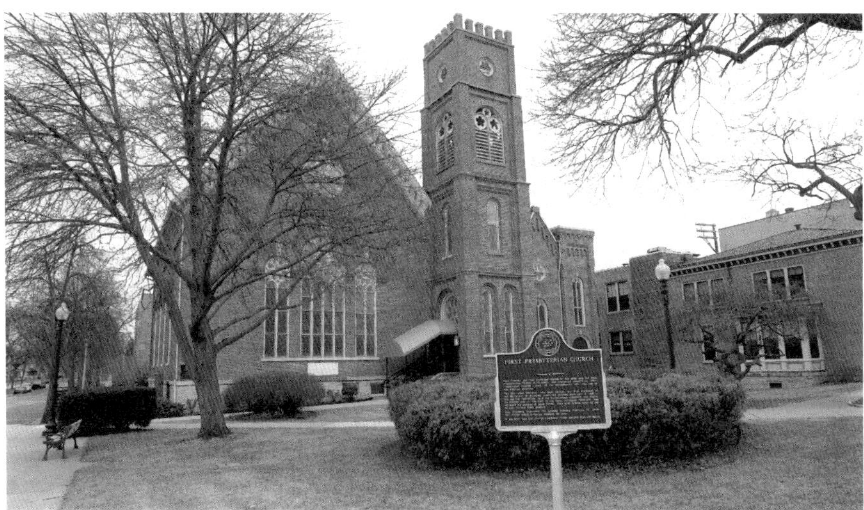

First Presbyterian Church, First Street.

to the Dorsch Memorial Library website.[183] Also, it is believed that there is a tunnel leading from his basement to the Presbyterian church next door. Talcott Wing says in his *History of Monroe, Michigan* that "with the head of a philosopher and heart of a poet, he worked or blended the two together in the most of his poetical works....[He was] carried away by the inspiration of his theme, throwing his entire soul into the subject in hand, and with an earnest desire to create in the reader the same determined opposition to slavery and ardent love for freedom which inspired him."[184]

The historical marker in front of Dorsch's former home, which now houses the Dorsch branch of the Monroe County Library System, says, "In Monroe his love of freedom led him to make his home a station on the Underground Railroad."[185]

An 1859 map of Monroe County and the City of Monroe shows the house as being next to the Presbyterian church, albeit much smaller, as it was later added on to.[186]

Colonel Oliver Johnson was also involved with the antislavery movement, as were other men in Monroe. William Hart Boyd, whose house was at the corner of East Fourth Street and Washington and called the "Irish Castle," was rumored to have been part of the Underground Railroad, concealing escaped slaves in his house.[187] In Marion Childs's 1960 interview with May Smith about the Presbyterian church, Smith said she was a good friend of Carrie Boyd, who actually told her that the Boyd house was a stop on the Underground Railroad.[188]

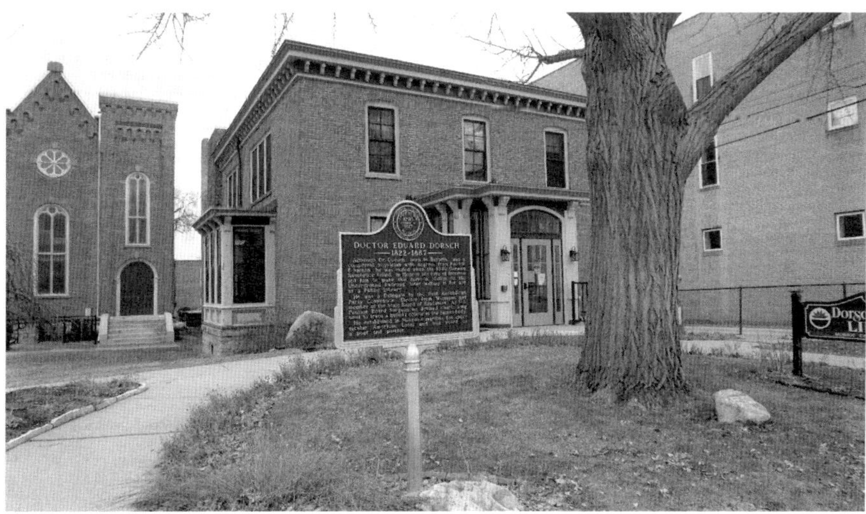

Dorsch Memorial Library, First Street.

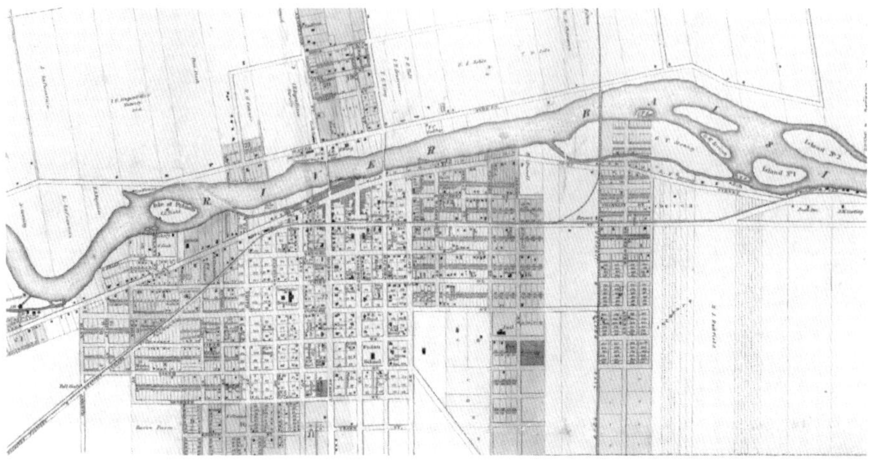

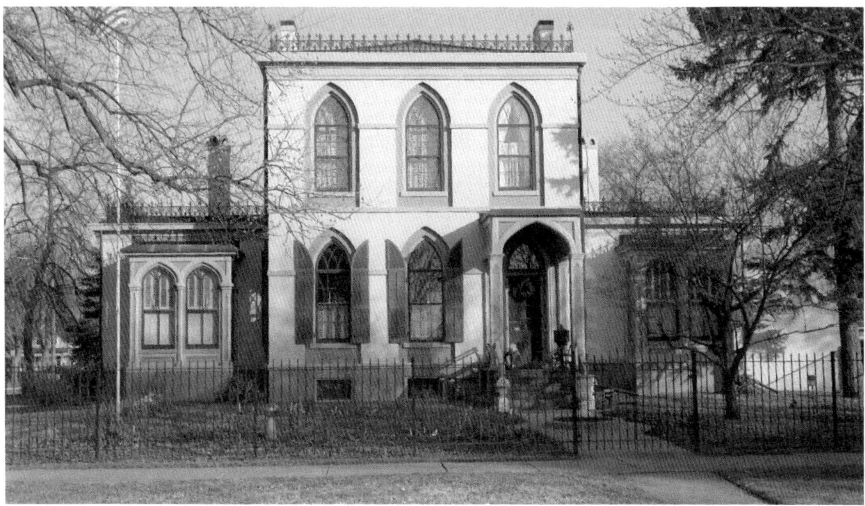

Top: Map of the city of Monroe, 1859 (cutout from a map of the county). *Library of Congress.*

Bottom: Boyd house today.

Erasmus Boyd, brother of William, was also against slavery and was a founder of the Republican Party. While running the Monroe Young Ladies Seminary, he hired Beverly Harris, a Black carpenter. Harris was previously a conductor in Perrysburg, Ohio, and it is thought he now was using the seminary as an Underground Railroad stop in Monroe.[189]

Other residents were also rumored to be involved in the Underground Railroad, such as Theophilus Osgood, who hid slaves at his farm in Monroe and then guided them to the next station during the night. There were rumors of the Dewey house in Brest and the Farnham house in Summerfield being part of the network.[190]

Quaker Amasa Atkinson built a farmhouse west of Monroe, and it was said that "one of the steps leading up to the attic was never nailed down, which created a cramped, but effective, hiding place."[191]

The Bradford family lived on a farm on Stein Road in LaSalle Township in the 1800s. Neighbors of the Bradfords, as well as owners of the home since, claim the house was a stop on the Underground Railroad.[192] Also, in an interview with Marion Childs, Elizabeth Godfried said her father-in-law's house was an original French homestead that was over 160 years old in the mid-1900s; he bought it in 1865. She said one of the most curious parts of the house was a trapdoor in the floor of a closet off the dining room. Under it was a tunnel over three feet deep.[193]

In the 1830s, John and Abigail Critchett moved to London Township in Monroe County. John knew only too well the heartbreak associated with separation. His father was a Connecticut sailor who was captured by the British and imprisoned on a British ship for two years. His mother thought she was a widow until his fateful return. John and Abigail used their home as a safe house for as long as necessary for slaves making their way to Canada.[194]

Although not a lot of information has come to be known about Monroe and the Underground Railroad, there is no doubt how strategic Monroe was to the route and how many residents were sympathetic to the cause. It would not be surprising in the future if more of Monroe's involvement comes to light from the underground.

Chapter 12

Monroe's Miami Beach

Monroe used to rival many of the finest beach communities of today. Back in the day, Monroe was synonymous with the Monroe Piers. The Monroe Piers was a destination. In its heyday, it used to offer a sandy beach, swimming area, bathhouse, clubhouse, hotel and even a casino. The Piers park, with its large grove of trees, provided plenty of shade and picnic and fishing areas. "It had extensive play grounds, recreational and amusement facilities. The Beach as it was called in the horse and buggy days was 'The Place' to go."[195]

Furthermore, part of the attraction of the Piers also lay in the ways to get there. The Piers was at the mouth of the River Raisin where it emptied into Lake Erie and developed because of the U.S. Ship Canal project. In 1834, Captain Henry Smith of the U.S. Army Corps of Engineers recommended straightening and dredging the River Raisin by cutting a canal through to Lake Erie. The canal was four thousand feet long by one hundred feet wide. The river also had a sharp turn in it that the city decided to straighten out at the same time. Once the canal was dug, wooden piers were put in that ran the length of the canal for about one-fifth of a mile.[196]

In 1849, a lighthouse was also built to aid in navigation. Its red light illuminated the water for a thirteen-mile stretch. A lightkeeper's house was built in 1860, but in 1893, it was damaged in a springtime storm. It was rebuilt the following year. In 1916, the government installed an automatic gaslight in the lighthouse, therefore eliminating the need for a lightkeeper's

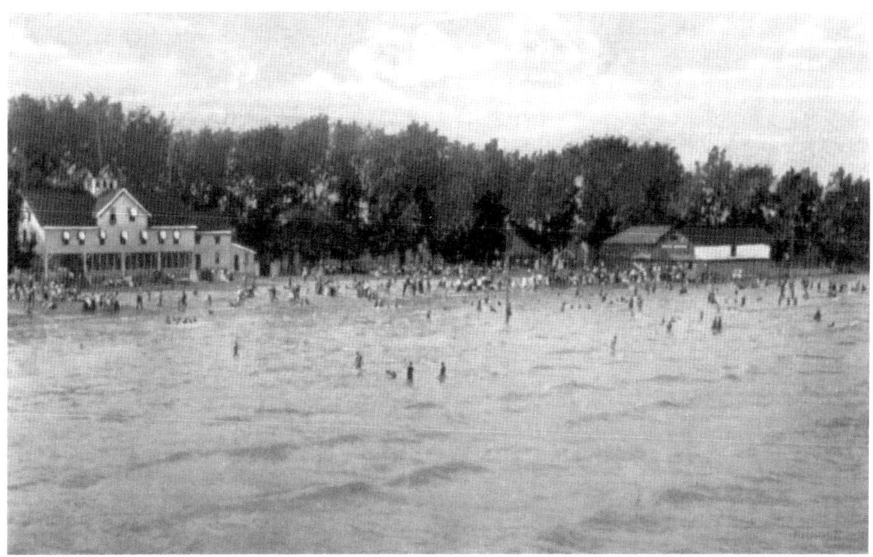

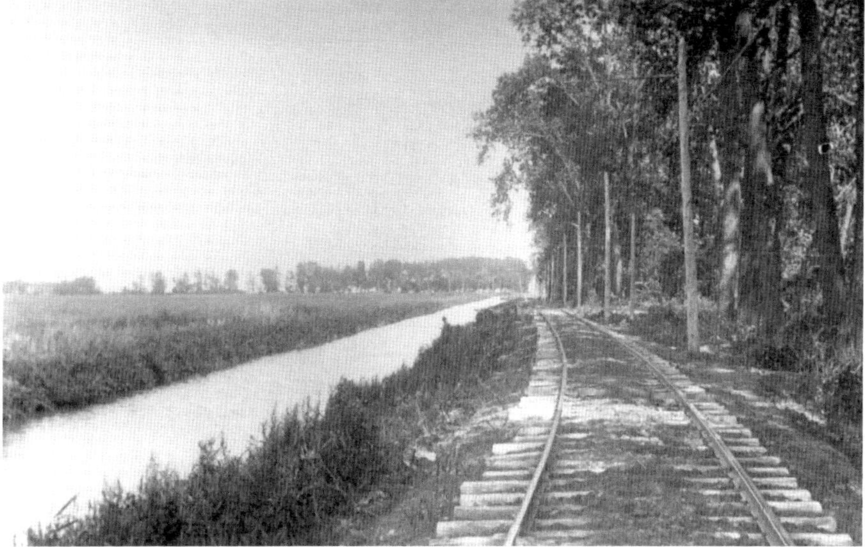

Top: Monroe Piers, Hotel Lotus and bathhouse. *Monroe County Library System.*

Bottom: Streetcar tracks to the Piers. *Monroe County Library System.*

house. But just a few years later, the lighthouse was sold to a Toledoan for a mere thirty-five dollars.[197]

The building of the canal opened up not only recreational possibilities but also commercial possibilities that ran alongside it. "A horse-drawn, strap-iron

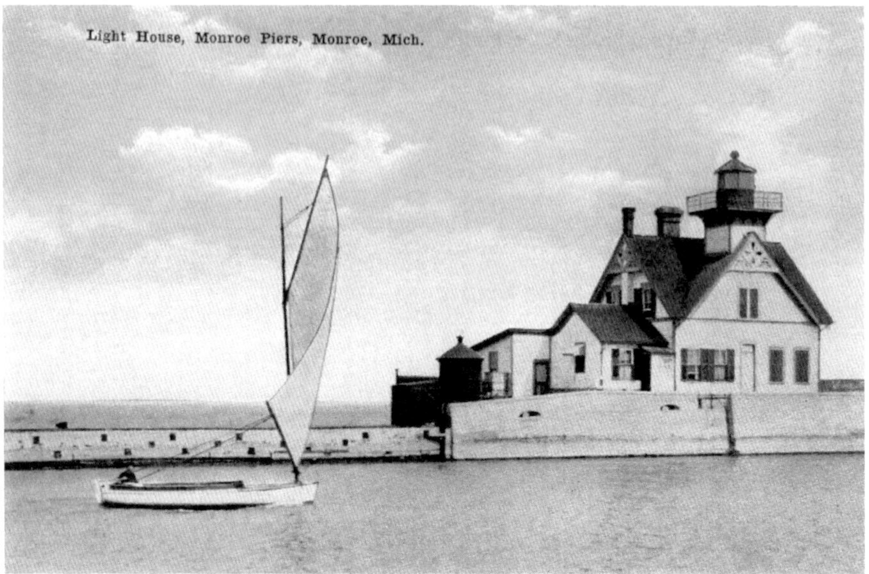

Lighthouse at Monroe Piers. *Monroe County Library System.*

railroad went from the harbor into town following the south side of the canal through the marshes."[198] Before long, in the 1850s, a boarding hotel and numerous warehouses sprang up along the south side of the canal. A sawmill and a plaster mill were constructed by Captain George Strong along the city docks. Shipping on Lake Erie was very hazardous, with Lake Erie being the shallowest of the Great Lakes. But the early demise of commercial shipping was not in the hazards of the lake but in the advent of the steam railroad.[199]

A revival of sorts came in the 1880s when brothers William Clark and Frank S. Sterling rebuilt and reinvested in the area with their cedar pole business. "The poles were piled on rafts and towed by steamer from Omer, Michigan, and stockpiled here, to be reshipped throughout the world."[200] The Sterlings even enticed Toledo's Western Union to move their pole yard here. In 1884, a fire destroyed many of the city canal warehouses but did not affect the pole yards. In 1898, the local newspaper, the *Democrat*, reported that a shipment of poles was sent all the way to Cairo, Egypt.

Meanwhile, recreation boomed as well. By the late 1880s, passenger boats were carrying boatloads of people to and from the Monroe Piers. An advertisement in 1889 lauded the locally owned steamboat *Jeanie* as a new, elegant side-wheel paddle boat to chauffeur up to five hundred passengers: "A sidewheeler, it's the neatest and trimmest little excursion boat ever seen. Her length is 125', her breadth is 38' and her draft is 4½'. Her three decks include a refreshment stand, kitchen, a cabin for dancing with an elegant Steinway upright piano, plush divans, reclining chairs and Brussels carpet."[201]

Another locally owned boat was the *F.S. Sterling*, built in 1893. It carried up to two hundred passengers and offered moonlight cruises. Other boats were *Douglas*, *Fuller*, *Messenger*, *Dove* and *Newsboy*. The available routes were to Monroe, Toledo and Detroit. Toledo residents were frequent visitors to the Monroe Piers. People interested in going to downtown Monroe were usually carried to the city docks, or "Steamboat Landing." Sometimes, passengers were dropped off at the Piers when the water was too low and made the voyage the rest of the way by canal tugs *Arbutus*, *Fred L.* or *Clara S.* To get into town, tourists could opt to take a "hack," a large horse-drawn carriage that could seat up to twenty-five people.[202]

In 1895, the Monroe Piers Hotel Company formed, and the Hotel Lotus was born. The lavish hotel was three stories tall, with seventy-six-foot-long verandas over the porches. It had twenty-five rooms and could sleep up to seventy people. The Hotel Lotus lured tourists from all over and became famous for its family-style chicken dinners. The backyard, framed by willow trees, became a favorite spot to picnic. A refreshment stand was set up by the picnic area. Soon, there was a saloon, amusements, a merry-go-round and games. Even those living in the city could hardly resist a trip to the Piers on the weekend.

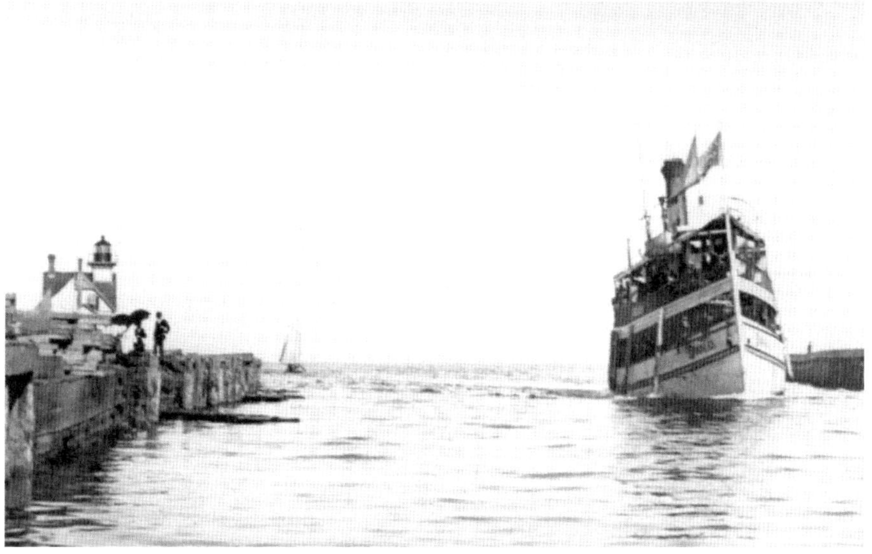

Steamer *F.S. Sterling* at Monroe Piers. *Monroe County Library System.*

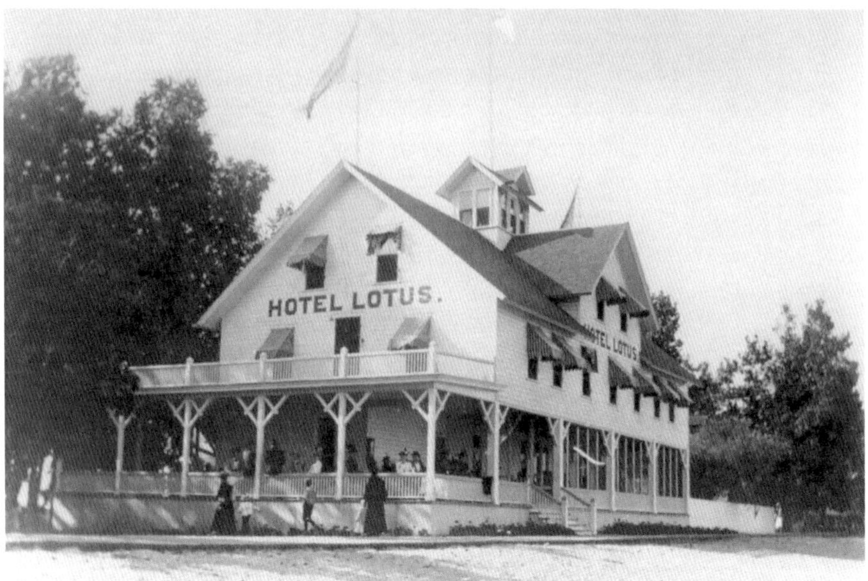

Hotel Lotus at Monroe Piers. *Monroe County Library System.*

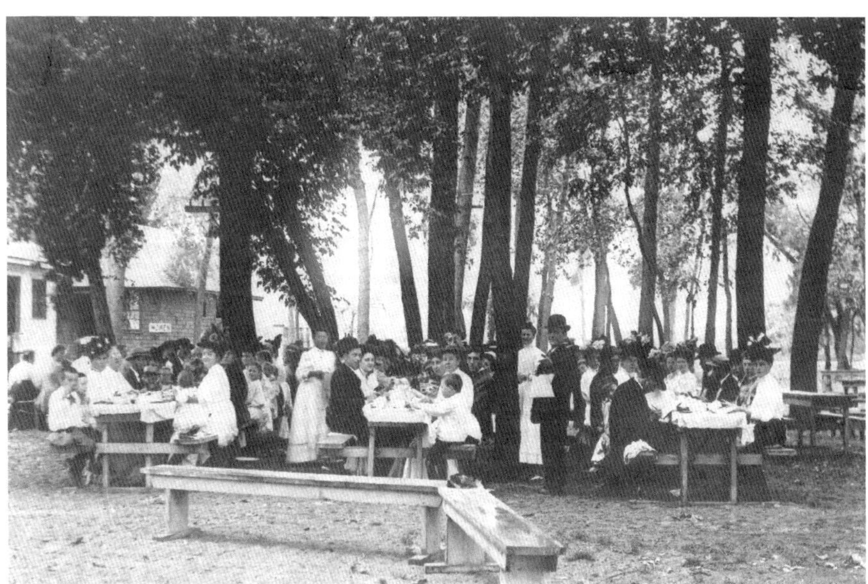

Monroe Piers picnic area. *Monroe County Library System.*

Around the same time the Hotel Lotus was built, so was the bathhouse. It contained fifty changing rooms. As the Piers grew more popular, the bathhouse was enlarged to two stories with over three hundred rooms. Tourists could actually rent a bathing suit, towel and locker. The bathing beach of Lake Erie was described as "like velvet, sloping so gradually that children can wade far out."[203] The beach was large and sandy. Benches were available for spectators, and there was also a seven-hundred-foot boardwalk alongside the beach and the hotel.[204]

In 1900, the Toledo and Monroe Railroad was granted a franchise to lay a pier line on Elm Avenue to run to the Piers. There was strong opposition to the line, but to no avail. Opening day of the new pier line was to be July 4, 1901: Independence Day. Eager to cash in on the popularity of the Piers, the T&M Railroad scheduled particular cars to run from Toledo to the Piers that day. Hundreds of people were eager to partake of the new venture. Onboarding at Monroe, the excited passengers were ready to hop on the new Beach Line, but owing to unforeseen circumstances, there was a malfunction at the powerhouse, and the pier line went down. Others who came to Monroe by other means, such as boats, could not even get close to the city owing to the throngs of people.

It also seemed Mother Nature was not on the side of the railroad either, for no sooner had everyone crowded into the town than a terrific thunderstorm hit. People wanting to return to Toledo were faced with yet another hazard, according to the *Monroe Democrat*: "And finally when the cars got under way for Toledo, that Jonah tunnel [at Alexis Road] was again filled with water. So there they stood, 500 passengers on board, all tired, hungry, thirsty, the women hysterical and fainting and the men profaning. Supper time passed and no relief. 9:00 p. m. and no change and the crowd clamored to get back to Monroe to catch the late Central train, but to no avail."[205] Some passengers were so angry they threw rocks at the train. The train finally got back to Toledo at 1:00 a.m. There were some passengers from Monroe wanting to go back; they did not arrive in the city until 7:00 a.m.[206]

Meanwhile, at the Piers, the Hotel Lotus served 360 people; it seemed people were everywhere. Extra steam railroad cars were sent from Detroit to carry the throngs back to Toledo since the electric cars had broken down and it was unsafe to travel by boat in the storm. The crowds might have broken records, but the only safe alternative was to board the steam trains, since the storm was heightening in its intensity. But when they were taken to their next destination, there were no cars available to take them into the city. They were given no choice but to walk in the stormy conditions. Once

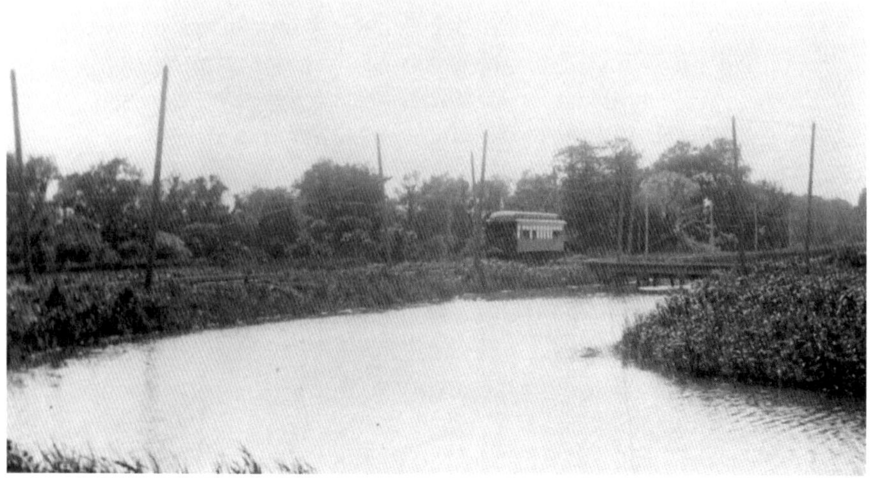

Above: Streetcar going to Monroe Piers. *Monroe County Library System.*

Opposite: Detroit, Monroe and Toledo Electric Railway (DM&T) 507 Pier Line. *Monroe County Library System.*

they reached the city, they found that the Toledo cars were not running either, and there were no buses or hacks anywhere. Their only alternative was to walk back through the mud to the depot in the pouring rain and wait to catch the steam trains. Certainly, a disastrous day for the opening of the new pier line![207]

The first successful trip by the new railcars was on July 11, 1901. Despite the July Fourth disaster, excited passengers paid their nickel fare to ride the new Beach Line and filled the tram, ready to make history. Almost as if history was repeating itself, another test came when the railcar tried to cross the other steam railroad tracks that existed on Elm. No arrangement had been made with the steam railroads to have a crossover line. The passengers suddenly became railroad workers as they tried to help the car get to the other side. Finally, after about thirty minutes, they were on their way.[208]

The interurban railroad increased the popularity of the piers immensely. All of a sudden, the gateway to the Piers was open, and anyone in Monroe could board the trolley for a nickel and, after a short, ten-minute ride, they would be immersed in the sun and sand. The demand was so high that on Sundays and holidays, extra cars were brought in to handle the crowds. Beachgoers from Toledo were desperate to get to Monroe, even arriving in gondola freight cars. In 1905, the newspaper reported, "70,000 passengers have been carried over the Beach Line during the season, an average of 700 a day."[209]

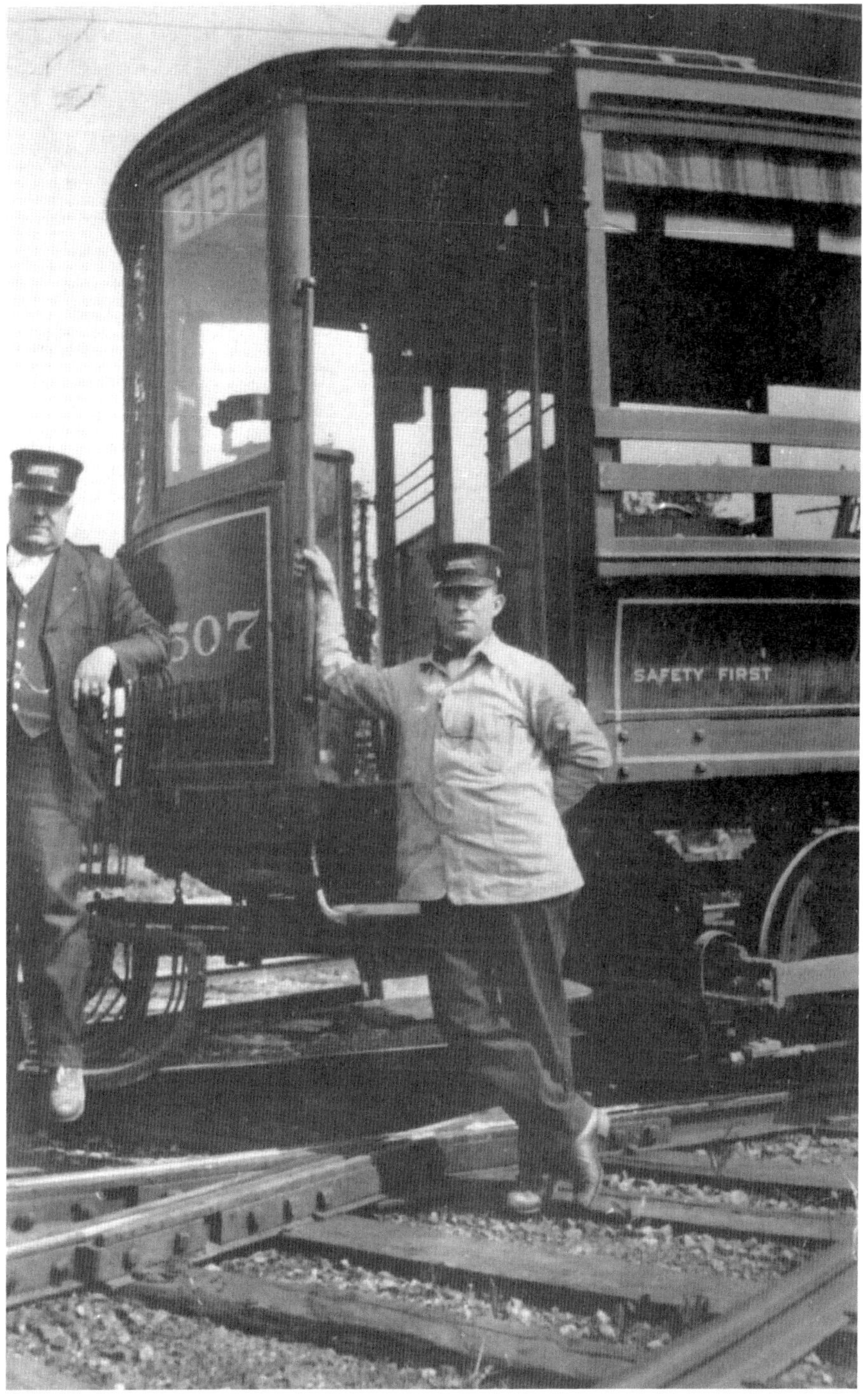
507
SAFETY FIRST

Even with all the activities at the beach, hotel, etcetera, another popular pastime at the Monroe Piers was boating. People loved to boat into the marshes to admire and pick the lotus flowers in the summer. In 1889, the newspaper reported, "Fully 100 acres of the marsh are covered with lotus this season."[210] Rowing on the river was another pastime, and rowboat races in the 1870s led to rowing clubs. Sailboating was another form of boating that had quite the history on the river. In 1886, the Monroe Yacht Club came into existence, with William Clarke Sterling as commodore (namesake of current-day W.C. Sterling State Park).[211]

In the early twentieth century, regatta fever hit Monroe, and it was determined a new clubhouse should be built on the south pier. On pilings, the building rose out of the water at thirty feet by sixty feet. It had twelve-foot verandas on all sides and a beautiful maple floor for dancing. The yacht club opened its doors in 1902. Access to the club could be gained only by a twenty-five-foot raft that held up to fifty people at a time. Once the club opened, boats swarmed into the Piers area. Regattas were held numerous times during the summer season and were a crowd-pleaser, with people coming from all over the state to participate in the races or simply watch them. In 1909, there were 131 entries! Yacht club dinners also took on a significance of their own. In the year 1903, seven hundred muskrats were served to dinner guests. This started a tradition that still exists to this day: the yacht club muskrat dinners.[212]

The Piers also had two notable islands in the area contributing to its popularity: Guyors Island (also known as House Island) and Johnsons Island. In the 1880s, "Uncle Joe's place" on Guyors Island on the south side was the place to go, especially when you desired a wild game dinner. Game was abundant in the marshes, notably ducks, geese, swan, muskrat and fish. Duck hunting became a favorite pastime for many a sportsman. The first hunting club was located in an old hotel on the south pier and was called the Golo Club, with local members such as George Armstrong Custer, Joseph M. Sterling and H.A. Conant. The clubhouse was destroyed in a storm in 1865. In 1882, the Monroe Marsh Club built a lavish two-story clubhouse on Guyors Island since Joseph Guyor sold the island shortly before he passed away. The exclusive club gained national notoriety as a hunters' retreat. Grover Cleveland was a visitor in the 1880s. Each man had his own boathouse for his duck boat and was provided a room to stay in. The clubhouse did not last long, however, due to a stove fire that burned it to the ground in the 1920s.[213]

Johnsons Island was owned by the Johnson family, who, in 1891, purchased the hamlet on the north side of the canal. The couple worked hard for four

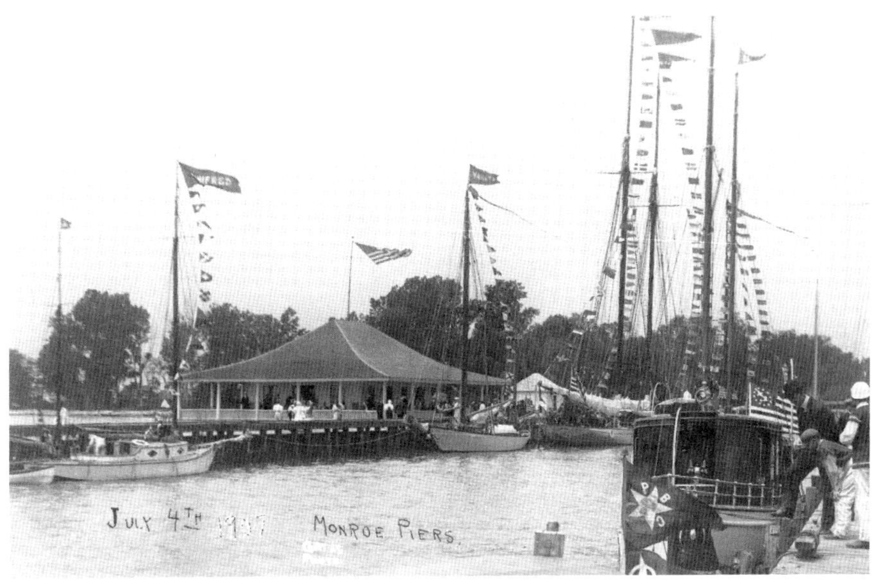

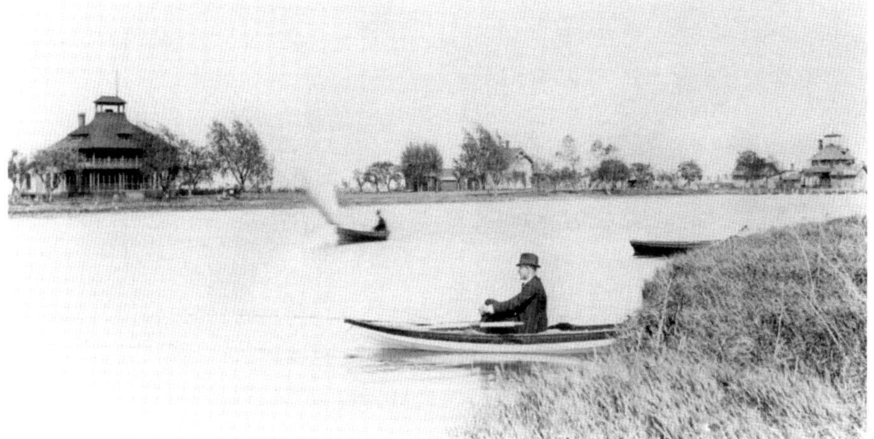

Top: Monroe Piers regatta, July 4, 1907. *Monroe County Library System.*

Bottom: Johnsons Island in the River Raisin. *Monroe County Library System.*

years to create a charming English-style home and gorgeous garden retreat area. In 1905, it was described by the local newspaper as follows: "Mr. Johnson's cottage is filled with curios and heirlooms brought from his home in England…now a speck of oasis in the midst of reeds and cattails. The electric railway crosses the island, and as one enters from where the cars stop, this romantic place shows itself to be a very practicable little farm."[214]

The Johnsons welcomed guests heading to the Piers with open arms. It turned out that their little oasis became a tourist stop in and of itself, famous for its lavish meals. In time, even a baseball park was added, and there were plans for a vaudeville playhouse and covered pavilion. Later, in 1911, when interest started to wane, Mr. Johnson took the position of manager at the Hotel Lotus. But shortly after, he died at fifty-nine years old while working in the dining room.[215]

The beginning of the twentieth century saw the Monroe Piers grow even larger when, in 1905, a building 225 feet by 50 feet rose up on the pilings to be christened the new casino. The two-story structure had a large dance floor with live music each night. The first floor had a luncheon area. In the same year, a roller coaster with a 75-foot tower encircled by incandescent lights turned the beach into a favorite nighttime swimming area. That same year, the yacht club also received its electric lights. Other improvements were made, including replacing the wooden planks on the boardwalks. Mini resort communities sprang up along the north and south pier areas, with families building beach houses and utilizing the beach area. Some had their own clubhouses.[216] With all the additions, it is not surprising that Monroe Piers recorded seventy thousand visitors for the year in 1905.[217]

Monroe also had a November gale to remember when on November 12, 1911, the Piers experienced "one of the worst and most disastrous that had been experienced in late years. So violent was the gale that swept out of the northeast and to such a height did the waves pile up and with such force."[218]

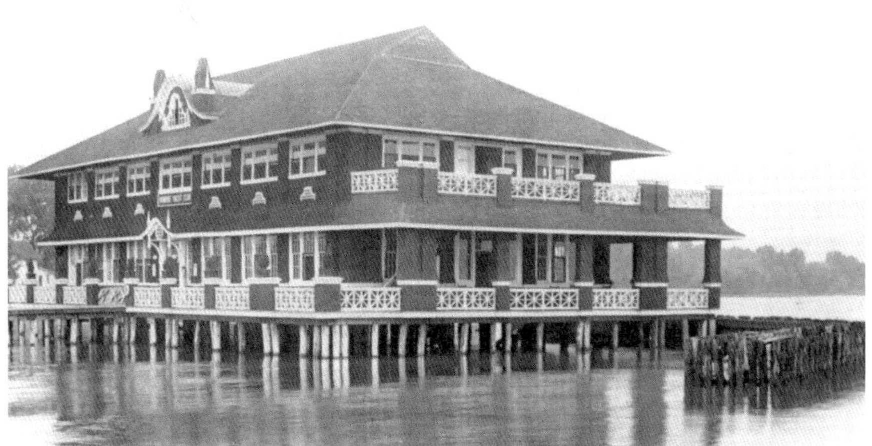

Monroe Yacht Club, 1917. *Monroe County Library System.*

The year 1913 was huge for Monroe, in that it marked one hundred years from the Battles of the River Raisin in the War of 1812. The Piers was at the center of the anniversary, with Commodore Oliver Hazard Perry's flagship the *Niagara* of Put-in-Bay fame making a stop in Monroe. The ship from which Perry coined his famous phrase "Don't give up the ship" caused immense crowds to flock to the Piers.[219]

In 1916, the casino was struggling financially, and the Monroe Yacht Club, which had outgrown its clubhouse, decided to purchase the building and improve it along with adding double porches.

During World War I, the Piers and remodeled casino/yacht club became a mecca of repose, providing a nice distraction. But the absence of younger men affected the boating activities and competitions. The Piers would never host the kinds of boating activities it did prewar. The now-vacant original yacht club building was bought and moved across the frozen lake to Pointe aux Peaux. But it did not quite make the trip, breaking through the ice and shattering into sections. Once it was salvaged, it was rebuilt into a private home.[220]

The advent of the automobile marked an end to the heyday of the Monroe Piers. People could now jump into a car and travel more quickly to new places they had never been before. The interurban lines could not compete with the automobile. The Piers was never accessible by car, and attendance waned. The Beach Line closed, and in 1932, the last electric trolley made its last voyage. The Monroe Yacht Club was also a victim of

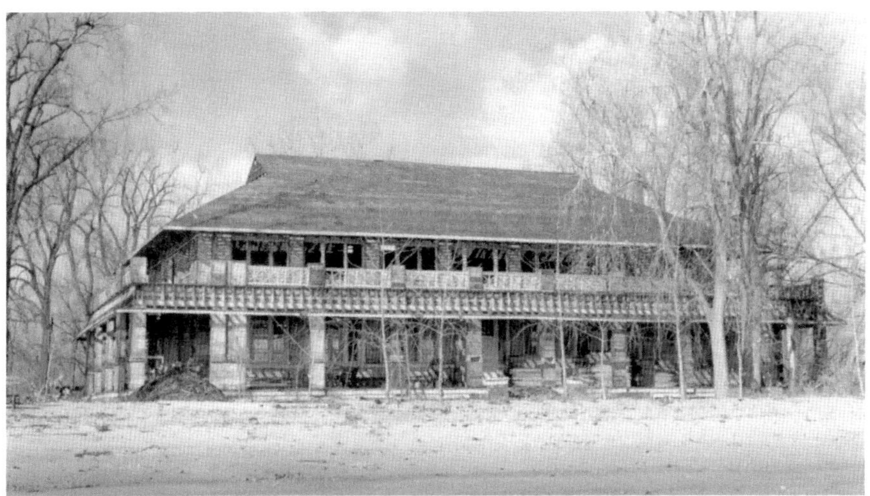

Old casino moved to Sterling State Park, 1948. *Monroe County Library System.*

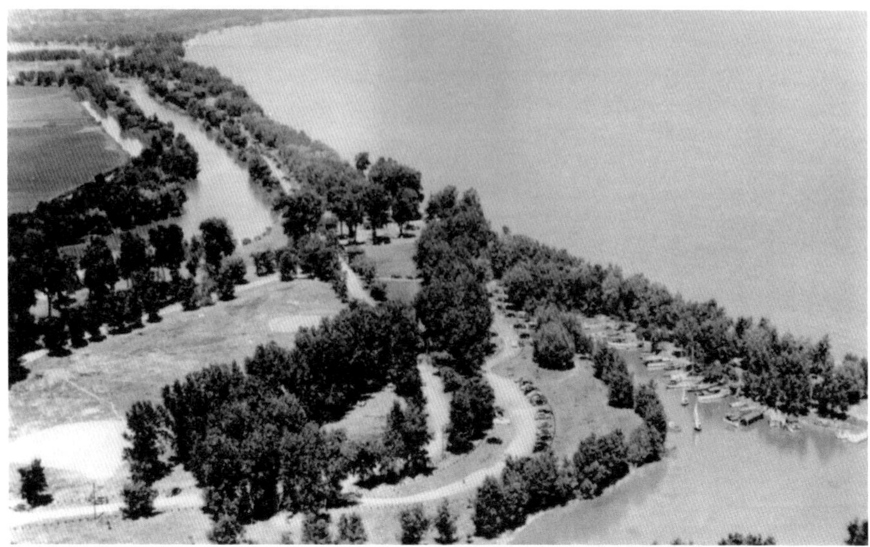

W.C. Sterling State Park. *Monroe County Library System.*

the automobile, and in 1927, it was "agreed to move the clubhouse (Casino) across the ice to a new private resort under development on the site of the present state park."[221] This building made the trip successfully, unlike the original clubhouse. The yacht club revived its popularity for a little while, but when the Great Depression struck, everything came to a halt. The club was dissolved, and the clubhouse/casino was given to the State of Michigan. The building became part of the state parks pavilion for a while but was eventually dismantled in 1948. In 1945, the Monroe Yacht Club and the Bolles Harbor Yacht Club reorganized to become the Monroe Boat Club.

The Monroe Piers and all its accompanying resorts are now just a memory. In 1927, the Newton Steel Company purchased 350 acres on what was the north side of the Piers to build a steel plant. Islands, marshes and buildings were all demolished to make way for the industrial age. The Hotel Lotus was no exception. Ford Motor Company became the next factory to erase any traces of the once-glamorous Monroe Piers. And the 1970s saw the once-famed Guyors Island become the home of an electrical company by way of Detroit Edison, which purchased the island in 1953.[222] Today, unfortunately, there is no trace of what was once Monroe's Miami Beach. The closest you can get to the Piers experience is the beach at William C. Sterling State Park.

Chapter 13

Dry Monroe?

In 1916, Michigan joined the revolution to become a "dry" state with a statewide prohibition. It was a slow process, with counties choosing to go dry on their own since 1907. The town of Temperance in Monroe County got its name from being on the forefront of the temperance movement. Temperance advocates Lewis and Marietta Anstead would only sell land to people who agreed to their clause of no selling or manufacturing intoxicants of any kind.

The movement gained momentum with the help of the Michigan Anti-Saloon League, churches and local groups. Of course, the owners of saloons, breweries, some restaurants and similar establishments vehemently opposed the idea.[223] In 1918, Monroe had thirteen saloons and had also been known as wine country since the 1860s.[224] Many of the residents' homes had vineyards in them. But the first winery was that of Joseph W. Sterling, who planted the first vineyard at Pointe aux Peaux in 1863. He had a limestone wine cellar constructed from limestone sailed in from Sandusky, Ohio.[225]

Michigan, in particular Monroe, gained quite a reputation before national Prohibition took effect in 1920 with the Eighteenth Amendment. Due to its location, Monroe was caught right in the middle, if you will, between Canada, Detroit and Toledo. Dixie Highway (US 25), running north and south between these locations, came to be known as "Avenue de Booze." Ohio was wet a full three years after Michigan was dry. No wonder smuggling was such a hot commodity; whiskey could be bought for $60 in Canada and sold for $200 in Michigan.[226] "Alcohol from Canada arrived in Michigan by every means imaginable—not just planes, trains, automobiles, trucks and boats, but also underwater sleds and at least one funeral hearse."[227]

Liquor could be exported to other countries from Canada due to a loophole in the law. So, smugglers simply said they were taking the cargo to a foreign country. The waters of the Detroit River, the River Raisin and Lake Erie had so many boats either transporting or policing the trade that they looked like water highways themselves. Large boats, up to thirty feet long, came from Canada, their destination the marshes at Stony Creek and Bolles Harbor in Monroe County. Many Monroe County residents found ways to participate in this illegal highway of booze for profit, as well as to simply keep themselves "wet." The local watering holes were known by all, especially those in Rockwood, Newport and Estral Beach.[228]

The term "bootlegging" originally came about because of the crafty, illegal technique of smuggling liquor in one's boots. Women strapped alcohol to their legs and covered it with their garments.[229] There was no shortage of ingenious ways to smuggle: split gas tanks, hollowed-out fruit, loaves of bread and eggshells, to name just a few.[230]

Some say Prohibition led to the development of the Mob. No doubt, rum-running was profitable; it led to rival gangs and caused all kinds of problems, especially with the law. Smugglers were not only in shoot-outs with the police but with rival groups, too. All kinds of lawlessness ensued. It got so bad that thirty state troopers were deployed to Monroe in June 1918. A month later, six hundred people were arrested, found guilty and thrown in the slammer for a month or so. "Court had to be held six days a week to deal with all the offenders. Confiscated liquor filled a jail cell. By July 8, 1918, $10,000 in fines had been collected."[231]

There were also just as many, if not more, ways to make the booze and hide it as there were to smuggle it. An intimate look at Monroe is given in a 1960 interview with Ed Steiner by Marion Childs. Steiner recalled, "For 3 days at one period there were a string of cars going thru Monroe, bumper to bumper, loaded with liquor."[232] He also remembered some of the curious ways citizens made the booze: "Sugar beets, from rotten tomatoes, from ensilage, from dandelions."[233] Ed's father, William Steiner, worked for William H. Boyd in those times. Steiner was entrusted with the job of "packing whiskey into barrels, labeled such inconspicuous names as 'crackers' or 'flour' to be taken to the Boyd barn."[234] When a friend of the Boyd family became ill and was advised to drink some whiskey, Boyd was able to help out by getting the contents from the barrel in his barn labeled

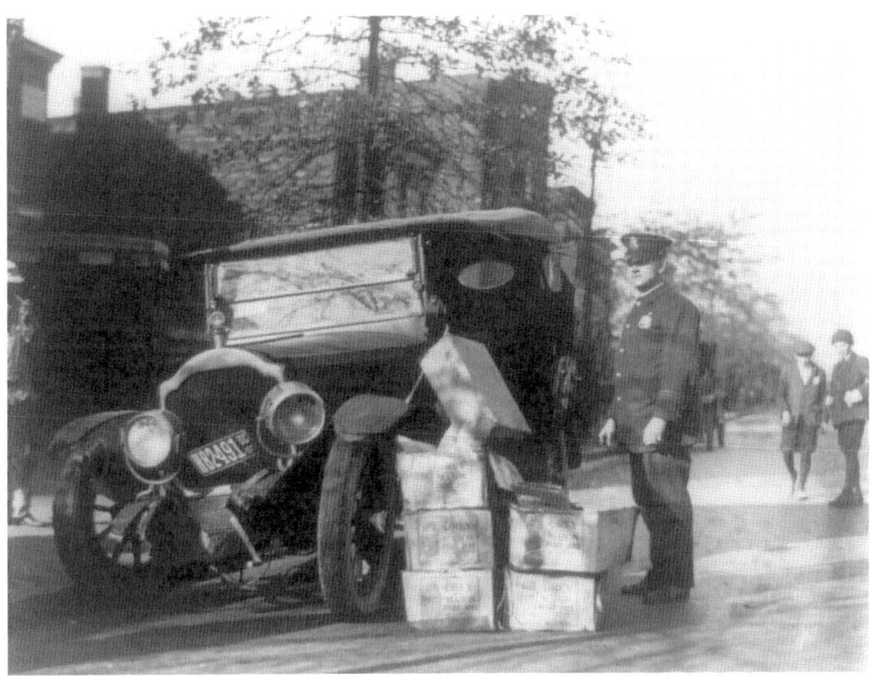

Above: Prohibition booty. *Library of Congress.*

Right: Clever concealment. *Library of Congress.*

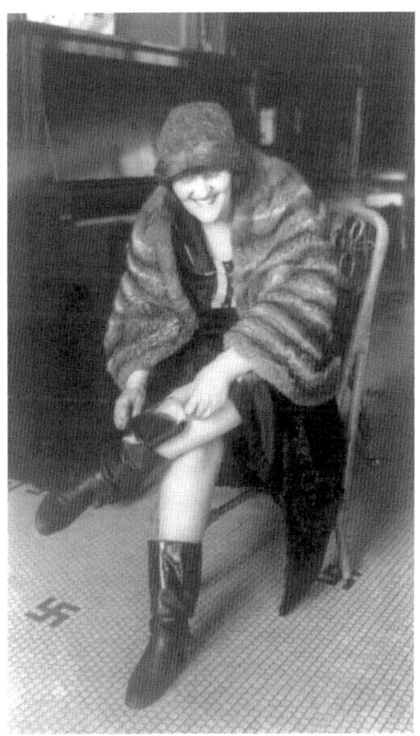

"crackers." In any case, "No one would think of reporting a rumrunner in those days," Ed confessed.[235]

Another interview Marion Childs conducted in 1958 was with Bernard Lazette. He had vivid memories of Prohibition in Monroe. He remembered how the river became an ice highway in the winter, with car after car heading to and from Canada loaded with illegal whiskey and beer. Every now and then a car didn't make it and went through the ice.[236]

In case they get caught, the bootleggers had several tricks up their sleeves. One of them was to pry off the top of the wooden crate and throw the crate overboard, letting it fill quickly with water and sink, a quick way to dispose of the evidence. If the Canadian runners spied a government boat with their binoculars, they would load empty crates into a decoy boat. The police boat would follow the decoy, while the real, loaded boat made its way freely to Monroe.[237]

Bernard recalled how mash, used for making whiskey, could be smelled all throughout the east end of town, with at least fifty places making it. Many of them were raided, but the mash makers were clever at evading the law. Many of the houses were rentals, so it was harder to find the responsible party. One "blind pig" (speakeasy) was run by a couple who owned the empty house next door, where they kept all the liquor. Some of the houses were not even occupied, with the only residents being large tanks full of mash. One on Winchester Street caught fire, and on the second floor was a still along with a room full of bottles with labels on them that said "rubbing alcohol." Yet, other than a canary on the first floor, the place was empty. Another empty house that was raided was on Third Street, and when the police entered it, they found nothing but a huge tank ten feet by five feet. They broke the tank open and let the booze spill to the floor. But they were absolutely horrified when not only the booze rushed out—but also dead rats.[238]

At one house, a big kettle of mash was in the backyard next to the pig pen. When the police questioned the owner about it, she claimed that it was food for her pigs and proceeded to give them a big scoop of it in their trough. The officers left, and no arrests were made, but the pigs were never quite the same.

Bernard worked as an electrician, and this gave him an intimate view into the bootlegging trade. On one job, he had to install push buttons under the front counter at a mom-and-pop grocery store. The buttons were not installed to call the police in the event of a robbery but were used to call the back room when the police arrived. Wooden shelves were rapidly put up and evidence stashed, all in quick order.

Another job found Bernard installing wiring on the ceiling of a huge room that was full of cases of liquor that reached almost up to the ceiling. Instead of using a ladder, he was able to lie down on the cases to reach the wiring. The booze-filled cases engulfed the room in the morning and by night were gone, but within a short time, a different load from Canada replaced them.

But just as Ed Steiner claimed, Bernard said, "No one would squeal to the police—there was absolutely no social stigma to being a bootlegger."[239]

In another interview, Marion Childs heard much the same thing from Clarence Durocher. He said that in 1917, the cars traveling on the ice between Amherstburg and Toledo were thicker than the cars on Dixie Highway! But police officers did not attempt to arrest any of the rumrunners unless they drove up on the land, despite the evidence being all over. Also, under the cover of darkness, rowboats would travel out to the big Canadian boats, get their bounty, proceed back to the shore in Monroe, unpack the bottles of booze from the crates and proceed to their next destination, leaving the wooden crates littering the whole shoreline.

Clarence also remembered someone nicknamed Rubbergut, who knew all the right places to go. One day, when a stranger asked him where he could find some whiskey, Rubbergut answered, "Why! Just stop at any house east of Kentucky Avenue!"[240]

The following article was published in the *Monroe Evening News*, February 1920:

> Sheriff Bairley Gets "White Mule"
>
> *Sheriff Bairley, Deputy Sheriff Mets and Castro raided a house at 1014 E. Third St. Wednesday and confiscated 50 gallons of raisin mash, 3½ gallons of white mule whiskey and a still.*
>
> *The owner of the house, a paper mill worker, was arrested and brought to the county jail. The raisin mash, white mule whiskey and still were brought to the jail.*
>
> *The still was found under the kitchen floor and was not in operation at the time of the raid. The house has been watched closely for some time by the officers.*
>
> *The homeowner was bound over to the circuit court and bail placed at $300.*[241]

In some cases, as we know, the officers did not do much to stop the rum-running, but in this case, it appears that the Monroe County sheriff was accused of a lot more than that:

> Supreme Court Orders Bairley from Office
>
> *Although he is still in charge of the office—at least he was at 3 o'clock this afternoon—Joseph J. Bairley is no longer sheriff of Monroe County. His removal was affirmed by the state Supreme Court in Lansing late Friday afternoon.*
>
> *According to Bairley's attorneys, no further effort will be made to retain the office.*
>
> *The Supreme Court's removal writ has not yet been served and until it is, Bairley will remain in the office.*
>
> *Bairley's removal grew out of charges preferred against him by State Food and Drug Commissioner Woolworth and Assistant Attorney General Thomas Baillie.*
>
> *The charges were to the effect that Bairley did not enforce the dry laws, that he sold liquor confiscated from the liquor violators to several drug and food inspectors and that he released several prisoners without authority.*[242]

Prohibition became increasingly hard to police, and by the 1930s, it was apparent the Eighteenth Amendment was a failure. With the United States entering the Great Depression in 1929, money became much more important, and there was a lot to be had in bootlegging. Thus, in February 1933, Congress passed the Twenty-First Amendment, which repealed the Eighteenth Amendment and legalized liquor again. In Temperance, it took another forty years, however.

Chapter 14
FORGOTTEN CITIES OF THE DEAD

FIRST CEMETERIES

St. Antoine's

St. Antoine's was the oldest cemetery established in Monroe in 1788. The cemetery was founded along with the first organized St. Antoine's Catholic Church. This church was the predecessor of modern-day St. Mary's Church. St. Antoine's was located on North Custer Road, and the first burial at the cemetery was in 1795. Four local victims of the Battles of the River Raisin were also interred there in 1813.

The cemetery filled up quickly, and it was decided to bring in dirt to cover the first layer of graves and establish a second layer. Thus, they buried people on top of each other. By 1829, the new St. Mary's Church and cemetery was built at Monroe and Elm Streets, which led to the St. Antoine's Cemetery being abandoned and the ground sold. It became farmland for almost a century and was virtually lost.

In 1957, a historical marker was dedicated, and two years later, a granite monument with a cutout cross in the middle was placed at the site of the old church. In the 1980s, the cemetery was researched by local historians and registered as an archaeological site.

By 1999, it seems the cemetery was lost in obscurity again, because everyone was stunned when in the midst of a construction project for a new

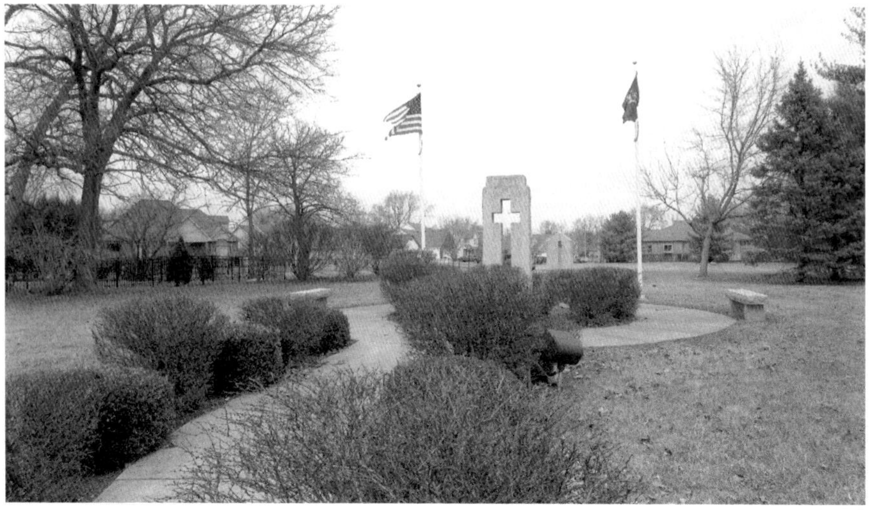

St. Antoine's Cemetery.

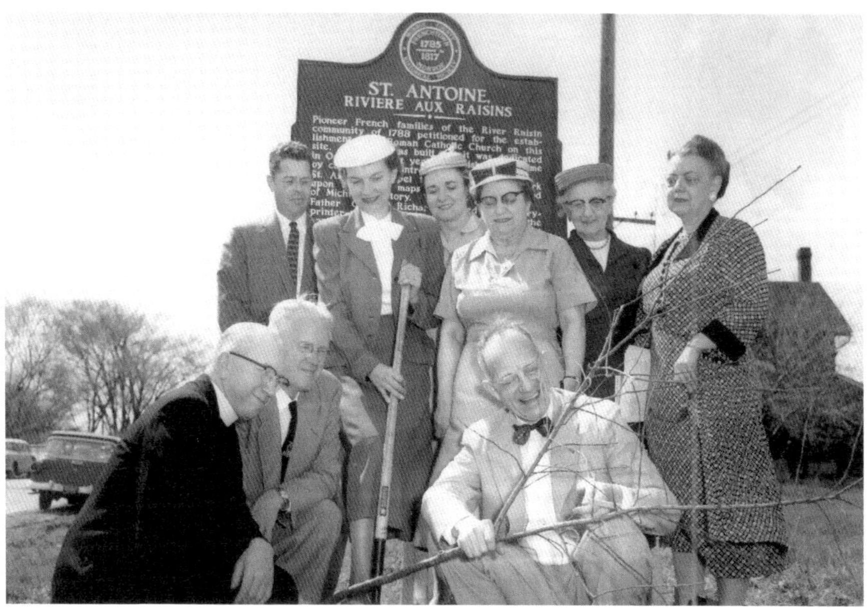

St. Antoine's plaque unveiling, 1957. *Monroe County Library System.*

subdivision, not only was soil turned up but so were graves. The owner hired an environmental firm to assess the impact. Archaeologists meticulously worked to expose the grave sites. But another shock was in store when it was discovered that many of the grave sites had already been disturbed. Coffins were caved in, and skeletal remains showed evidence of plow scars from farming. Before it was over, forty-five graves were found, but it was believed there could be up to five hundred.

Monroe County, the City of Monroe and the new Friends of St. Antoine's group worked to save the cemetery by purchasing the land and covering the graves up again. A new memorial was added to the site with the names of those believed to be buried there.[243]

First Protestant Cemetery

How can two cemeteries right in the heart of downtown Monroe be forgotten, even though they keep revealing grim reminders?

The oldest Protestant cemetery in Monroe was founded in 1810 and was largely forgotten over time. Yet, its contents have managed to reveal themselves throughout the decades.

In 1808, Samuel Egnew (Agnew) purchased farmland at six dollars per acre that included a large plot of land along Monroe Street. Two years later, he donated one-quarter acre to the District of Erie (as the settlement was called then) for the purpose of establishing a Protestant burial ground. The cemetery was on Monroe Street between Front and First Streets.

The first interments were those of soldiers from the Battles of the River Raisin. The cemetery quickly outgrew its confinements, however. Documents say some soldiers were removed in 1818 to a cemetery in Detroit, but not necessarily all of them. Perhaps some of the soldiers, as well as other burials, were moved to a larger cemetery down the same road.

Through the years, the area was built up as the main downtown Monroe area, and structures were built right over the cemetery. Not surprisingly, that would not be the last we hear of it.

Preparing for the Fourth of July celebration in 1848, workers digging post holes for sunshades along Monroe Street had the surprise of their lives when they unearthed a mass grave. Thirteen skulls, showing evidence of "tomahawk markings," and various bones revealed themselves, leaving the *Monroe Advocate* to publish an article titled "A Place of Sculls [*sic*]."[244] Although some elderly residents remembered a tale about two families murdered by

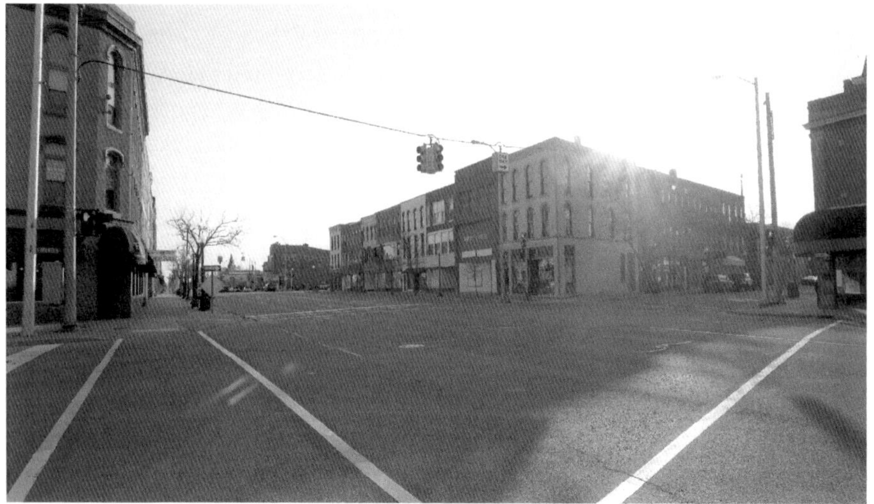

First Protestant cemetery, Monroe Street.

Native Americans in that area, chances are that these were the bones of soldiers buried there in the cemetery in 1813—but everyone seemed to have forgotten there was a cemetery there.[245]

Decades later remains were still revealing themselves. The newspaper reported on a discovery made on April 19, 1894. Contractors were working in the area, putting sidewalk curbs in where the old cemetery was, when they dug up remains they identified as possibly being Native American (no forensic examination was done, however). Then, in the same location, only three years later, on June 10, 1897, more "Native American" bones were revealed under the sidewalk in front of George Kronbach's store. When Kronbach closed the store in 1930, the *Monroe Evening News* said that the "old building occupies burial ground used for soldiers of the massacre."[246]

It would not be long before the cemetery was forgotten again. The last reminder would be July 6, 1966. Michigan Bell Telephone Company was digging a trench for phone lines when suddenly, under the sidewalk, about five feet down, bones were discovered yet again on Monroe Street, between Front and First Streets. The town went into a frenzy when it was determined the bones were human remains. Local historians were consulted, and with research, it was discovered—yet again—that there had actually been a cemetery there. It was during this time that the deed from Samuel Agnew was discovered.[247]

Kentucky Memorial Place

Another cemetery associated with Samuel Agnew and right on Monroe Street is Kentucky Memorial Place. The land for this cemetery was donated by Samuel Agnew as well, although there is actually a lot of confusion over this. Some accounts claim it was donated by Daniel Mulhollen, Samuel's son-in-law, and yet other accounts claim different entities entirely.

In any case, the graves were supposed to be removed from Front and First Streets and relocated to this cemetery, which is on Monroe Street, between Sixth and Seventh. There is no specific date of its founding, but it seems to have been established around 1815–20.

Noted Monroe historian Talcott Wing writes, "At this time and for many years thereafter, the land between First and Front streets, and joining Monroe Street on the west, was occupied as a burying ground, and a number of our citizens well remember the time when the bodies were exhumed and removed to the old cemetery between Sixth and Seventh streets, on the west side of Monroe Street."[248]

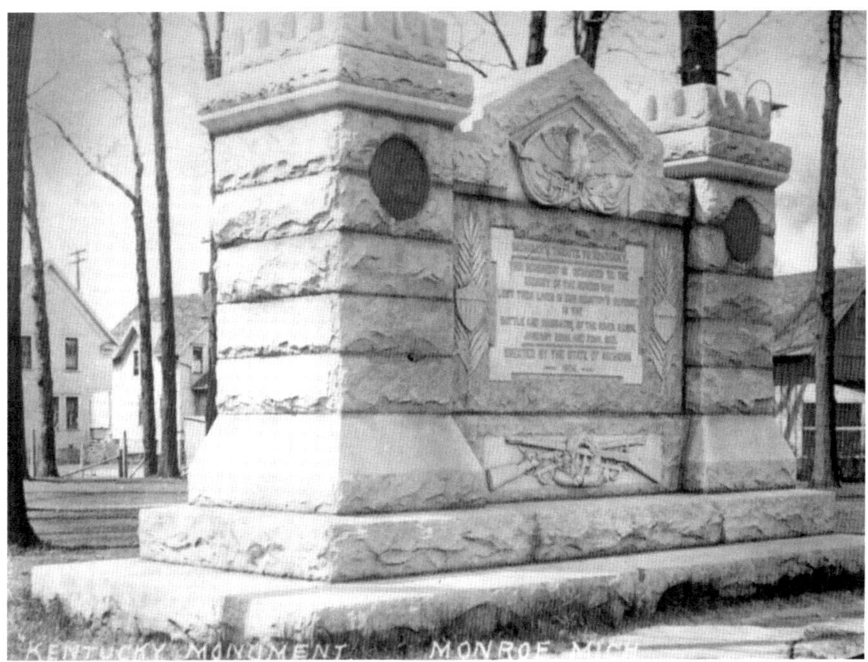

Soldiers monument, Memorial Place. *Monroe County Library System.*

In 1834, a cholera epidemic swept through Monroe, and many of the victims of the epidemic were buried in the Seventh Street cemetery. Over the years, many of the graves, which were probably marked by wooden markers, became no longer locatable. Even many of those that were marked by cement tombstones were lost, since the stones were laid down on the ground and many were overtaken by the soil.

At the turn of the twentieth century there were numerous letters to the editor published in Monroe newspapers regarding the old cemetery, and a petition was circulated to abandon the cemetery altogether, especially since the last burial there was in 1838. No one could agree on whether to leave the bodies where they lay and cover them up or have them relocated. In any case, seventy-nine people signed the petition.

Thirty-two years earlier, at the Battles of the River Raisin veterans' anniversary, it was proposed to erect a monument to the Kentuckians who fought in the battle and those who were buried there. In his speech, the mayor of Monroe, the Honorable H.J. Redfield, said to the Kentucky dignitaries, "Remember the Raisin, and you and your dead in our care and keeping, we will build a monument."[249] Yet, nothing was ever done, and now some people were proposing, instead of a monument, to erase the sacred soil altogether.

In the midst of all this, a civic-minded women's society called the Monroe Civic Improvement Society was born. Focusing on Monroe's history and the promise made in 1872, Josephine Van Miller, president of the society, "begged the members to lend not only enthusiasm to herself, but to one another. That the markings of these places must be done now or it never would be accomplished."[250]

September 1, 1904, was a banner day for Monroe; the dedication of the new, long-promised monument to honor the Kentuckians had finally come to fruition. Now, the ashes of those who gave their lives for freedom have one large tombstone to remember their sacrifice. Over ten thousand spectators and numerous dignitaries, as well as officials from Kentucky, were there to witness the dedication of the memorial.

In the century since that fateful day, the cemetery once again fell into obscurity, with the tombstones succumbing to the natural elements. The monument itself became the identifier known as Memorial Park and later, Memorial Place. A few times, the tombstones were reclaimed from the elements again by volunteers, just to succumb again. Then, in 2019, the City of Monroe reerected the tombstones that still survived. Many of the town's residents were amazed to suddenly see tombstones, having never realized a cemetery existed there. There are many more burials there than depicted by the stones, however, which were discovered when the city did a ground-penetrating radar scan. Hopefully, this cemetery will not be forgotten again.

Later Cemeteries

Altenheim Cemetery

Many people utilize the Monroe Shopping Center on South Monroe Street; it is a typical shopping center with a grocery store, hardware store, gas station, fast food restaurant and a cemetery. A cemetery! That is anything but typical. Why is there a cemetery in the shopping center, and how many people realize there is?

The shopping center is actually the former Lutheran Old Folks Home, or the Altenheim. The home was built in 1893, and the cemetery was constructed with it. The home was torn down to make way for the shopping center in 1955. The cemetery was left intact and is located behind the mall. It has a cement brim and a large fence around it to protect it, along with a locked gate. There are 237 people buried there; the last burial was

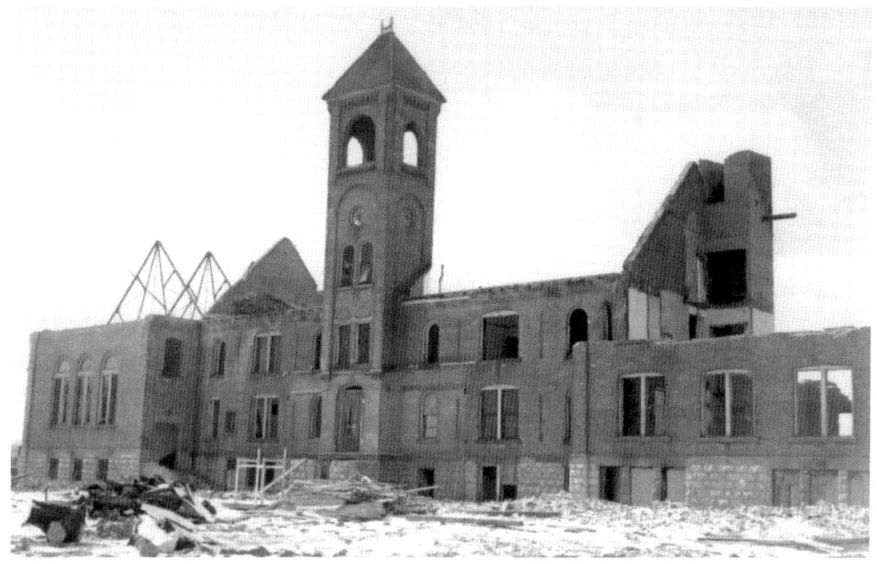

Demolition of the Altenheim. *Monroe County Library System.*

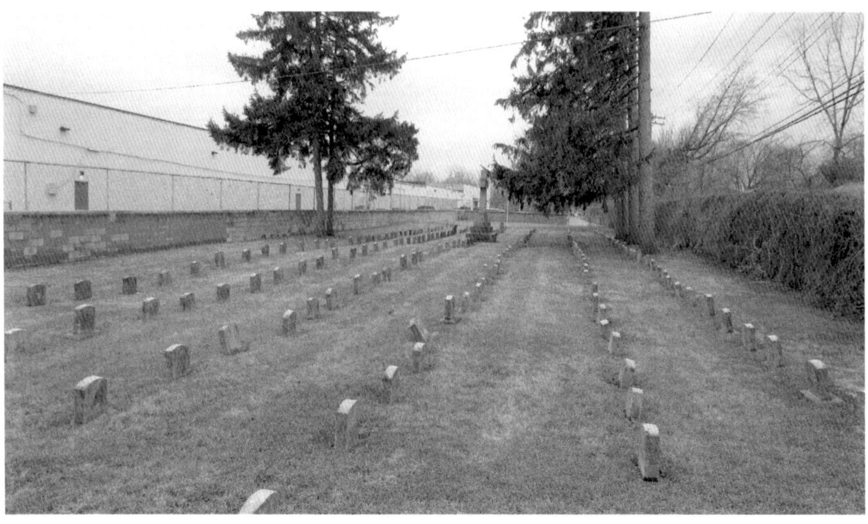

Altenheim Cemetery.

in 1979. There is a large granite cross among the tombstones, which has a German inscription on it that translates to "All that die in the lord are blessed souls."[251]

Bradford Cemetery

The Bradford family cemetery is located on private property on the north side of Stein Road in LaSalle Township between Suder and Strasburg Roads. It is about one hundred feet square and is on a slight hill covered with some big oak trees and a few smaller trees. There are no markers, fence or anything to reveal it as a cemetery.

The Bradford family lived on the farm in the 1800s, and the cemetery was to the west side of the lane going back to the house, which was a long way off the road. Eliza Bradford died in 1840 and was buried in the cemetery; there used to be a stone marking her grave. John Bradford was still living on the farm in 1859, but at some point after that, he moved to Kansas and left the farm to his three sons.

Neighbors say that there were at least forty to fifty graves there, all with monuments, including hickory wood crosses and very crudely cut stones. But over time, many fell over, and some might have even been used as steps for a local farmhouse. At the turn of the twentieth century, many stones could be seen on the south side of the road but have long since disappeared.

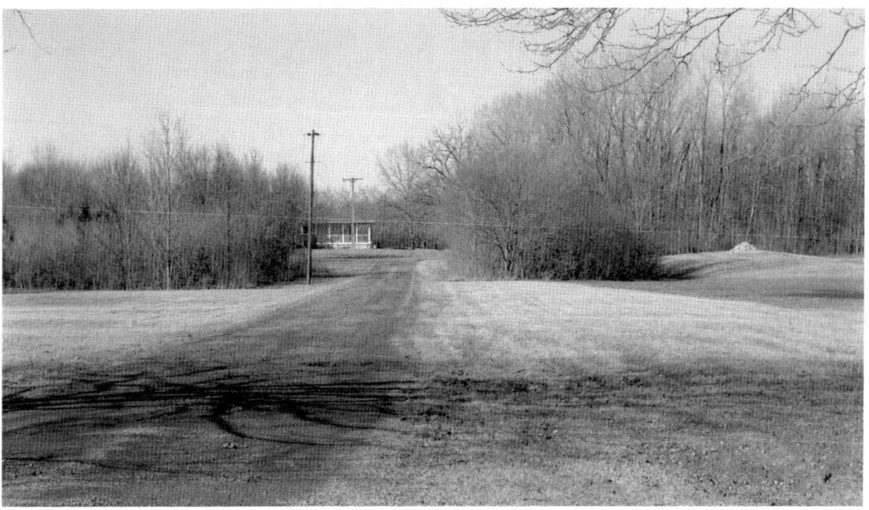

Bradford Cemetery area.

Rumors abound about some of those interred in the cemetery having been slaves owned by the Bradford family. Property owners since the Bradfords have fueled such rumors, also saying that the property might have been a stop on the Underground Railroad.[252]

Brest Cemetery

Just west of North Dixie Highway on North Stony Creek Road, by the waterway, was a cemetery that contained one of the earliest possible residents of the area, other than the Native Americans: a Revolutionary War soldier by the name of Gideon Badger. The Brest Cemetery, as it was known, has no existing records but plenty of tales. Local legend has it that the gravestones were used for steps in a house on Stoney Creek Road that has since burned. Over time, a new house was built where the old one was. Today, there is no evidence of a cemetery ever existing there.[253]

Heck Family Cemetery

Imagine a cemetery on the property of an elementary school; that could definitely be a child's nightmare. In Monroe, the nightmare is all too real. In 2001, the county investigated claims about a cemetery located on Albain

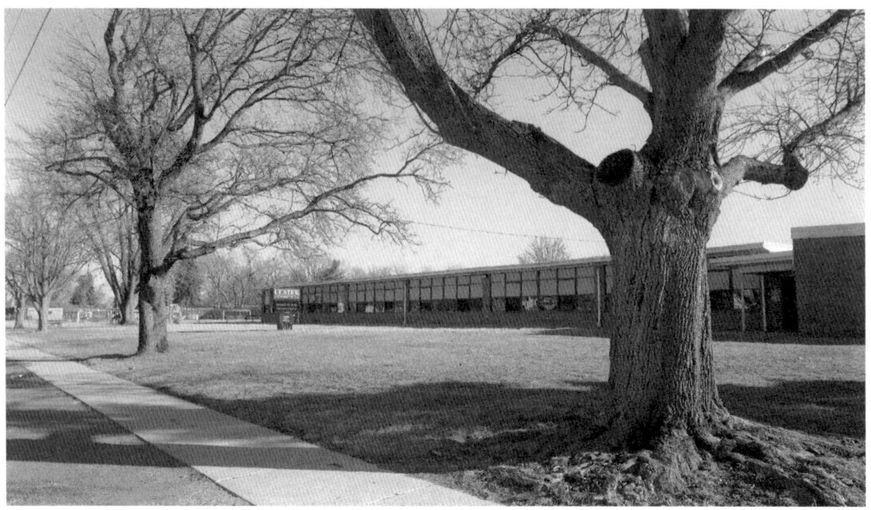

Custer Elementary School, area of the Heck family cemetery.

Road, east of South Telegraph (US 24) on the property of the Custer Elementary School.

The cemetery was called the Heck family cemetery, but the family says they believe no Hecks were buried there or ever owned the property. There are no tombstones or markers, but remains were verified by a cadaver-sniffing dog. Technically, the cemetery is owned by the Monroe Public School System.[254]

Immanuel Lutheran Cemetery

In Raisinville Township on Saum Road, east of Strasburg Road and south of West Dunbar Road, used to be the Immanuel Lutheran Cemetery. It was also known as the East Ida Lutheran Cemetery.

The Immanuel Lutheran Church and Cemetery occupied the site long ago. In the 1830s, a cholera epidemic swept through Monroe County, and many of the church's parishioners died from the disease. They were buried in the church cemetery. When a new cemetery site was chosen, it was decided not to relocate the bodies for fear of disease. The area was abandoned and sold at some point. In the 1920s, the owner of the land discovered some tombstones as he was plowing and brought them to the new cemetery. The bodies remained, however.

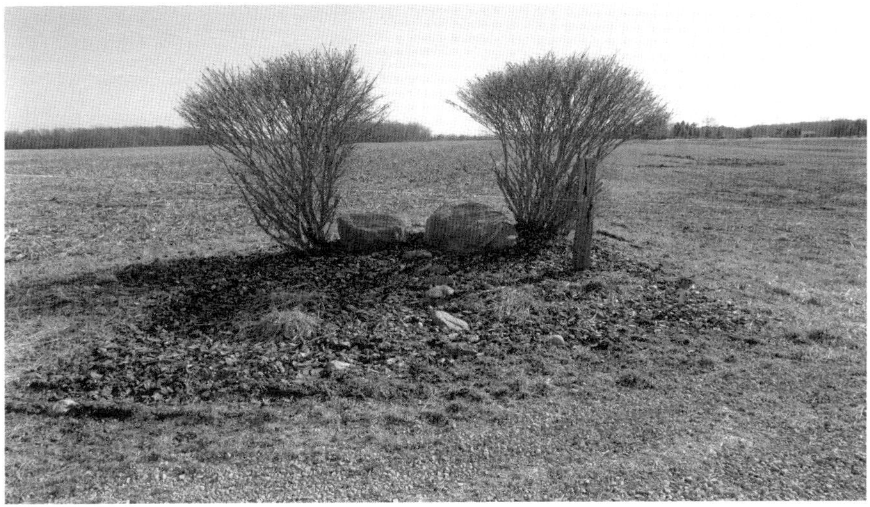

Immanuel Lutheran Cemetery.

Today, all that remains are two large boulders with plaques on them; one denotes the site of the former church and cemetery, and the other has the names and dates of the forty-eight people who were formerly buried there and—lest we forget—still remain.[255]

Keeney Cemetery

In Erie Township, there used to be an old cemetery marked off by an iron fence. The cemetery was known as the Keeney Cemetery, even though many members of the Larrow family were buried there. It is believed that the last burial was performed in 1900 and was, incidentally, that of a Larrow.[256]

Noble's Pond Cemetery

The Legacy Golf Course in Whiteford Township is not your run-of-the-mill golf course. Wander to the sixteenth hole by Noble's Pond and, in contrast to the manicured beauty of the lawn and trees, you will see broken-up tombstones where a cemetery still exists. Thus far, there have been two confirmed burials by the pond; investigation is ongoing.[257]

Pioneer Cemetery

In Dundee Township, at the intersection of Petersburg and Kent Roads, used to be a wrought-iron marker that said "Pioneer Cemetery." Over the years, the marker and, it is believed, at least sixty graves, have disappeared. Any evidence of a cemetery having existed there has been completely wiped out. The stones were taken out, and the graves were filled in with dirt. Around 1958, the land was sold, but was the history of the land passed on with it? One has to wonder if the homeowners know they are living on top of numerous graves.[258]

Potter Cemetery

In 1860, Mr. and Mrs. Royal Potter and Mr. and Mrs. John D. Flint donated land to make up the one-acre Swan Creek Cemetery, which would later become known as the Potter Cemetery. The cemetery is located at Labo and Swan Creek Roads in Ash Township. Surprisingly, however, the first burial was that of Mr. Flint's father, Roswell, in 1847, before the cemetery was officially established. The last burial took place in 1930. It is believed there are eighty-four people buried there, including six Civil War veterans.[259] There is also a marker in the cemetery for Royal Potter, even though he died in Libby Prison and his remains were never recovered.

The graveyard was looked after until the 1940s, then it fell into deplorable shape. Stones were broken, buried and covered in weeds; trees had fallen, etcetera. The State of Michigan declared Potter Cemetery abandoned in 1968. But in 1998, the families of those buried there formed the Friends of Potter Cemetery Association to work on restoring it. The cemetery is on private property, and permission must be granted in order to enter through a locked gate. These restrictions made it very difficult for the restoration project.

In 2000, however, access was denied to the Friends group. For seven years, the group tried to regain access but was unsuccessful, so in 2007–8 they pursued litigation to gain access and ensure that people have access to all landlocked cemeteries in the future. Finally, in 2010, Ash Township bought some land next to the cemetery and constructed an easement for access. In 2008, the group began legislative efforts to ensure access to all Michigan cemeteries. In 2012, Public Act 525 of 2012 unanimously passed and was signed into law, prohibiting cemeteries from being landlocked.[260]

For the Friends group and the cemetery, 2017 was a banner year. A historical marker and a flag were installed, and the graveyard was finally a suitable resting place for those that repose there. "The historical significance of Potter Cemetery is important to Monroe County as several Civil War veterans are interred here," said state senator Dale Zorn. "While this cemetery was abandoned and lost for nearly 90 years, it once again honors the final resting place of some of Monroe County's earliest settlers and war dead."[261] The relatives of those buried there, the Friends group and Sue Donovan, one of the Friends organizers, were thrilled the cemetery was finally getting the recognition it deserved. "This is all about honoring the veterans," Donovan said. "It's a celebration."[262]

Potter's Field

Monroe County Community College has many claims to fame, but an unusual one is that it is the home of a cemetery! As soon as you enter the college, located at 1555 South Raisinville Road, you cannot help but see the little knoll with a historical marker noting the County Poor Farm or Potter's Field Cemetery. Land was purchased by the county in 1832 and 1871 for the county's infirm. People who could not afford to pay for a plot were provided a place for burial in an unmarked grave. Potter's Field had burials in it up to the 1940s and has about 198 graves, although none are marked. When the college purchased the land, it left the cemetery intact.[263]

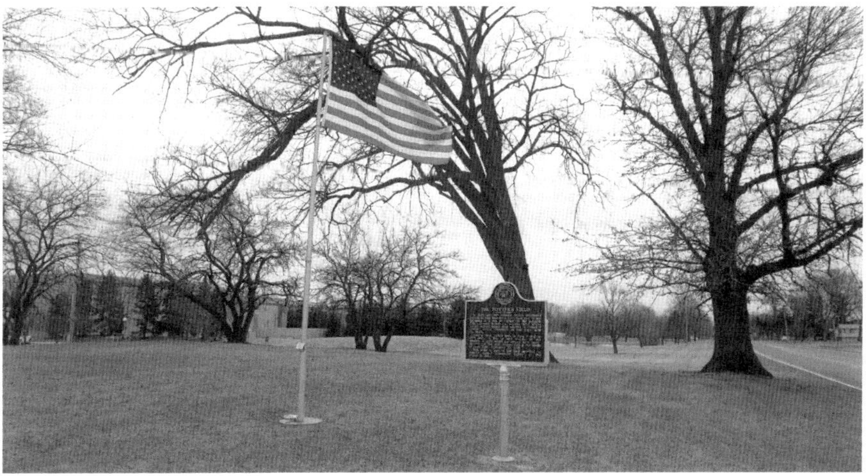

Potter's Field at Monroe County Community College.

Samaria Burial Ground

The Samaria Burial Ground is located south of Samaria Road and on the east side of Jackman Road. The abandoned cemetery is currently on private property. There is no clue that there once was an old cemetery there; today, the only item still visible from the cemetery is a large, old tree. A November 15, 2002 article in the *Bedford Now* newspaper reported that there might be up to forty burials there. In the past, the cemetery was located next to the Samaria School, which was destroyed in 1920 by a tornado.

Local historian Donald Adams believed there were seven burials, but when Sandra Anderson and her cadaver-sniffing dog, Eagle, investigated the area in 2002, they identified many more possibilities. It appears the burial ground was a family plot in a field where some of the family died of smallpox. The burial ground grew from there. Adams believes that there could be as many as twenty more abandoned burial grounds in Bedford Township.[264]

Private Cemeteries

Back in the day, many families simply buried their loved ones in the backyard and had a family cemetery. There is no doubt that many old homesteads probably have resting places in their yards. A couple examples that had monuments were on farms near Ida and Maybee. One was on the Bullock farm near Bigelow Road, another was on Yensch Road near Henry Mulheisen's farm. Yet another exists on Doty Road and still has a tombstone marker right next to the road.

Chapter 15
To Arms!

Monroe County men, and later women, were eager to enlist when called on to defend their country. They participated in every war and almost every major battle of those wars. In fact, Monroe County often provided more people per capita than many of its neighboring counties. It would take volumes to cover every war and the men and women who sacrificed for and in them. It is not in the scope of this work to be able to do so. So, we will look at a just a few of the thousands of extraordinary stories. But the author encourages the reader to continue to learn about the men and women who sacrificed so much.

War of 1812

Ezra Younglove

Ezra Younglove served in the War of 1812 as chief gunner for Oliver Hazard Perry on the *Niagara* in the Battle of Lake Erie on September 10, 1813. He received a gold medal from the state of Kentucky for his valiant conduct in the battle. He was also a spy during the same war. According to his wishes, he was buried at the county's poor farm, Potter's Field. Today, that cemetery is on the grounds of Monroe Community College on Raisinville Road. Younglove's headstone was moved to Lulu Cemetery, although his remains

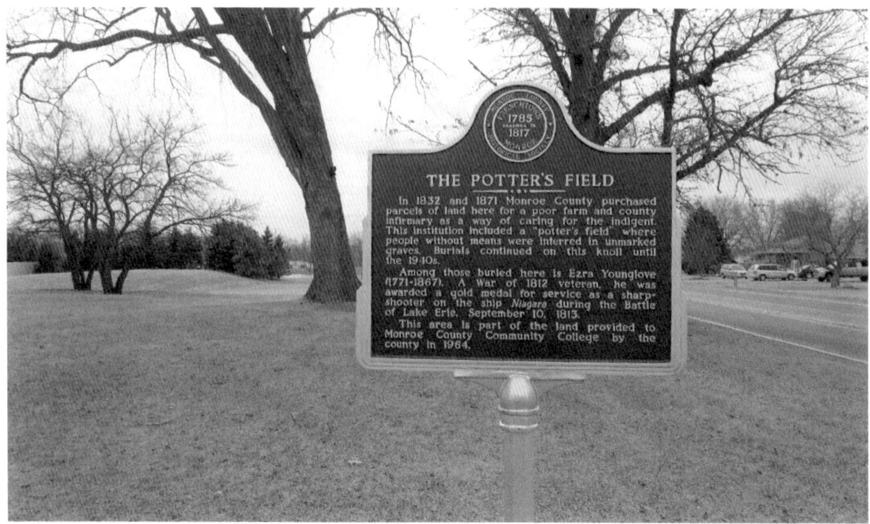

Potter's Field at Monroe County Community College.

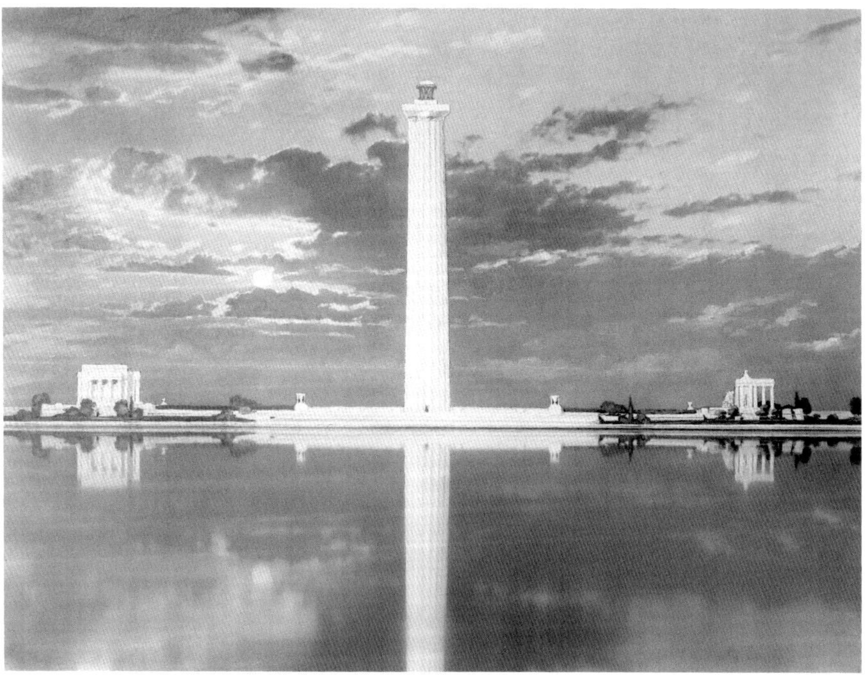

Perry's Victory Monument at Put-in-Bay. *Library of Congress.*

are still at Potter's Field. Potter's Field had burials in it up to the 1940s and has about 198 graves, although none are marked. It was established as the county's poor farm and infirmary for the county's indigent population.

Unfortunately, there is not much to honor Younglove in Monroe, but he and his fellow seamen were honored at the Perry's Victory and International Peace Memorial, located at Put-in-Bay, Ohio. The monument honors those who fought and died during the Battle of Lake Erie and the War of 1812.

Ezra was born in New York originally, the son of Samuel and Anna Younglove. He was married to Catherine Chabert Lafontaine and then to Margaret Russell. He lived in Kentucky and was a blacksmith by trade. After the war, he settled in Monroe, where he died in 1867.[265]

The Civil War

During the Civil War, Monroe County had the highest enlistment per capita of any county in the nation. Almost 10 percent of the county's population fought in the Civil War and were in every major engagement of the war. Monroe men were represented in almost every regiment in Michigan, but especially the Fourth, Seventh, Fifteenth and Eighteenth Michigan

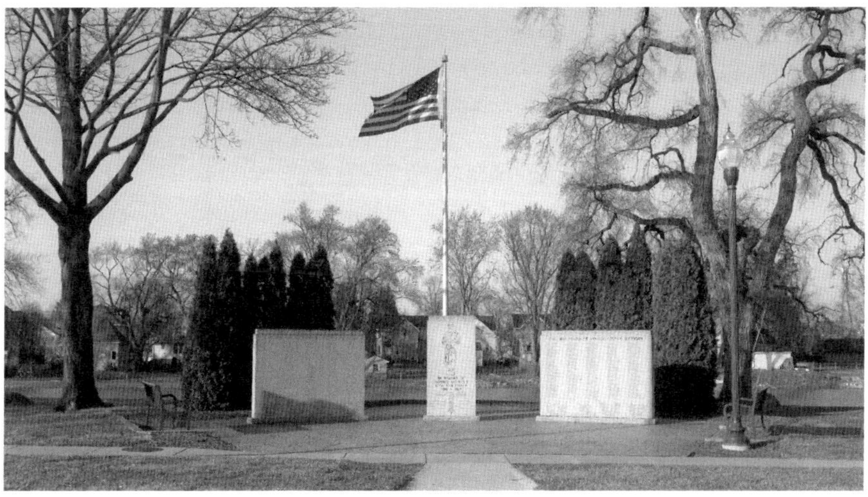

Civil War Soldiers and Sailors Monument, Soldiers and Sailors Park.

Infantries. The Smith Guards was the first regiment to organize, and when the war was over, only 18 out of 101 had not been wounded or killed. Of 2,270 Monroe men who fought in the Civil War, nearly 300 were killed. More than half died of disease. At Andersonville Prison Camp in Georgia, twenty-one Monroe men died of disease.[266]

Ira R. Grosvenor

Colonel Ira R. Grosvenor was forty-four years old when he was asked to raise a regiment, which became the Seventh Michigan Infantry. Only fifty days after the first Battle of Bull Run, he was promoted to commander. At the battle of Fair Oaks, he was resting under a tree due to illness when he heard his infantry firing out on the field. Even though scurvy filled him with pain, making it difficult for him to ride his horse, he mounted it nonetheless and headed straight out to his men. He also managed to fight in a few more battles before he was forced to resign in 1862 because of his advancing illness.[267]

Norman J. Hall

Norman Hall resided in Raisinville Township and attended the Papermill School. At the age of seventeen, he enrolled at West Point. He was the only soldier from Michigan at Fort Sumter when the Confederates bombarded the fort on April 12, 1861. The attack on Fort Sumter in South Carolina was considered the official start of the Civil War. On the second day of the attack, Hall noticed a shell had knocked down the flagpole, leaving the flag dangling. He could not have that and dashed through the shot and shell reigning down all around him to rescue the stars and stripes. He managed to grab the flag and run back to the fort, only to discover his hands, hair and even his eyebrows were burned. "The epaulets of his uniform had to be removed because they were so hot."[268] Yet, that didn't stop him; despite his injuries, with a little help, he managed to create a new flagpole and once more raised the flag high.

In July 1862, Hall was put in charge of the Seventh Michigan Volunteer Infantry, replacing Colonel Ira R. Grosvenor. Hall and his men fought at Antietam, Fredericksburg and Gettysburg. At Fredericksburg, it was Hall's brigade that that crossed the Rappahannock River in pontoon boats under a hail of gunfire in a mission to reach the city on the other side and clear out

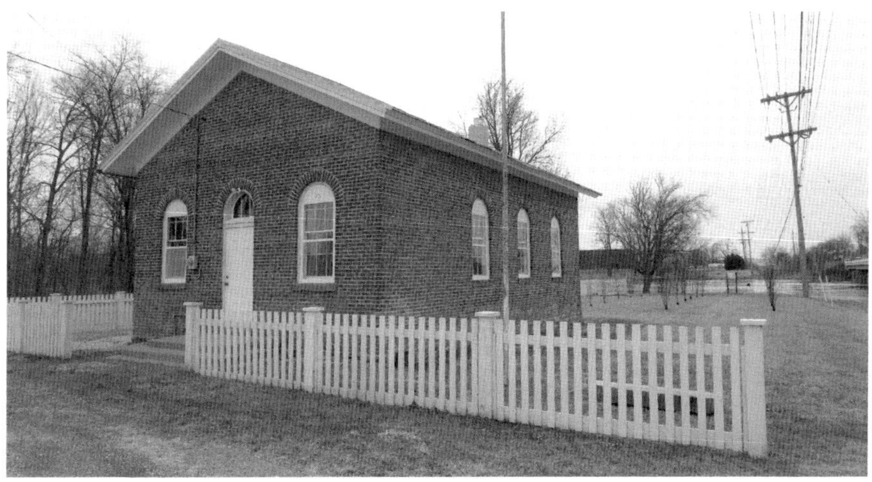

Papermill School.

the Confederate sharpshooters. The action earned the Seventh Michigan the nickname "the Fornlorn Hope."

The following year, the Seventh Michigan was at Gettysburg. They helped hold the Union line during Pickett's Charge at the Angle.

Shortly after Gettysburg, in 1864, Hall had to go on disability because of typhoid fever he had contracted previously at Fort Sumter. He wrote a farewell letter to his men:

> *The emotions that possess me at this moment are profound beyond my words to describe, side by side with the bitterly painful realization that I cannot return to the war-worn companions I have learned to trust and love.... With a heart sincerely mourning the brave dead full of sympathy for the wounded and suffering, and the bereaved and helpless ones, with earnest prayers for your welfare, and a deep and lasting regard for every one of you and my hearty GOD SPEED, I have the honor to be Your late commander and sincere friend.*[269]

He ended up dying of typhoid in Monroe at only thirty years old.[270]

George Spalding

Colonel George Spalding enlisted in Company A, Fourth Michigan Infantry in June 1861. He rose through the ranks to captain of Company B in just a few months. In the summer of 1862, he was severely wounded in the neck, and it was reported that he had died in the Battle of Malvern Hill. Yet, he went on to become lieutenant colonel of the Eighteenth Michigan Infantry. He was promoted to brigadier general after winning the Battle of Nashville as colonel of the Twelfth Tennessee Calvary.[271]

THE SULTANA TRAGEDY

In 1865, after the Civil War was over, twenty-two Monroe County men were anxious to get home to their families and friends. They had been held in Confederate hospitals, prison camps such as Andersonville and other places. Their ordeal was finally over. They boarded the ship *Sultana* at Memphis, Tennessee, on April 27, 1865. The 260-foot wooden steamboat *Sultana* normally transported passengers from St. Louis and New Orleans.

In all, 2,000 soldiers boarded the ship, which was not supposed to carry more than 376 passengers. Unbeknownst to the soldiers, the *Sultana*, just four days earlier, on April 24, had docked at Vicksburg on its journey from New Orleans because of a problem with the boiler. Eager to transport the soldiers and honor the ship's contract with the U.S. government, the captain opted for a quick fix and patched up the boilers. He also decided to take all the soldiers in one trip, even though he was advised numerous times against it.

Not long after leaving Tennessee and heading up the Mississippi River, the boilers were struggling under the extra strain of the weight of too many passengers and the force of swift currents due to the spring thaw. No longer able to withstand the extra pressure, they suddenly exploded into a huge plume of fire that left a gaping hole in the middle of the ship. Many of the men died instantly in the explosion; those who didn't tried to swim to shore, but most did not make it. Of those who did survive, 200 later succumbed to their injuries.

Out of the 2,000, 1,800 men perished and would never make it home despite surviving the war and the prison camps.[272] The incident was the "deadliest maritime disaster in U.S. history—worse than the Titanic," according to *Smithsonian Magazine*.[273]

Twenty-two Monroe County men were aboard the *Sultana*; fifteen survived, and seven perished. Six of the men who perished on the Sultana had previously been captured at Athens, Alabama, on September 24, 1864. They were on their way home after being held as prisoners, only to ultimately die before they could get there. They were:

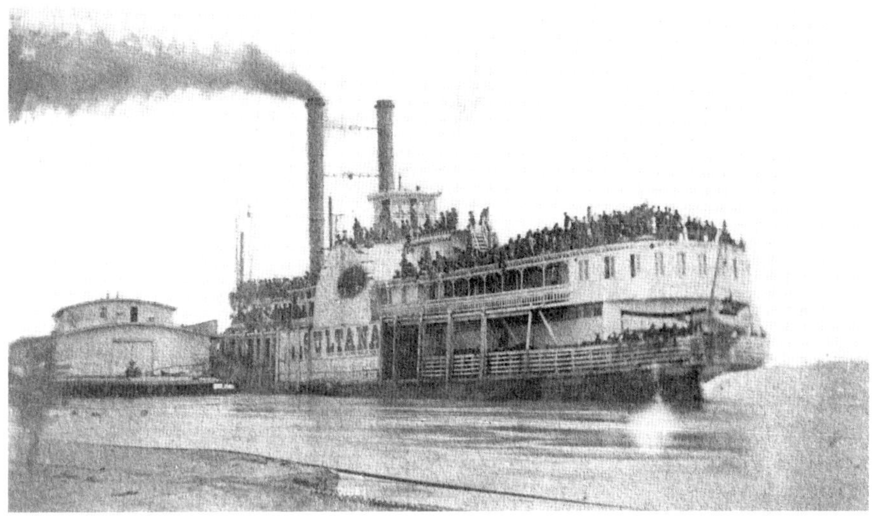

Steamboat *Sultana*. *Library of Congress.*

Thomas J. Hinds (or T.F. Hines), enlisted at twenty-four years old on August 9, 1862, at Whiteford. He was a corporal in Company K, Eighteenth Michigan Infantry for three years. He mustered in on August 26, and became a sergeant on January 1, 1864.

Andrew J. McEldowney, enlisted at twenty-five years old on August 14, 1862, at Erie. He was a corporal in Company K, Eighteenth Michigan Infantry for three years. He mustered in on August 26, 1862.

Anthony R. Metta, enlisted at twenty-six years old on August 13, 1862, at Monroe. He was in Company K, Eighteenth Michigan Infantry for three years. He mustered in on August 26, 1862.

Conant Nichols, enlisted at nineteen years old on August 9, 1862, at Dundee. He was in Company H, Eighteenth Michigan Infantry for three years. He mustered in on August 26, 1862. On September 25, 1862, he was taken prisoner and paroled at Snow's Pond, Kentucky.

Harrison D. Plank, enlisted at twenty-one years old on August 11, 1862, at Dundee. He was a corporal in Company H, Eighteenth Michigan Infantry for three years. He mustered in on August 26, 1862.

David L. Snyder, enlisted at twenty-three years old on August 13, 1862, at Dundee. He was in Company H, Eighteenth Michigan Infantry for three years. He mustered in on August 26, 1862.

The seventh man to perish on the Sultana was Jasper R. Decker. He enlisted at eighteen years old on April 11, 1863, at Whiteford. He was a private in Company L, First Michigan Engineers and Mechanics for three years. He mustered in on April 29, 1863, and was taken prisoner on December 15, 1864, and was eventually paroled.[274]

The Spanish American War

The Spanish American War was declared on April 25, 1895. The Light Guards from Monroe County answered the call to arms with 110 men; they eventually became Company M, Thirty-First Michigan Volunteers.

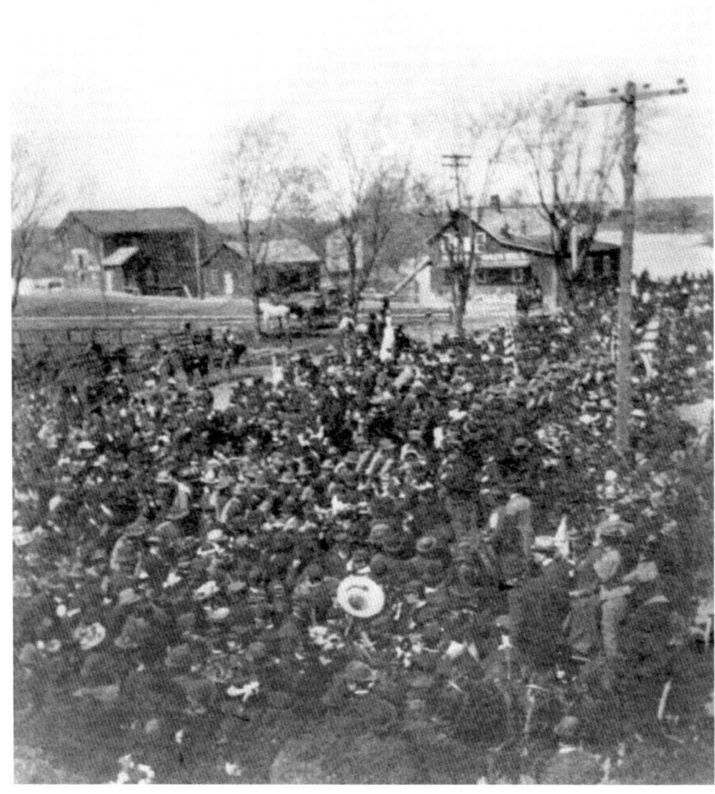

Monroe soldiers off to the Spanish American War, April 26, 1898. *Monroe County Library System.*

John Gutmann

Captain John Gutmann was the first leader of the Thirty-First Michigan Volunteers. He was reluctant to leave his wife and three children but felt an obligation toward the men he trained with in the National Guard. Unfortunately for Gutmann, only a couple months later, he contracted typhoid fever and died at the age of forty-two years.[275]

World War I

In 1917, the United States entered the "war to end all wars," as World War I was called. By the end of it, Monroe County had lost fifty of its men.

Russell A. Galbraith

Russell Galbraith was only twenty when he enlisted in Company E, 128th Infantry, 32nd Division. His family resided in Monroe and received news that their son had perished in France on October 30, 1918. He had just achieved the rank of corporal. It turned out that he was wounded in the hand but had not died. He left behind his pack and identification when he went to find the first aid station. Another soldier was killed right next to his pack, however, leading to the confusion. When he was finally discharged and came home to Monroe, his parents were utterly shocked, thinking they were seeing a ghost.[276]

Charles K. Wesley

Charles Kenneth Wesley was only twenty-one years old when he entered into the American Field Service. The service provided drivers and ambulances to tend to the wounded. Wesley wrote of his experiences, describing how the ambulance had to travel with its lights off and creep along so as not to be detected. He wrote of one particular night: "As I remember it was a moonlit night and we could see the Boche planes flying low and dropping their bombs. They were evidently trying to destroy some big French guns that were being transported to the front.…Our motor had conked out and we

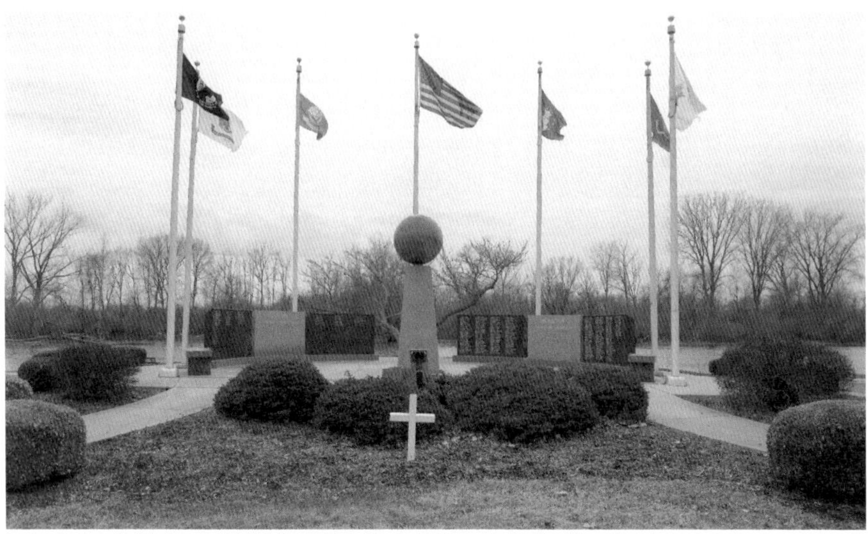

World Wars Monument. *Veteran's Park.*

were trying to repair it with the aid of a flashlight. When the bombs dropped we scattered into the fields next to the road and fell flat on the ground. No one in our group was injured, but all were shaken by the experience."[277] Wesley survived the war and returned to Monroe.

WORLD WAR II

The United States entered World War II on December 11, 1941. From Monroe County, a total of 6,200 men volunteered and/or were drafted for the war. At the war's end, 220 of them did not return. Five pairs of brothers and a father and son were among the casualties.

Ozzie Gaynier

Ozzie Gaynier reported for combat duty in 1940 and served as a pilot. In the Battle of Midway on June 4, 1942, Ozzie flew a Grumman Avenger torpedo bomber. In the very first hour of the battle, Ozzie and six other torpedo planes fired on a Japanese aircraft carrier. Even though they rained down machine gun fire and torpedoes, they didn't hit any ships. The attack managed to stall the Japanese navy, giving the Americans more time to prepare for the land assault. But Ozzie and his team soon found themselves covered in a storm of antiaircraft fire. Only one plane survived the mission, and it was not Ozzie's. He and his wife had been married less than a year. After his death, he was awarded the Navy Cross for heroism and had a warship named after him.[278]

Robert Slaughter

Monroe resident Robert Slaughter was at the Battle of the Bulge. At that battle, his antiaircraft unit was overtaken by the Germans; although he escaped, he was lost in hostile territory. He was on his own for two weeks trying to get back to the American lines. He said he often thought about his wife and son at home as he made his way through the farm country of Luxembourg by night. He survived on beets he scavenged from the local farms. More than once, he came upon German tanks within close range: "I made up my mind that either they were going to kill me or something was going to happen. I just walked by those tanks and kept going."[279] When he finally made it back to the American lines, he was fired upon by American paratroopers who believed he was a spy. After that, he was put on the front line at Bastogne, where he was "hit by mortar fire and was wounded five times in the leg, back, arm and chest."[280] He was sent to a hospital to recover. When he finally made it back to Monroe, he was stunned to see the doctor in Monroe, who had been in charge of the hospital he was in in Paris.[281]

Marian Wojciechowski

Marian Wojciechowski, who was in a cavalry brigade, was sent to his native land of Poland in August 1939 as a platoon leader. It wasn't long before he was on the front fighting the German army, including tanks, from horseback. Somehow, his unit managed to push them back. "It was bad, it was very bad," he remembered.[282] At one point, the situation in Poland was so desperate, with the Russians on one side and the Germans on the other, that the army had to discard their uniforms and weapons and try to look like civilians. Marian and some friends fled to the Romanian border but realized they couldn't get through, so they headed toward Warsaw but were captured. Somehow, they managed to escape the barbed-wire cage and set out again. This time, Marian made it to Warsaw and for three years blended in and worked as a farmer to produce food under the eyes of the Germans. Despite being watched, he somehow managed to get involved with the Polish underground resistance and help other Polish people obtain new identities. He just barely missed getting caught by the Gestapo and being sent to a death camp when a meeting he was supposed to attend got raided. But his luck ran out when a letter to him from a friend in Berlin got intercepted. In 1942, he was arrested, tortured and beaten in order to get him to talk, but he held out and never revealed a thing. Somehow, friends managed to bribe the Gestapo agents to send him to Auschwitz to work. He worked at the prison for a few years and, unfortunately, was a witness as "Jews were murdered by the thousands."[283] During his time there, he came down with typhus, and the Germans were just going to kill him. But unbelievably, a Jewish doctor lied and told them to spare him, saying he was part of the human experiments. With the help of strangers and many miracles, Marian says he was able to survive.

When the war was almost over, he was able to rejoin the American army, where he met his wife in a displaced persons camp in Germany. He made it back to Monroe in May 1950.[284]

THE KOREAN WAR

The Korean War broke out on June 25, 1950. Twenty-seven Monroe men served in this war, most of them in their teens.

Rufus Miller

Rufus Miller was only sixteen years old when he joined the army. He said he was taught, "If you can't go in front of the enemy, you jump on them."[285] He became a paratrooper, one of the 850 paratroopers fighting in Korea. The "troop would literally drop on top of the enemy, shooting as they came down and then engage in hand to hand combat behind the enemy line."[286] In Pusan, "the Marines and Army couldn't get off the beaches, so they called in for paratroopers. This time we jumped in behind them. In that particular jump we lost 68 percent of the men. It was a calculated

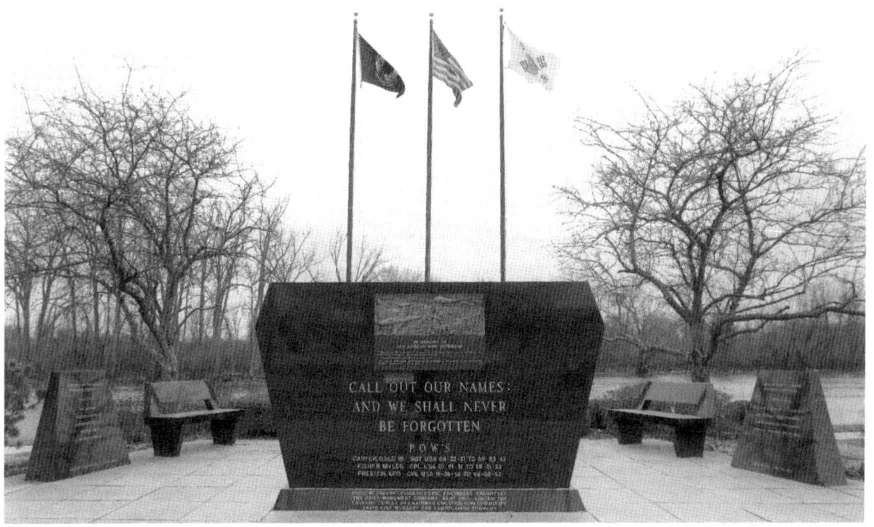

Korean War Monument. *Veteran's Park.*

risk. The ones that made it were very lucky. That was very devasting."[287] Miller fought for thirteen months but said the cold could be more trouble than the enemy at times. After Korea, he spent twenty-one more years in the army.[288]

The Vietnam War

The Vietnam War broke out on November 1, 1955. There were forty-five Monroe County men killed in the war.

Leo B. Abramoski

Captain Leo B. Abramoski was a veteran in the Army Corps of Engineers and thus was in Vietnam before the United States fully committed to the war. He was dedicated to helping the war-torn area's children by having clothing drives at home and helping with the construction of schools and airports in Vietnam. Yet, on July 28, 1964, he was traveling with some companions outside of Saigon when, suddenly, the military vehicle they were in was hit by a land mine. It exploded right in front of the truck. They swerved to avoid

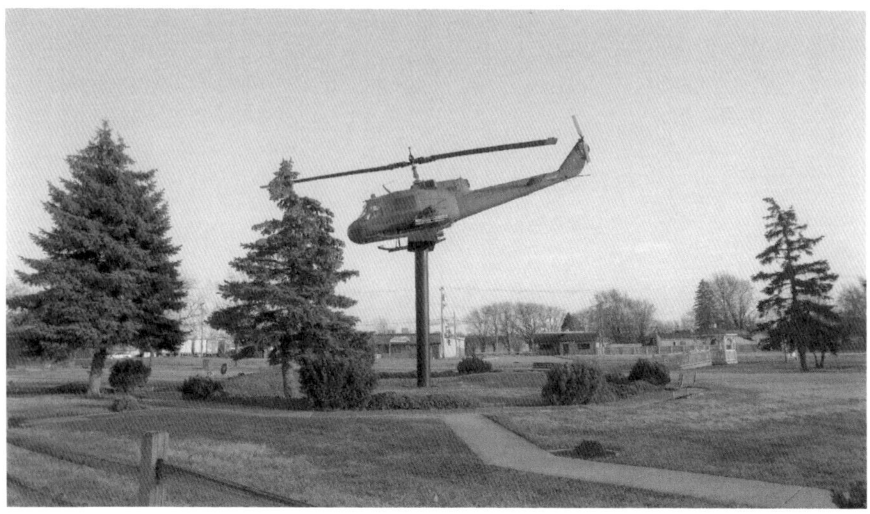

Vietnam War Memorial. *Vietnam Veteran's Park.*

the crater it formed and found themselves caught in a crossfire. It turned out to be a trap, and at only thirty-one years old, Abramoski was shot and killed. He became the first Monroe County man to be killed in Vietnam and was buried at Arlington National Cemetery. His widow got the following letter from a Vietnamese woman after his death: "Throughout his stay here, Capt. Leo B. Abramoski proved himself a faithful and devoted friend of our people….In fighting Viet Cong and at last dying so courageously for our cause, he has simply endeared himself to every one of us as a brother. Now that he is gone, his blessed memory remains forever lively in our hearts and it will last with this land."[289]

Darryl Ansel

At twenty years old, Corporal Darryl Ansel was part of the Fourth Division mechanized infantry unit. Around the area of Plei Mrong, on October 20, 1969, their unit was ambushed, and one of their armored personnel carriers was destroyed. A nineteen-year-old soldier was killed, and in the rushed retreat, they had to leave the body behind. The next day, they quietly approached the area on foot to retrieve the body. But to their surprise, a sniper was waiting for them. The Vietnamese fired a rocket but was killed in doing so. Yet, the rocket managed to blast into all eight men standing there, including Ansel. Ansel was wounded by shrapnel in his back, while the soldier behind him was killed. Despite their wounds, the men knew they had to make a run for it. Ansel decided to stay back and cover the rest of the men's retreat by firing his machine gun repeatedly. He was able to hold back two companies of Vietnamese while the men escaped. Still not deterred, Ansel and his men went back the next day to get the body. The whole group was awarded the Purple Heart and Ansel got a Bronze Star with a V pin for his bravery that day.[290]

Chapter 16

Monroe Takes Center Stage

Monroe became the center of the world's attention more than once in its history. Each time was completely unexpected and, unfortunately, was not for a good reason. The first time was the Battles of the River Raisin in the War of 1812. The Toledo War, the Newton Steel Strike and Enrico Fermi II were the others. How does a little town in the lowest corner of the state sandwiched between the two giants, Detroit and Toledo, end up with all eyes watching its every move?

Battles of the River Raisin

The War of 1812 was fought along many fronts in the United States. How was it that Monroe (then known as River Raisin or Frenchtown) became a key player in the war?

After the American Revolution, the area ceded to the United States by Great Britain was now part of the Northwest Territory. River Raisin (Monroe) was included in this area, and shortly after the United States declared War on Great Britain in July 1812, General William Hull surrendered Detroit and areas south, including River Raisin.

Most of the French Canadians that settled along the River Raisin came from Detroit and Canada. They made friends with the local Potawatomi who resided along the river, and the community thrived. Founded in the

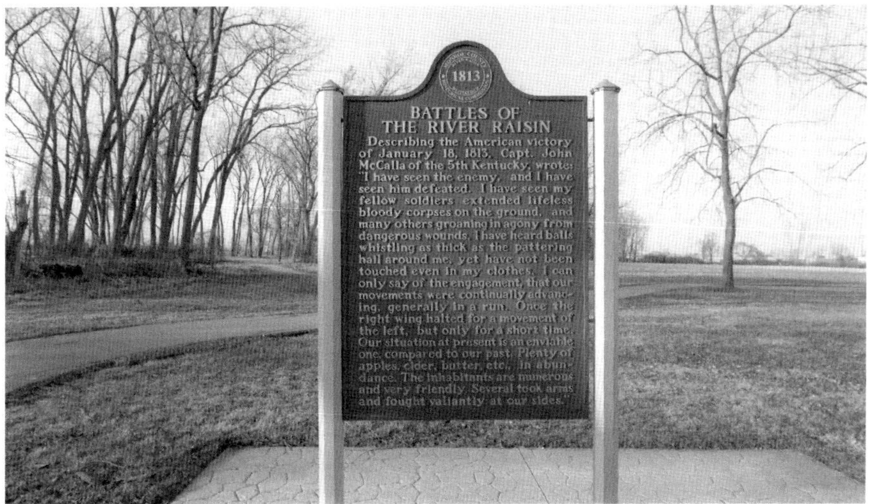

Battles of the River Raisin marker.

late 1780s, by 1812, the settlement was sprawling, with homes all along the river for twelve miles. The peaceful community was to be thrust into a war they really did not want and would be forced to choose sides between their families, their friends and even between Canada and the United States.

Many of these French Canadian settlers did not consider themselves U.S. citizens, either, and had families on the other side of the border. In the end, they chose to defend their settlement and fight with the Americans. The Native Americans were in much the same predicament. They did not wish to fight alongside their French Canadian friends, either. But ultimately, Shawnee warrior chief Tecumseh formed a confederation of tribes that decided to join with the British in the War of 1812, in the hopes that they could retain their lands and their way of life.

After Hull surrendered Detroit to British colonel Henry Proctor, the settlers were considered prisoners of war, and the British sent militia and Native nation allies to police the area. The settlers' farms were looted, and the local militia stockade burned to the ground. If the settlers showed even the slightest resistance, they would be taking their lives in their own hands. Thus, when they heard that the American army under General James Winchester, mostly Kentuckians, was heading north to retake Detroit, they asked for help in liberating their settlement.

The result was the Battles of the River Raisin. The first battle, on January 18, 1813, was an American victory, with a force of about 650 Kentuckians and 100 local militia facing a force of only about 260 British soldiers and

Native warriors. Everyone knew that this was not the end, and tensions rose with each passing day, knowing sooner or later, the British and their allies would return to reap revenge.

The counterattack happened in the predawn hours of January 22, 1813. A reinforced U.S. army of nearly 1,000 soldiers fought against 1,400 or so British soldiers and Native warriors. This time, the Americans were not so lucky, and the Battles of the River Raisin turned out to be their worst battles in the entire war. Out of the 1,000 soldiers, only 33 escaped. One out of every five soldiers killed in the war were at the Raisin, losses the American army could not afford. On the other hand, for Tecumseh and his Native American confederation, the Battles of the River Raisin proved to be the high tide of the alliance.

Despite the twenty-second being an unequivocal British and Native confederation victory, everyone was surprised when on January 23, 1813, the killing commenced yet again. Wounded Kentuckians convalescing in the homes of the settlers were shocked to find Native warriors once more attacking the settlement. It was not clear if these were warriors from the battles or not. Furthermore, the reasons for the attack were muddied as

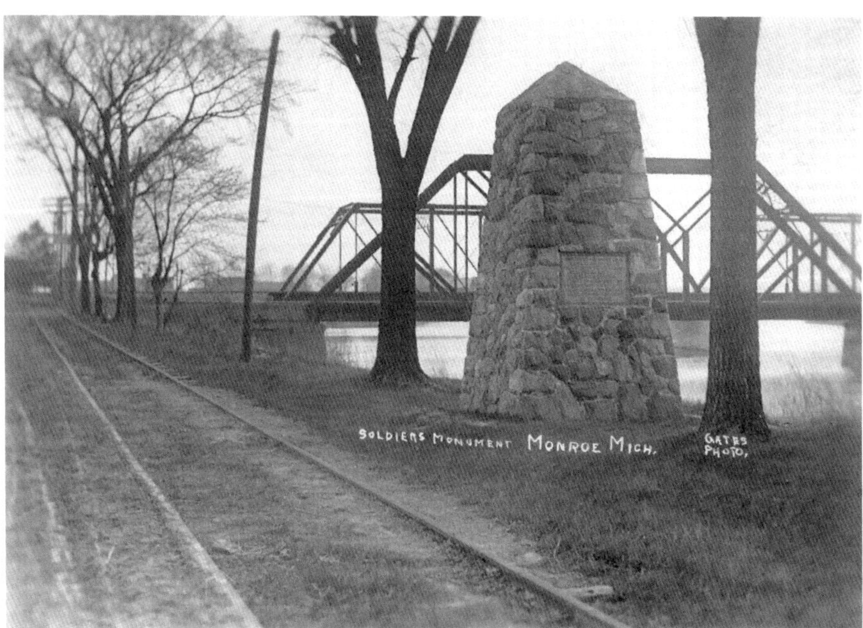

Battles of the River Raisin cairn monument.

well. But there is some evidence that the long, violent history between the Kentuckians and the Native nations was playing out again. Especially when Thomas Jefferson receives a letter in 1815 accusing the Kentuckians of mutilating a dead Native warrior after their victory on January 18.[291]

January 23, 1813, became known as the River Raisin Massacre by the Americans and cemented the settlement and the event in the nation's consciousness for good. The commander of the American forces, General William Henry Harrison, described the events at the River Raisin as a "national calamity." When he became president, he called it a monumental disaster.[292]

Yet, in the fall of 1813, at the Battle of the Thames, when the Americans started to struggle, someone shouted, "Remember the Raisin!" That war cry became a national rallying cry for the rest of the war and even later wars. Shawnee warrior chief Tecumseh was killed at the Battle of the Thames, and the confederation was no more. President Harrison had the epitaph "Avenger of the River Raisin" put on his headstone.

Even though the confederation dissolved after Tecumseh's death, the Battles of the River Raisin upheld the notion that the Native nations were a force to be reckoned with. Thus, Native American removal in the Northwest Territory started much earlier than the Cherokee Trail of Tears and is still having effects even today.[293]

The Toledo War

In 1833, Michigan petitioned for statehood, and the state of Ohio stood up and took notice. Ordinarily, this would not be a problem between states, but Ohio had a lot to lose in this case, most notably the city of Toledo. The Northwest Ordinance of 1787 established the southernmost edge of Lake Michigan as being in Michigan Territory. But when Ohio became a state in 1803, it also claimed the same strip of land. The disputed land was an area of about five to eight miles. Now that Michigan was seeking statehood, the "Toledo Strip," as it would come to be known, could be lost to Michigan forever, and Monroe County could be changed forever as well.

It turned out that the United States senate and the house of representatives could not agree on the issue. Michigan's governor, Stevens T. Mason, wanted to set up a commission to formally look into the issue. Ohio's governor, Robert Lucas, however, refused to go along with Mason's

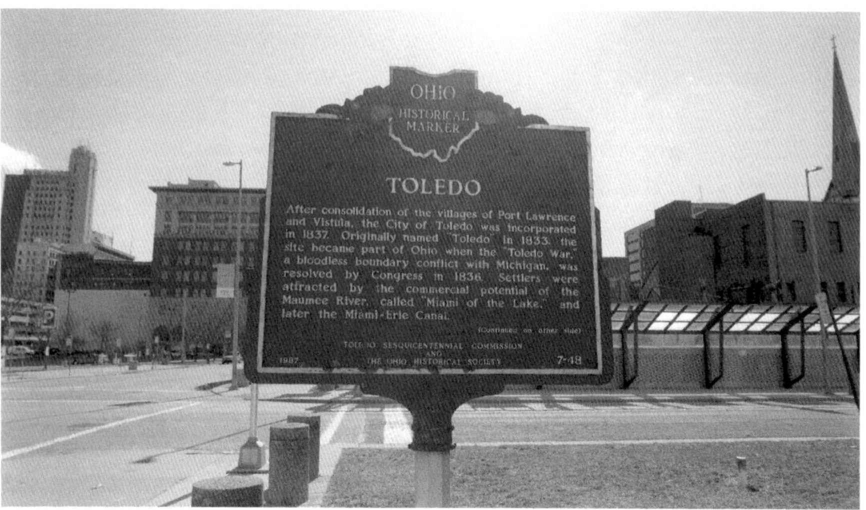

Toledo War marker.

idea. Ohio's legislature took it a step further by carving Lucas County out of the strip. Governor Mason's response to this action was a letter to General Joseph Brown of the Third Michigan Militia on March 9, 1835:

> *You will perceive that a collision between Ohio and Michigan is now inevitable, and you will therefore be prepared to meet the crisis. The Governor of Ohio has issued a proclamation, but I have neither received it, nor have I been able to learn its tendency. You will use every exertion to obtain the earliest information of the military movements of our adversary, as I shall assume the responsibility of sending you such arms, &c., as may be necessary for your successful operation, without waiting for an order from the Secretary of War, so soon as Ohio is properly in the field.*[294]

On March 31, Governor Lucas and eighteen of his military staff and the Ohio boundary commissioners reached Perrysburg on their way to re-mark the Harris line as directed by the legislature. Previously, William Harris was commissioned to survey the line by the State of Ohio. Governor Lucas, anticipating a possible clash on their journey, made provisions for military support. General John Bell, of Lower Sandusky (now Fremont), then commanding the Seventeenth Division of Ohio militia, soon arrived and mustered into service a volunteer force of some six hundred men. They set up camp at old Fort Miami, on the west side of the Maumee River and below Maumee City.

Michigan governor Mason, with General Brown, reached Toledo with a force estimated from 800 to 1,200. This was about the same time Governor Lucas arrived at Perrysburg. Mason anxiously awaited a move from the enemy.

> *The two commanders-in-chief were brought almost face to face in hostile array. The condition of excitement throughout the entire region was most intense. The active partisans of the antagonists were daily growing more belligerent and threatening, while others stood appalled with a sense of impending bloodshed. Throughout the spring and summer Toledo was the center of incessant excitement, greatly stimulated by frequent incursions of Michigan officers in pursuit of citizens holding office under Ohio authority or otherwise recognizing the same. Arrests made were almost wholly of Ohio adherents. Attempts were made by Wood county officers to capture adherents of Michigan, but in some way they got information of such purpose and kept out of sight.*[295]

President Andrew Jackson sent some commissioners to call a truce until everything could be ironed out. Lucas agreed to the stipulations, but Mason refused to. This resulted in Mason losing his position and being replaced by John Horner. Horner worked with the commissioners and Lucas to come to an agreement on the dispute. Michiganders were not too amicable, however, and hung Horner in effigy. On June 15, 1836, President Jackson settled the conflict once and for all when he gave the Toledo strip to Ohio and the Upper Peninsula to Michigan. At that time, the Upper Peninsula (UP) was considered very wild territory. Yet, throughout the decades, the UP revealed itself to be a very valuable resource in commodities. The Toledo War was finally over—or was it?[296]

A tiny island called Turtle Island was still being disputed until 1973. Even though Michigan controlled it, Ohio still claimed it. It was finally resolved when the island was cut in two by the U.S. Supreme Court on February 22, 1973. One half resides in Monroe County, Michigan, while the other half is in Lucas County, Ohio.

Turtle Island is about one and a half acres, although some accounts say it is up to seven acres. Earlier in its history, the island was utilized by the Native Americans, then by the British, who built a fort there in 1794 to guard the entrance of the Maumee River. Later, when the United States gained control of the island, they erected a lighthouse there in 1866. The lighthouse was used until 1904. During the border war, the island was forgotten, and it wasn't until 1973 that it came back into the forefront. Today, the island is privately owned and uninhabited, although several abandoned structures, including the decaying Turtle Island lighthouse, still cast shadows over the dark waters of Lake Erie.[297]

Newton Steel Strike

In 1930, Newton Steel opened an $8 million plant in Monroe, on what was then known as Johnsons Island (at the corner of Elm Street and Detroit Avenue, where the historical marker is today). This was at the mouth of Lake Erie and in the vicinity of the Battles of the River Raisin during the War of 1812. Monroe was a peaceful community and never thought it would again witness any violence like it had during the battles so long ago.

The 1930s were tumultuous years for the United States. In the labor movement, the Committee of Industrial Organizations (CIO) gathered over two hundred thousand steelworkers under its union wing in 1937. It was looking to organize more labor workers. That year saw seven states and over seventy thousand steelworkers strike, including workers at the plant in Monroe. There were already two steelworkers' unions in Monroe, the CIO SWOC (Steel Workers Organizing Committee) which decided to strike, and the SWA (the independent company union of the Newton Steel workers) which did not want to strike.

SWOC picketed the plant on May 28, 1937. That same night, the plant decided to shut down, putting its non-striking workers on hiatus. Just two days earlier, there had been bloodshed and violence in Chicago over a strike. No one could imagine that Monroe might be next.

For ten days, all seemed fine, with the picket line staying fairly calm. Thus, it was decided to reopen the plant two days later. The city was not taking any chances, however, and began deputizing residents and patrolling all areas by the plant. The opening was scheduled for June 10 at four o'clock in the afternoon. Eight hundred workers were ready to report to work as they waited in their vehicles. The strikers held their line, however, and two hours later, at six o'clock, two tear gas bombs were thrown into the picket line, and everyone held their breath. Spectators fled, but the line, although disrupted, was still intact. Fifteen minutes later, more tear gas was thrown into the line, and this time:

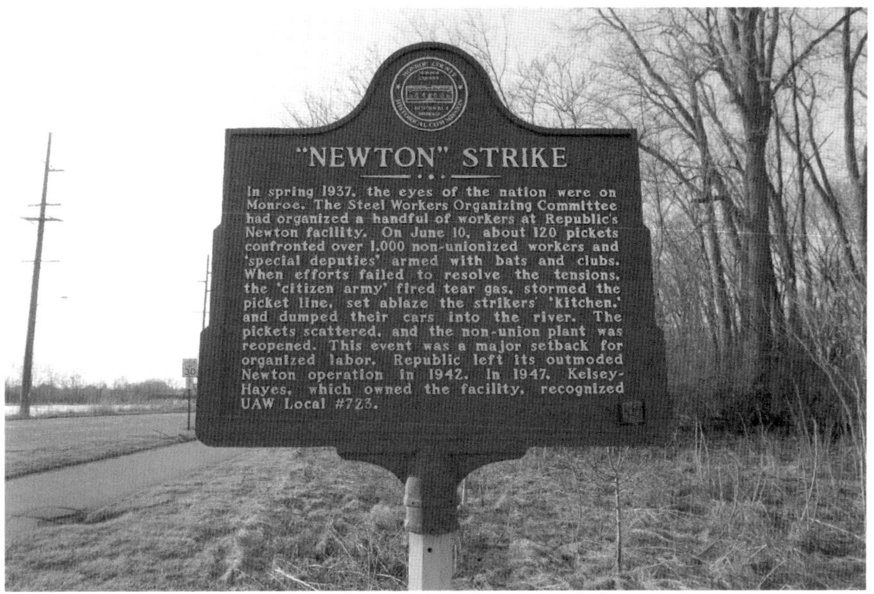

MAYOR'S OFFICE
CITY OF MONROE
DANIEL A. KNAGGS, MAYOR
MONROE, MICHIGAN

June 28, 1937

Sarah I. Spencer & family,
Mrs. Carl C. Spencer,
725 Oakridge Drive.,
Jackson, Michigan

Dear Madam:

I wish to extend my appreciation for your letter sent me during the recent labor trouble in our City.

I feel that the two thousand letters and telegrams from those living outside of Monroe, advising that they were supporting the principles for which the City of Monroe was fighting, were of invaluable aid in maintaining the courage and spirit of the citizens of Monroe.

We feel that we have won our fight to maintain law and order, to keep our streets open to the public and to give the 90 per cent of our citizens at the Newton Steel Company the right to go to their place of employment if they wished to work.

The City has adopted a set of rules governing peaceful picketing, some of which have never been used before. As head of the law enforcement branch of the City, I have demanded that these rules be strictly observed and believe that we have worked out a proper solution for labor troubles in our City.

Again thanking you for your kind interest in our City, and assuring you a welcome at any time you might be in our midst, I remain

Very truly yours,
D A Knaggs
D. A. Knaggs
Mayor

DAK:ID

Above: Newton steel strike marker.

Left: Letter from Mayor D.A. Knaggs of Monroe.

> *Special deputies advanced toward the line, and a sizable force of workers from inside the factory attacked it from the rear. The CIO line was broken and in the melee that followed, union supporters were chased and beaten. By 6:22 p.m. the tent at the corner of Detroit and Elm, which was used as the strikers' kitchen, was set ablaze. Eight people were injured and hospitalized. Sixteen cars were vandalized, five cars were overturned, and eight more were dumped into the River Raisin. Cars filled with non-strikers drove through the battlefield toward the Newton mill. The road to the plant had been re-opened. For now, the picket line had been eliminated.*[298]

According to the Monroe County Labor History Museum:

> *Monroe was involuntarily cast into the national spotlight from late May through July. It was a position for which Monroe was woefully unprepared. Even so, the city had fared well. Breaking the picket line had not turned into another Chicago. In its aftermath, a union backlash was averted or defused. The remaining question was "Would peace in Monroe hold?" It was likely that people around the country, as well in Monroe, were still waiting for the other shoe to drop. Monroe's picketing rules, though not perfect, were effective enough to be adopted and adapted for use in other strike-torn areas of the U.S.*[299]

Fermi I

As you can imagine, not everyone was too happy about the idea of a nuclear reactor being built in small-town Monroe. The plant was named after physicist Enrico Fermi, creator of the first nuclear reactor. It was scheduled to start operations by the end of 1959 but was stalled until 1963 because of litigation and a sodium explosion accident.

In 1966, Fermi I had the distinction of being the worst United States nuclear disaster until Ohio's Three Mile Island in 1979. Since it was early in the development of nuclear power, Fermi I served as a good example against the idea of radio fusion, even though no radiation had actually been released. It did not help matters when rumors circulated that "a crushed beer can in the works had caused the partial meltdown. The Fermi accident had many of the trappings of a Hollywood drama, including shadowy informants and a purported cover-up. Even then–vice president Hubert

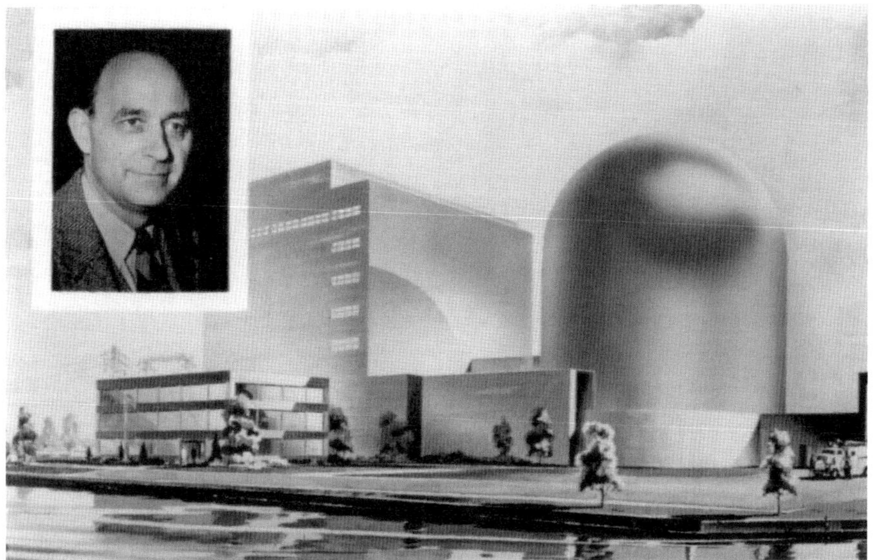

Enrico Fermi I.

Humphrey was in town at the time of the partial meltdown to dedicate the new Monroe County Public Library."[300]

The Enrico Fermi power plant employed a breeder reactor, and in the 1960s, it was considered experimental. The idea behind the breeder reactor is that it can generate more nuclear fuel than it uses. It relies on liquid sodium, which is very flammable and cannot be exposed to water or air; otherwise, it can explode. This kind of reactor allows very little time to fix a problem; thus, today's nuclear plants employ the water-cooled design. It turns out Fermi I was only one of two commercial breeder reactors ever built in the United States.

> *The Fermi 1 accident occurred when a metal object broke loose inside Fermi's reactor vessel and blocked sodium coolant from reaching a portion of the fuel, allowing about 1% of the total fuel to melt. The accident investigation lasted months and involved speculation that the errant object might be a beer can.*
>
> *The official time of the incident is recorded as 3:09 p.m., when radiation alarms sounded and the reactor building automatically sealed shut. Control room instruments showed temperatures rising inexplicably in the reactor's core and radiation leaking out into the containment building. Shortly afterward a phone call purportedly came into the Monroe County*

> *Sheriff's Office. The unidentified caller said he was with Detroit Edison and reported that something unknown had gone wrong at Fermi 1. However, the caller said the situation should not be publicized and no public alert be given.*[301]

The whole affair lasted only about twenty minutes because employees were able to shut it down. It took several weeks, however, before the incident could be investigated.

> [Forty] *pounds of nuclear fuel had melted, about 1% of the total fuel. And months passed before they learned the cause: an unknown metallic object had blocked the liquid sodium coolant from reaching the fuel. Almost a year later, in September 1967, investigators managed to lower a periscope to the bottom of the reactor and, to much astonishment, discovered what looked like a crushed beer can. Finally, in early 1968, the errant metal was fished-out and identified as a zirconium metal plate that was installed in the reactor as a safety measure but had broken loose....*
>
> *Fermi 1 stayed offline until July 1970, when the reactor was started up again. It went on to produce a modest amount of electricity before it was permanently shut down in 1972 for financial reasons. Fermi I's reactor*

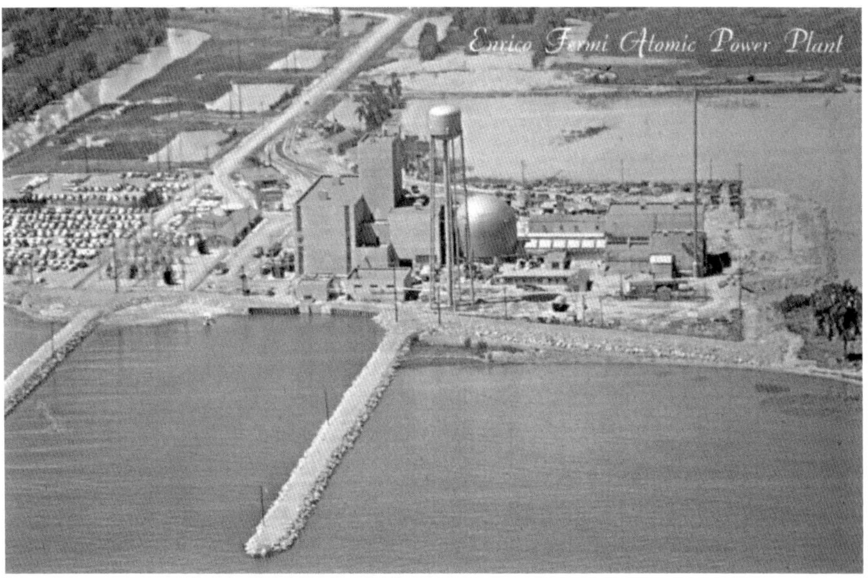

Enrico Fermi I at Lagoona Beach, 1950s.

was welded shut and its nearly 80,000 gallons of radioactive liquid sodium placed into giant 55-gallon drums and shipped out in 1984. The sodium coolant was originally slated to go to a planned breeder reactor in Tennessee, but that plant never got built. Fermi 1's reactor was cut up and also removed in 2012....A photo provided by the utility shows several gray buildings still standing along with the plant's containment dome. Situated nearby is Fermi 2, a boiling-water nuclear plant reactor that began commercial operations in 1988.[302]

Chapter 17
Tragic Turn of Events

Train Crashes

September 2, 1926

On September 2, 1926, two Detroit United Railway municipal passenger trains violently collided into each other, causing 66 percent of their lengths to lie crumpled in a heap on top of each other. The horrific accident was the result of both trains being on the same track at the same time. The crash happened at the large two-thousand-foot curve at the end of Maple Boulevard and Michigan Avenue. Eleven people were killed and twenty-six injured. Renowned local doctor Charles Stacy Southworth was killed in the accident.

The southbound train was running behind schedule and reeved up its engines to fifty miles per hour just as it was reaching the curve. The northbound train was stunned when it saw the southbound train rounding the curve, hurtling right toward them. In a stunning admission, the crew of the southbound train claimed responsibility, saying they forgot orders to pull off onto a side rail to let the northbound train pass.[303]

November 18, 1955

From the *Monroe Evening News* on November 18, 2015,

> *Sixty years ago today was a tragic day for Monroe County. Nine railroad workers were killed when their truck was hit by a train in Newport. Three others in the truck were injured. Railroad workers were in the truck on their way to make repairs to the tracks in Newport when it crossed the tracks at South Road and in the path of a speeding northbound NY Central passenger train. 7:12 am in morning. All nine sitting on the benches in the back of the truck were killed the other three injured were in the cab.*[304]

June 25, 1964

On June 25, 1964, a train riding on the Detroit and Toledo Shore Line Railroad crashed at Cousino Road in LaSalle at one o'clock in the morning. The train was northbound to Detroit when the wheels suddenly left the track. Fifteen freight cars were hurled on top of each other in a huge, mangled mess. Giant rolls of steel, coal, sand and other detritus were all intermingled

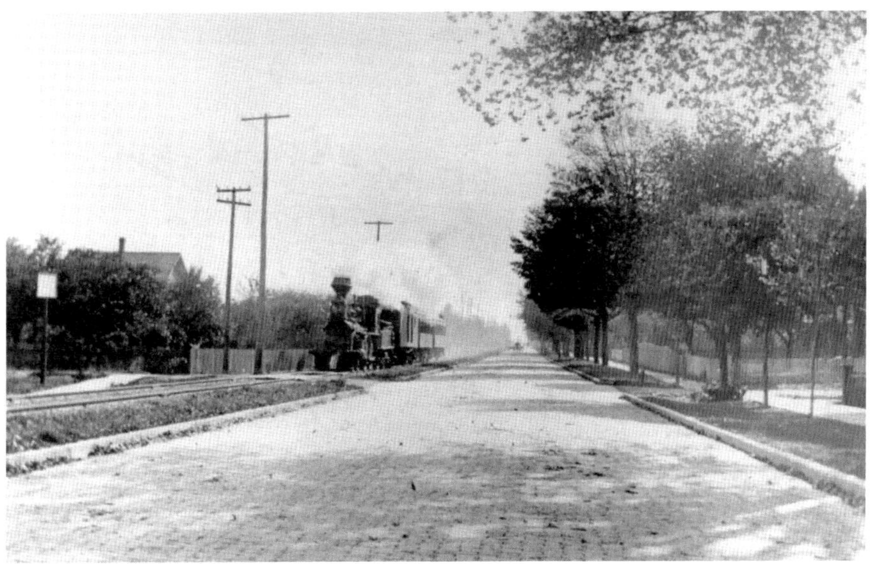

Steam train. *Monroe County Library System.*

in a huge, unrecognizable pile. The solid steel rails were bent into *S* curves. Miraculously, no one was injured. Damages were estimated to be around $110,000. No cause was ever determined.[305]

Plane Crashes

June 14, 1935

Leong Chee, owner of the Chop Suey Inn, died piloting his Eagle Rock biplane when the plane crashed near Post Road, Newport. Chee was flying the plane when it started to nosedive. He tried to parachute out, but his parachute did not open. Chee was thirty-six years old and had lived in Monroe for some time.[306]

January 9, 1997

The worst aviation accident to happen in Monroe County was on January 9, 1997. Comair Flight 3272, a twin-engine commuter plane traveling from Cincinnati, Ohio, to Detroit, Michigan, crashed into a farm field in Raisinville Township, just north of M-50 at Ida Maybee and Dixon Roads, right by

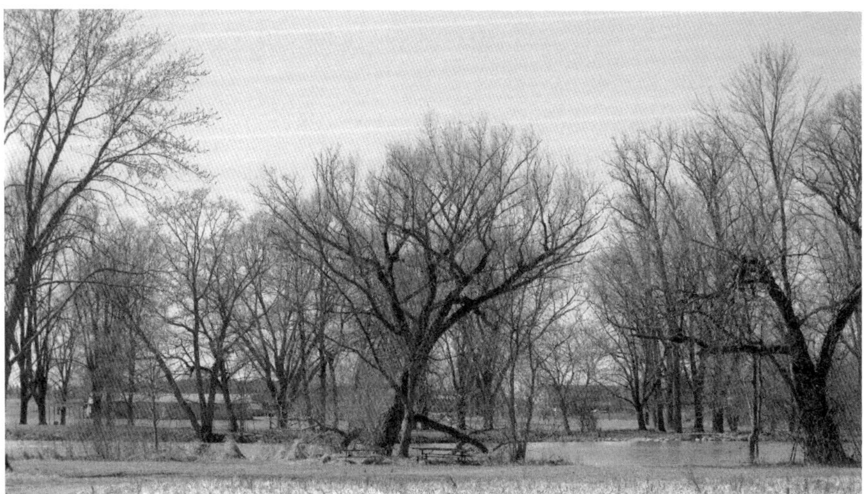

Dixon Road area plane crash by River Raisin.

the River Raisin. Flying through a snowstorm at 3:56 in the afternoon, the plane appeared to just nosedive into the ground. The plane was obliterated, leaving pieces all over the ground and in the woods. Fire and rescue vehicles rushed to the site, only to find the wreckage scattered all over in the snow and down the hillside by the river. All twenty-nine souls aboard were killed in the crash, twenty-six passengers and three crew members. The plane was only four years old and had a good service record. In fact, it was flown earlier that day by a different crew with no incident. Ironically, the crashed happened by a large wooden cross that had been erected years before by the church that used to occupy the area. The crash was later determined to have been caused by ice accumulating on the plane's wings.[307]

March 29, 2011

One girls' tennis team will never forget its spring practice on March 29, 2011. Busy hitting the ball back and forth on the court, they hardly noticed the plane flying overhead, since Munson Park, on Elm Avenue in Monroe, is right next door to the small Monroe Custer Airport. But when the plane tried to pass over the runway at too high a speed, the propeller struck the ground, and it was the beginning of the end. The Piper Malibu Mirage lost its airspeed when the propeller struck repeatedly and could no longer fly. The girls were stunned when they realized the plane was in trouble and

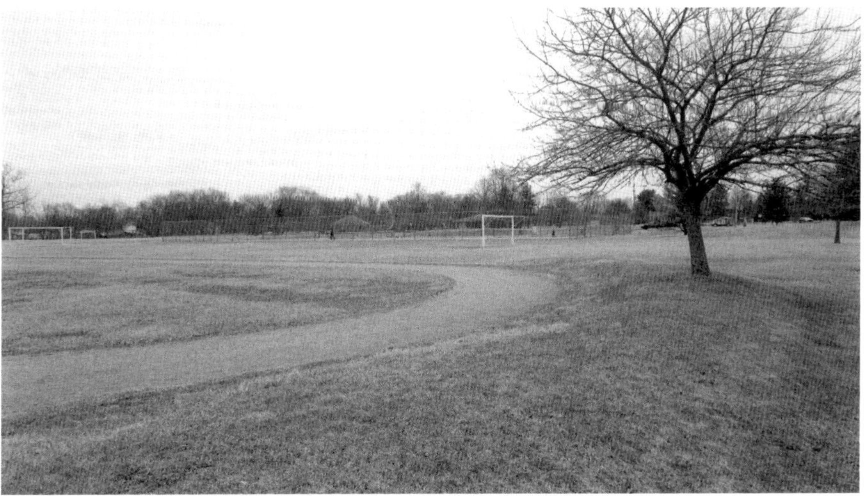

Munson Park area plane crash by tennis courts.

heading right toward them. Then it suddenly managed to veer off and ultimately crashed in the soccer field not far from them. Upon impact, the plane burst into flames.

The pilot, who was from LaSalle in Monroe County, and two other passengers were killed. They were returning from a business trip to Pennsylvania. Later, it was determined the crash was caused by pilot error.[308]

Shipwrecks

Lake Erie, the tempest of the Great Lakes, is known for its waxing and waning moods, especially because it is the shallowest of the Great Lakes.

> *Surprisingly, of all the shipwrecks on the Great Lakes, the lake that has the greatest concentration of them is Lake Erie....Lake Erie has an astonishing 2,000-plus shipwrecks which is among the highest concentration of shipwrecks in the world. Only about 400 of Lake Erie's wrecks have ever been found. There are schooners, freighters, steamships, tugs and fishing boats among them. There are more than 40 miles of Lake Erie coast in Monroe County from the Ohio state line to the Wayne County line. There have been a number of shipwrecks off the shores of Monroe County over the centuries.*[309]

On November 9, 1846, a seventy-foot-long schooner named the *Lexington* sank in a storm with a crew of thirteen men four miles off of Point Mouillee. Everyone perished. The *Lexington* was made of wood and had two masts. The ship's cargo actually washed ashore several days later and consisted of one hundred barrels of whiskey. Two boilers and coal were lost. Local legend has it that there was a safe full of gold aboard.[310]

Heavy westerly winds often push the water off the shores of Lake Erie and, every now and then, reveal its real hidden treasures. On December 7, 1948, close to the shoreline, the remnants of "Cap" Dandron's ship *Plow Boy* were revealed. On January 17, 1950, it was reported that "about 200 yards North of the Monroe channel...lie the remains of this approximately 60-foot schooner, believed to be 'Cap' Dandron's three masted lumbar schooner, the *Vernia M. Blake.* The double-planked craft, with heavy wooden stakes of still stout lumbar, had a 15-foot stern. She succumbed to a storm about 1898, when heading for refuge at the Monroe Piers."[311]

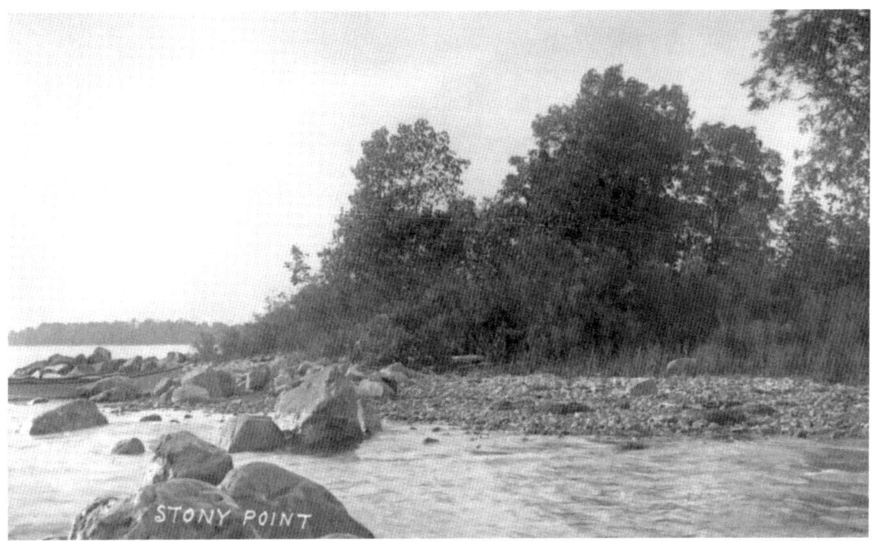

Stony Point. *Monroe County Library System.*

Probably the most famous shipwreck near Monroe took place on November 12, 1853. A schooner named the *Favorite* left port in Buffalo with three hundred barrels of whiskey, one hundred barrels of apples, one hundred stoves and other merchandise. The vessel was only ten years old and worthy of sailing on the Great Lakes. But on account of delays, the schooner was late leaving the port. The weather on Lake Erie appeared to be taking a drastic turn, so part of the crew abandoned the voyage. Many felt an uneasy apprehension about making the journey on such a foreboding night on the shallowest of the Great Lakes, which was known for its ability to weave up a tempest in a matter of seconds. The captain, however, was undaunted; he scrounged up enough men to make a crew and set off, despite the dark, ominous skies and bone-chilling temperature.

> *When open water was reached, a snow storm greeted the adventurous mariners—accompanied by a thirty-six mile gale; ice formed on deck and rail, and the outlook was not promising; but the skipper kept a stiff upper lip and held his course steadily towards the head of the lake. The sailors were hardy fellows, and clung to their task bravely, so that at the end of a week's buffeting in the high seas, Raisin Point, at the mouth of River Raisin, was sighted, perhaps two miles distant from the present lighthouse on the government piers. A gale was blowing, the waves were rolling mountain high, and from the lookout it was plainly seen that it was not*

> *a hospitable harbor of safety towards which they were being driven, but a vast field of ice extending out from the shore a considerable distance. Upon the unyielding mass of ice they were rushing helplessly before the howling northeaster. As there seemed to be no way of averting their inevitable fate, preparations were made for leaving the vessel in her small boats, before she should strike. They were made none too quickly, for the captain and crew speedily found themselves, scantily supplied with provisions, upon the bridge of ice that stretched away toward shore, and as they looked back they beheld the schooner pitch, stern first, into the depths of Lake Erie. The shipwrecked crew made their dangerous and difficult journey over the ice field, reaching the snow covered shore half frozen.*[312]

The wreck was a matter of intrigue for over sixty years and had its share of treasure hunters; the treasure, however, wasn't jewels or coins but whiskey. Many attempts were made to locate the valuable cargo, but to no avail, and thus it still sits at the bottom of the lake, corked.

FIRES

1868

In 1868, Monroe was devasted by a fire that destroyed nearly all the buildings in the half block west of Washington Street between First and Front Streets, including the Episcopal church and Strong Hotel on the square and the post office.[313]

1889

Early in the morning, Emma Monk woke up to see flames high in the sky from her bedroom window; little did she know it, but she was witnessing one of the largest fires in history. The fire was raging across the creek in Azalia and "men were carrying pails of water from the little stream and pumps but weren't able to do much to stop the flames."[314] Winds made it worse, fanning the flames to the stores at the corner of Dundee and Ostrander. Emma said, "It looked as though the whole town might burn."[315] The Star Bender factory and Del Reynold's General Store were engulfed in flames.

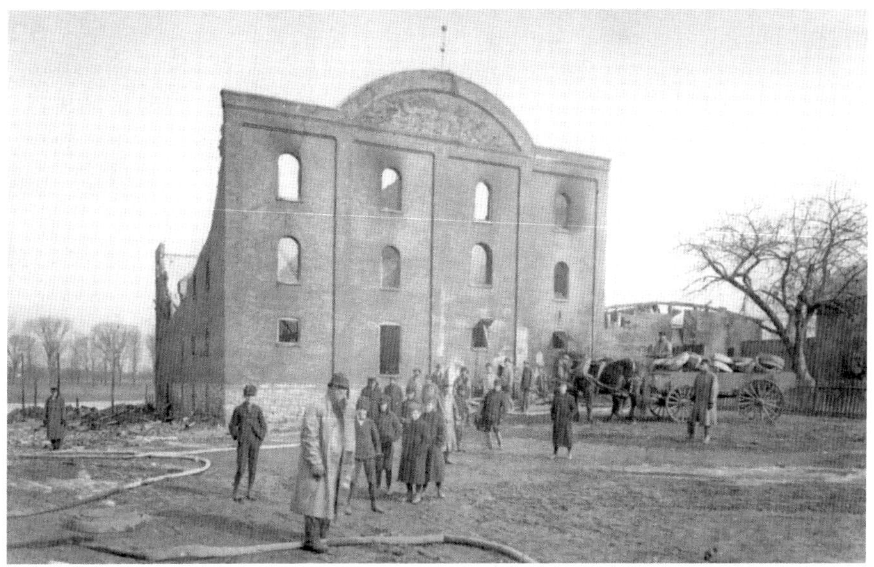

Wahl's Brewery fire, O'Brien Street. *Monroe County Library System.*

1890

The city of Monroe experienced a large fire in 1890 when a spark from the railroad ignited the icehouse. The fire then spread to the Waldorf Mill and ended up devasting the area for half a mile.[316] The fire department used the River Raisin to its advantage in fighting the Waldorf Mill fire and put its hand pumper right down into the river. Andrew Fragner was injured fighting the fire when the chimney collapsed and a brick fractured his skull. Dr. Lipke ended up removing a piece of Andrew's skull that was the size of a quarter. The family kept it in a button box and often retold the story. The doctor's instructions for recovery were "Keep him covered up and make him sweat. Tie him down to his bed if you have trouble keeping him in it."[317] Back then, doctors thought "sweating out" was a good way for someone to heal. In any case, Andrew did, indeed, recover.

September 20, 1916

"The Great Fire of 1916" is how the fire of September 20, 1916, came to be known. The headlines that day read: "100.000 FIRE AT ERIE TODAY! NEARLY ALL OF THE BUSINESS DISTRICT REDUCED TO SMOLDERING ASHES...SLIGHT SHIFT

OF WIND SAVED ST. JOSEPH CHURCH."[318] At that time, Erie was a bustling place with a church, hotel, bank, post office, saloons, general store, grocery stores and several other large stores. The business section of the town was wiped out, other than a few stores on the west side of Dixie Highway. The windy day fueled the flames, which ultimately resulted in "sixteen buildings, several dwellings and a half dozen barns"[319] destroyed.

The fire originated in a blacksmith shop and quickly spread due to the wind. Numerous bucket brigades were formed to drown the flames, but the fire was too intense. By the time the fire truck arrived, the wells were already pumped dry. In the end, only six buildings were spared on the other side of the street.[320]

February 23, 1923

"On February 23, 1923, a bucket brigade saved the town of Ida. The New York Central railroad depot caught fire and was completely destroyed. The depot is only a short distance from the town, and luckily the weather cooperated since there was very little wind. Citizens gathered to form a bucket brigade and although they failed to save the depot, they managed to keep other buildings from catching on fire too."[321]

February 4, 1929

"Formerly the National Guard Armory, turned Monroe Lodge 27's Masonic Temple, sustained a loss of over $100,000 in a fiery inferno at East Second and Washington Streets, on February 4, 1929. The blaze threatened many other downtown buildings, but owing to the little wind, the flames shot mostly upright."[322]

June 3, 1929

On June 3, 1929, St. Mary's Academy on West Elm Avenue was destroyed in an astounding fire that left only the brick wall in the front of the five-story building standing. Everything inside was reduced to ashes. Two hundred boarding pupils and thirty nuns escaped the fire. Sparks were blown for miles south of the river and set many buildings and homes on fire.[323]

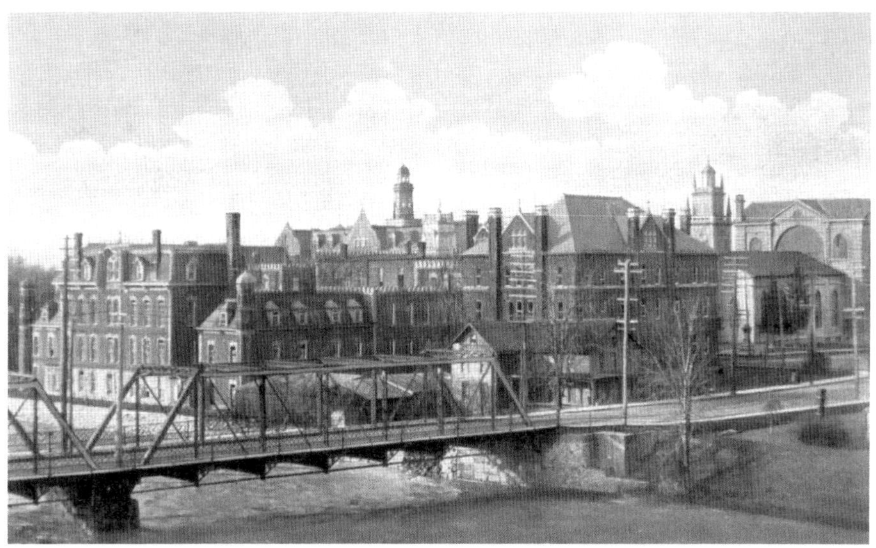

St. Mary's Academy complex, 1910. *Monroe County Library System.*

May 26, 1939

On May 26, 1939, the Monroe Co-Operative Oil Company, on West Front and Smith Streets, suffered $80,000 in damages from a horrific fire that is thought to have been caused by spontaneous combustion. The fire and subsequent explosions destroyed over twenty trucks, two cars, tires and more.[324]

1941

The Amendt Milling Company on 317 West Front Street was left in ruins after a fire in 1941. The company was first established in 1895 and processed wheat into flour.[325]

February 23, 1945

The Bullock School in Temperance was completely destroyed in a fire on February 23, 1945. It was believed the fire started in the furnace. The one-room schoolhouse was constructed in 1892 and named after an early resident of Temperance.[326]

February 4, 1946

Historian Donald Adams recalled a fire at Temperance School when he was a pupil there:

> *At 10 am on February 4, 1946, the fire alarm sounded and the 282 students, including myself, cleared the Temperance School building to safety at that moment did we realize this would be the last day to attend classes in the building? Fifteen minutes later the building was in flames and burned to the ground, despite efforts of eight fire departments from Temperance and surrounding villages. There was no water supply at that time and the Temperance Volunteer Fire Department was organized just ten months earlier. The wood floor hallways were oiled to reduce wear and this provided a wick for the fire, right down the middle of the building.*[327]

September 5, 1947

The tallest four-story building in downtown Monroe was consumed by fire on September 5, 1947. The Hubble Building apartments were located on Washington Street, and twenty people were injured from smoke inhalation or trying to escape the fire. The janitor had to be rescued by firefighters using a ladder. It is believed the fire started in the apartments on the second floor, but offices on the first floor were also damaged.[328]

May 29, 1962

On May 29, 1962, the most fearsome fire seen in two decades happened at Harry May Chevrolet-Cadillac Sales, located at 15180 South Monroe Street. The dealership was completely destroyed by flames that shot over two hundred feet in the air and injured seven people.[329]

February 16, 1974

Sacks Furniture Warehouse at 230 West Front Street was engulfed in flames on February 16, 1974. The fire was relentless, restarting several times, and ultimately destroyed the building.[330]

August 10, 1976

A famous nightclub at 111 South Monroe Street in downtown Monroe, the Mad Hatter, caught fire on August 10, 1976. The entire historic brick building was destroyed and had to be torn down.[331]

June 1, 1989

On June 1, 1989, a spectacular fire started in a restaurant, Duff's Smorgasbord, in the Monroe Shopping Center on South Monroe Street. The fire was actually out, then restarted several hours later in adjacent buildings, causing over $3 million in damages.[332]

OTHER TIDBITS

PLUM CREEK BRIDGE collapsed in 1929.[333]

TWO BUILDINGS in downtown Monroe were destroyed not by natural causes but by a construction project that went horribly wrong on July 15, 1946.

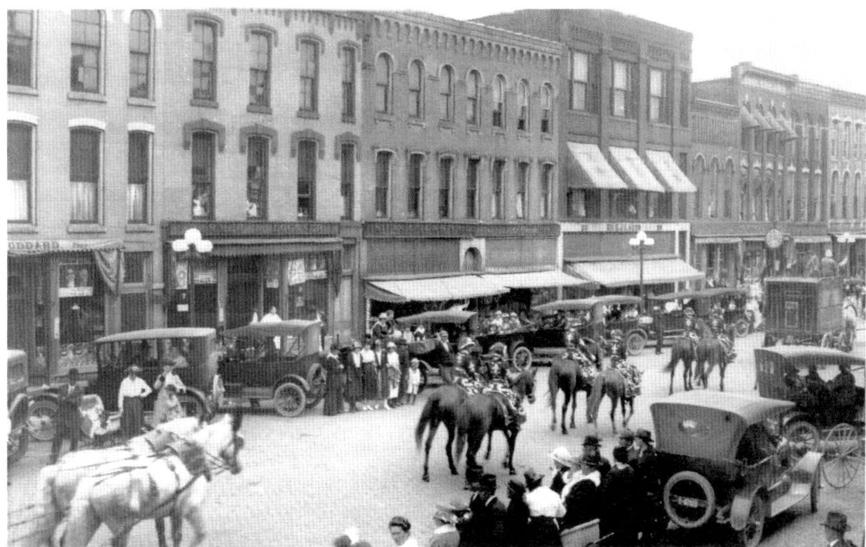

Downtown Monroe. *Monroe County Library System.*

The building being fixed up suddenly collapsed, taking the building next to it down with it in a pile of dust and debris.[334]

A METEORITE, about one foot in diameter, was found in Monroe while a tunnel was being dug between the old and the new St. Mary's academy buildings on November 4, 1904.[335]

Notes

Chapter 1

1. Bulkley, *History of Monroe County*, 54–55.
2. LaVoy, *Bay Settlement*, 40.
3. Bidlack, *Monroe County History*, 5–7.
4. Ibid., 7.
5. Ibid., 17.
6. Ellis, *Michigan Sentinel*.
7. LaVoy, *Bay Settlement*, 41.
8. Naveaux and Gruber, *Floral City*, 16–18.

Chapter 2

9. Strass, *French Canadian Folklore*, 34.
10. Ibid.
11. Au, *State of the Oral Traditions*, 12.
12. Strass, *French Canadian Folklore*, 35.
13. Ibid., 48.
14. Ibid., 42.
15. Hamlin, *Legends of Le Détroit*, 139.
16. Ibid., 140–41.
17. Ibid.

18. Childs, interview with Mrs. Edward Sieb, in *Recollections of Life*, 487.
19. Ibid.
20. Childs, interviews with Lulu Sieb and John Clark, in *Recollections of Life*, 530–31.
21. Childs, interviews with Mrs. Cron and Ambrose LaFountain, in *Recollections of Life*, 346–47.
22. Ibid.
23. "Lasalle," *Monroe Commercial.*

Chapter 3

24. Hinsdale, *Archaeological Atlas of Michigan*, 7–10.
25. Ibid.
26. Wyckoff, "Michigan's Indian Reservations."
27. Adams, *Bedford Township*, 7.
28. Ibid.
29. Heinlen, "Native Americans in Monroe County."
30. Ibid.

Chapter 4

31. Lossing, *Pictorial Field Book*, 283.
32. Ibid., 284.
33. Wing, *History of Monroe County*, 53.
34. Ibid., 53–54.
35. Ibid.
36. Ibid.
37. Ibid.
38. Ibid.
39. Naveaux, *Invaded on All Sides*, 55.
40. Antal, *Wampum Denied*, 112.
41. Ibid.
42. Ibid., 198.
43. Au, *War on the Raisin*, 17.
44. Naveaux, *Invaded on All Sides*, 26–27.
45. Ibid.
46. Ibid.

47. Ibid.
48. Bulkley, *History of Monroe County*, 69.
49. Ibid., 69–70.

Chapter 5

50. Naveaux, *Invaded on All Sides*, 229.
51. Ibid., 122, 145, 150, 154, 170, 221, 229–30.
52. Ibid., 127–29.
53. Ibid., 206–8; VanWasshenova and Naveaux, *Women on the Raisin*, 71–78.
54. Naveaux, *Invaded on All Sides*, 207.
55. Ibid.
56. Ibid.
57. Ibid., 202–3; Naveaux, *Invaded on All Sides*, 53–59.
58. VanWasshenova and Naveaux, *Women on the Raisin*, 66–67.
59. Ibid.
60. Ibid.
61. Naveaux, *Invaded on All Sides*, 214–15, 251.
62. Ibid.
63. Ibid., 235.

Chapter 6

64. "Attention Soldiers of 1812," *Monroe Commercial.*
65. Frost, *General Custer's Libbie*, 194.
66. Bulkley, *History of Monroe County*, 127.
67. "1812, Reunion," *Monroe Commercial.*
68. Frost, *General Custer's Libbie*, 194.
69. "Grand Celebration," *Monroe Commercial.*
70. "Fourth of July," *Monroe Commercial.*
71. Bulkley, *History of Monroe County*, 129.
72. Ibid., 128.
73. Wing, *History of Monroe County*, 82.
74. "Massacre at the River Raisin," *Monroe Evening News.*
75. Bulkley, *History of Monroe County*, 129.
76. Wing, *History of Monroe County*, 89.
77. Bulkley, *History of Monroe County*, 131.

78. Childs, interview with W.C. Sterling, in *Recollections of Life*, 512.
79. Childs, interview with Katherine Nims, in *Recollections of Life*, 395.
80. Frost, *Custer Album*, 19.
81. Ibid., 2.
82. Ibid.
83. Childs, interview with Charles Verhoeven, in *Recollections of Life*, 545.
84. Childs, interview with Bernard Verhoeven, in *Recollections of Life*, 545.

Chapter 7

85. *Monroe Democrat*, July 31, 1884.
86. "Historic Relic Preserved," *Monroe Commercial*.
87. "The Old Cannon," *Monroe Commercial*.
88. "Obituary for Joseph Steiner," *Monroe Democrat*.
89. Ibid.
90. "Obituary for Christian F. Beck," *Monroe Democrat*.
91. Bulkley, *History of Monroe County*, 136.
92. "Mrs. C. W. Beck: Reminiscences," *Monroe Democrat*.
93. *Observer*, May 1942.
94. Ibid.
95. "Obituary for Christian F. Beck," *Monroe Democrat*.
96. Garcia, "Cannon."
97. Trollope, "Cannon."
98. *Observer*, May 1942.
99. Harrison. "Monroe Courthouse Cannon."
100. Harrison, "Frontier Arms Race."
101. Harrison. "Monroe Courthouse Cannon."
102. MacKay, "Bruce Museum."

Chapter 8

103. Bulkley, *History of Monroe County*, 328.
104. Naveaux and Gruber, *Floral City*, 8–9, 17; *Pageant of Historic Monroe*; Bulkley, *History of Monroe County*, 481–94; Wing, *History of Monroe County*, 578–84.
105. Naveaux and Gruber, *Floral City*, 9–10.
106. Ibid., 10–11.

107. "Milan Area," Milan Area Historical Society.
108. "Old Tavern and Stage Coach Stop," *Monroe Evening News.*
109. Childs, interview with Ned Younglove, in *Recollections of Life*, 432.
110. "Old Tavern and Stage Coach Stop," *Monroe Evening News.*
111. Ibid.
112. Monroe County Library System, "Havre—Lost Town."
113. Ibid.
114. Childs, interview with Bruce Agnew, in *Recollections of Life*, 132.
115. Menard, *R.F.D. Newport.*
116. "Milan Area," Milan Area Historical Society.
117. "Steiner, Michigan," Wikipedia.
118. "Stoney Creek Settlement," *Monroe Commercial.*
119. "Vistula," *Monroe Commercial.*

Chapter 9

120. Bidlack, *Monroe County History*, 22.
121. Ibid., 20.
122. Ibid.
123. Ibid.
124. Ibid., 19.
125. Ibid.
126. Childs, interview with Dr. Sawyer, in *Recollections of Life*, 624.
127. Bidlack, *Monroe County History*, 22.
128. Ibid., 21–22
129. Ibid., 22.
130. Childs, interview with Wesley Rauch, in *Recollections of Life*, 486.
131. Wisler, "News Reports Show Monroe."
132. Childs, interview with Vincent Barker, in *Recollections of Life*, 440.

Chapter 10

133. Bulkley, *History of Monroe County*, 545.
134. Ibid.
135. Ibid.
136. Ibid.
137. Ibid.

138. Ibid.
139. Bidlack, *Monroe County History*, 24–25.
140. Ibid.
141. Ibid.
142. Ibid.
143. Ibid., 27–28.
144. Ibid.
145. Bulkley, *History of Monroe County*, 358.
146. Ibid.
147. Ibid.
148. Ibid.
149. Ibid.
150. Ibid.
151. Ibid.
152. Ibid.
153. Bidlack, *Monroe County History*, 65.
154. Ibid.
155. Ibid.
156. Ibid.
157. Childs, interview with Tillie Marie Sancrant, in *Recollections of Life*, 299.
158. Childs, interview with Mr. Munch, in *Recollections of Life*, 156.
159. Ibid.

Chapter 11

160. Naveaux and Gruber, *Floral City*, 22.
161. Mull, *Underground Railroad in Michigan*, 126.
162. Knabenshue, "Underground Railroad," 397–400.
163. Gindy, *Underground Railroad*, 26, 34, 46, 56.
164. Knabenshue, "Underground Railroad," 400.
165. Ibid.
166. Gindy, *Underground Railroad*, 39–40.
167. Ibid.
168. Bulkley, *History of Monroe County*, 127.
169. National Archives, "War of 1812."
170. Bidlack, *Monroe County History*, 25–26.
171. Ibid.
172. Ibid.

173. Mull, *Underground Railroad in Michigan*, 14.
174. Bidlack, *Monroe County History*, 26.
175. Mull, *Underground Railroad in Michigan*, 7–8.
176. Ibid., 19.
177. Ibid., 40.
178. Childs, interview with May Smith, in *Recollections of Life*, 599.
179. Ibid.
180. First Presbyterian Church of Monroe.
181. Mull, *Underground Railroad in Michigan*, 100.
182. Naveaux and Gruber, *Floral City*, 20.
183. "Old Home of Pioneer," *Record Commercial*.
184. Wing, *History of Monroe County*, 433.
185. Monroe County Library System, "Dorsch Memorial Library."
186. Library of Congress, "Map of Monroe County, Michigan."
187. Naveaux and Gruber, *Floral City*, 23.
188. Childs, interview with May Smith, in *Recollections of Life*, 599.
189. Naveaux and Gruber, *Floral City*, 23.
190. Ibid., 22.
191. Ibid., 23.
192. Childs, interview with Wesley Rauch, in *Recollections of Life*, 484.
193. Childs, interview with Elizabeth Godfried, in *Recollections of Life*, 614.
194. Mull, *Underground Railroad in Michigan*, 52.

Chapter 12

195. LaVoy, *Bay Settlement*, 156.
196. Vollrath, *Memories*, 1.
197. Ibid., 2–3.
198. Ibid., 3.
199. Ibid.
200. Ibid.
201. Ibid., 6–7.
202. Ibid., 7.
203. Ibid., 19
204. Ibid.
205. LaVoy, *Bay Settlement*, 157–58.
206. Ibid.
207. Ibid., 158.

208. Ibid., 157; Vollrath, *Memories*, 28.
209. Vollrath, *Memories*, 30.
210. Ibid., 15.
211. Ibid., 19.
212. Ibid., 19–28.
213. Ibid., 9, 11, 13.
214. Ibid., 32.
215. Ibid., 32, 34.
216. Ibid., 34, 37, 40.
217. Naveaux and Gruber, *Floral City*, 29.
218. Bulkley, *History of Monroe County*, 462.
219. Vollrath, *Memories*, 37.
220. Ibid., 40–41.
221. Ibid., 43.
222. Ibid., 45–46.

Chapter 13

223. LaFaive, Fleenor and Nesbit, "Appendix B," 85.
224. Wisler, "Monroe County's Location."
225. Childs, interview with Joseph Sterling, in *Recollections of Life*, 191.
226. Wisler, "Monroe County's Location."
227. LaFaive, Fleenor and Nesbit, "Appendix B," 85.
228. Wisler, "Monroe County's Location."
229. LaFaive, Fleenor and Nesbit, "Appendix B," 87.
230. Ibid.
231. Wisler, "Monroe County's Location."
232. Childs, interview with Ed Steiner, in *Recollections of Life*, 426.
233. Ibid.
234. Ibid.
235. Ibid.
236. Childs, interview with Bernard Lazette, in *Recollections of Life*, 264.
237. Ibid.
238. Ibid.
239. Ibid.
240. Childs, interview with Clarence Durocher, in *Recollections of Life*, 436.
241. *Monroe Evening News*, February 1920.
242. Ibid.

Chapter 14

243. Au, *Maps and Archaeology*; Tucker, "Saint Anthony's Parish," 21–25.
244. "A Place of Sculls," *Monroe Advocate*.
245. Ibid.
246. "George Kronbach to Close," *Observer,* (Monroe, MI).
247. "Bones Found in City," *Monroe Evening News*; "Bones May Be Remnant," *Monroe Evening News*.
248. Wing, *History of Monroe County*, 41.
249. "First Public Recognition," *Monroe Democrat*.
250. "Deserved Tributes," *Observer*.
251. Keehn and Kellie, *History of Cemeteries*, 21.
252. Childs, interview with Wesley Rauch, in *Recollections of Life*, 484.
253. Keehn and Kellie, *History of Cemeteries*, 18.
254. Ibid., 23.
255. Ibid., 114.
256. Childs, interview with Elizabeth Rosselle, in *Recollections of Life*, 430.
257. Keehn and Kellie, *History of Cemeteries*, 131.
258. Ibid., 65.
259. Ibid., 43.
260. Adamich, "Monroe County History."
261. Kisonas, "Ash's Potter Cemetery."
262. Ibid.
263. Adamich, "MCCC Home."
264. Adams, *Bedford Township*, 16–17.

Chapter 15

265. Adamich, "MCCC Home"; Find a Grave, "Ezra Younglove."
266. *Monroe Evening News*, *In the Rockets' Red Glare*, 7–8.
267. Ibid., 9.
268. Ibid., 8.
269. Ibid., 9; Find a Grave, "Col Norman Jonathan Hall."
270. Find a Grave, "Col Norman Jonathan Hall."
271. Ibid.
272. American Battlefield Trust, "Sultana Disaster."
273. Eschner, "Civil War Boat Explosion."
274. Michigan Family History Network, "Michigan Men on the Sultana."

275. *Monroe Evening News*, *In the Rockets' Red Glare*, 18–19.
276. Ibid., 34.
277. Ibid., 30–31.
278. Ibid., 71.
279. Ibid., 64–65.
280. Ibid.
281. Ibid.
282. Ibid., 76–77.
283. Ibid.
284. Ibid.
285. Ibid., 100.
286. Ibid.
287. Ibid.
288. Ibid.
289. Ibid., 113.
290. Ibid., 115.

Chapter 16

291. Strachan, "To Thomas Jefferson."
292. River Raisin National Battlefield Park, "History & Culture."
293. Ibid.
294. Wing, *History of Monroe County*, 184–85.
295. Ibid., 185–86.
296. Bulkley, *History of Monroe County*, 137–61; Wing, *History of Monroe County*, 181–99.
297. "Turtle Island (Lake Erie)," Wikipedia.
298. Monroe County Labor History Museum, "Eyes of the World."
299. Ibid.
300. Reindl, "Almost Lose Detroit."
301. Ibid.
302. Ibid.

Chapter 17

303. *Monroe Evening News*, *Monroe County, 1876–1941*, 67.
304. "Looking Back: Newport Michigan," *Monroe Evening News*.
305. *Monroe Evening News*, June 25, 1964.
306. Menard, *R.F.D. Newport*, 284–85.
307. "2011 Monroe plane crash," *Toledo Blade*; "Feds Rule Monroe Plane Crash Resulted in High-Speed Maneuver," *Monroe Evening News*.
308. Ibid.
309. Eby, "Shipwrecks of Monroe County."
310. Ibid.
311. Menard, *R.F.D. Newport*, 74–75.
312. Bulkley, *History of Monroe County*, 547–49.
313. *Pageant of Historic Monroe*.
314. Childs, interview with Emma Monk, in *Recollections of Life*, 87.
315. Ibid.
316. Childs, interview with W.C. Sterling, in *Recollections of Life*, 29.
317. Childs, interview with Walter Fragner, in *Recollections of Life*, 222.
318. LaVoy, *Bay Settlement*, 107–8.
319. Ibid.
320. Ibid.
321. *Monroe Evening News*, September 24, 1923.
322. *Monroe Evening News*, *Monroe County, 1876–1941*, 72.
323. Ibid.
324. Ibid., 69.
325. Ibid., 70.
326. Adams, *Bedford Township*, 114.
327. Ibid., 115.
328. *Monroe Evening News*, *Monroe County, 1941–1969*, 55.
329. Ibid., 57.
330. *Monroe Evening News*, *Monroe County, 1970–1999*, 90.
331. Ibid.
332. Ibid., 91.
333. *Monroe Evening News*, *Monroe County, 1876–1941*, 73.
334. *Monroe Evening News*, *Monroe County, 1941–1969*, 58.
335. *Monroe Democrat*, November 4, 1904.

Bibliography

Books

Adams, Donald R. *Bedford Township Monroe County, Michigan: Then and Now.* Temperance, MI: self-published, 2003.

Antal, Sandy. *A Wampum Denied: Procter's War of 1812.* Ottawa, ON: Carleton University Press, 1998.

Au, Dennis M. *Maps and Archaeology: The French Colonial Settlement Pattern to the River Raisin Community in Southeastern Michigan.* Monroe, MI: Monroe County Historical Commission, 1991. Addenda 2012–13.

———. *The State of the Oral Traditions among the French-Canadians of Monroe County, Michigan.* Monroe, MI: Monroe County Historical Museum, 1976.

———. *War on the Raisin.* Monroe, MI: Monroe County Historical Commission, 1981.

Bidlack, Russell E. *Monroe County History, 1780–1830.* Monroe, MI: Monroe County Historical Commission, 1986.

Bulkley, John McClelland. *The History of Monroe County, Michigan; a Narrative Account of Its Historical Progress, Its People, and Its Principal Interests.* Chicago, New York: Lewis, 1913.

Childs, Marion. *Recollections of Life in Monroe County Vol. 1 and 2, 1956–62.* Monroe, MI: Monroe County Library System, n.d.

Frost, Lawrence A. *General Custer's Libbie.* Seattle, WA: Superior, 1976.

———. *The Custer Album: A Pictorial Biography of George Armstrong Custer.* New York: Bonanza Books, 1984.

Gindy, Gaye E. *The Underground Railroad and Sylvania's Historic Lathrop House.* Bloomington, IN: AuthorHouse, 2008.

Hamlin, Marie Caroline Watson. *Legends of Le Détroit.* Detroit: Nourse, 1884.

Hinsdale, Wilbert B. *Archaeological Atlas of Michigan.* Ann Arbor: University of Michigan Press, 1931.

Keehn, Shirley, and Frieda Kellie. *The History of Cemeteries and Family Burial Plots in Monroe County, Michigan 1795–2011.* Monroe, MI: Monroe County Historical Commission, 2005 (revised 2011).

LaVoy, Lambert M. *Bay Settlement of Monroe County, Michigan.* Monroe, MI: self-published, 1971.

Lossing, Benjamin. *Pictorial Field Book of the War of 1812.* New York: Harper & Brothers, 1868.

Menard, T. Victor. *R.F.D. Newport: A History of Newport and Berlin Township, Michigan.* MI: Monroe County Library System, 1995. Accessed via Monroe County Library System digital collections: https://library.biblioboard.com/content/239b8b63-d51c-4357-896c-ac18660312cc.

Monroe Evening News. In the Rockets' Red Glare: Recollections of Monroe County Veterans. Monroe, MI: Monroe Publishing, 1997.

———. *A Pictorial History of Monroe County, 1876–1941.* Monroe, MI: Monroe Publishing, 1995.

———. *A Pictorial History of Monroe County, 1941–1969.* Monroe, MI: Monroe Publishing, 1996.

———. *A Pictorial History of Monroe County, 1970–1999.* Monroe, MI: Monroe Publishing, 2000.

Mull, Carol E. *The Underground Railroad in Michigan.* Jefferson, NC: McFarland, 2010.

Naveaux, Ralph. *Invaded on All Sides: The Story of Michigan's Greatest Battlefield Scene of the Engagements at Frenchtown and the River Raisin in the War of 1812.* Marceline, MO: Walsworth, 2008.

Naveaux, Ralph, and Shana Gruber. *The Floral City: A Brief History of the City and County of Monroe, Michigan, 1830–1930.* Monroe, MI: Monroe County Historical Museum, 2001.

Pageant of Historic Monroe, June 23–24, 1926, Monroe, Michigan. Monroe, MI: Lamour Printing, 1926.

Strass, Anne-Marie. *French Canadian Folklore from Monroe County, Michigan.* Monroe, MI: Monroe County Museum, 1982.

VanWasshenova, Mary Ellen, and Ralph Naveaux. *Women on the Raisin during the War of 1812.* Monroe, MI: Monroe County Historical Society, 2008.

Vollrath, J.A. *Memories of the Monroe Piers*. Monroe, MI: Monroe County Library System, 1972. https://library.biblioboard.com/content/46029e16-d6ca-4a15-b3c5-a6a39ce2f02f.

Wing, Talcott Enoch. *History of Monroe County, Michigan*. New York: Munsell, 1890.

Periodicals

Adamich, Tom. "MCCC Home to Historic Potter's Field." *Monroe (MI) News*, December 19, 2021.

———. "Monroe County History: Access to Potter's Cemetery Hard-Fought Battle." *Monroe (MI) News*, January 26, 2022.

Eby, Dave. "The Shipwrecks of Monroe County." *Monroe (MI) News*, March 1, 2021.

Ellis, Edward D. *Michigan Sentinel* (Monroe, MI), February 21, 1829.

Harrison, Daniel F. "Frontier Arms Race: Historical and Archaeological Analysis of an Assemblage of Eighteenth-Century Cannon Recovered from the Detroit River and Lake Erie." *Historical Archaeology* 48, no. 4 (October 19, 2016).

Heinlen, Dorothy. "A History of Native Americans in Monroe County What Became of Our Indians." Monroe County Historical Museum, 1976.

Kisonas, Ray. "Ash's Potter Cemetery Rededicated." *Monroe (MI) Evening News*, September 18, 2017.

Knabenshue, S.S. "The Underground Railroad." *Ohio Archaeological and Historical Publication* 14, no. 3 (1905): 397–400.

LaFaive, Michael D., Patrick Fleenor and Todd Nesbit. "Appendix B: Prohibition in Michigan and the Avenue de Booze," in *Cigarette Taxes and Smuggling: A Statistical Analysis and Historical Review*, 85–88. Midland, MI: Mackinaw Center for Public Policy, 2008.

Monroe (MI) Advocate. "A Place of Sculls." July 1848.

Monroe (MI) Commercial. "Attention Soldiers of 1812." June 1, 1871.

———. "1812, Reunion of Veterans-Survivors of the River Raisin Massacre-Dinner, Toasts and Speeches." June 22, 1871.

———. "Fourth of July—The Meeting Monday Evening." May 30, 1872.

———. "Grand Celebration. Re-Union of Veterans of 1812—Perry's Victory and Massacre of River Raisin, and Military Encampment! Monroe Patriotically Aroused!!" May 15, 1872.

———. "Stoney Creek Settlement." April 27, 1876.

———. "A Historic Relic Preserved." August 1, 1884.
———. "Lasalle." August 29, 1879.
———. "The Old Cannon." August 8, 1884.
———. "Vistula." June 15, 1876.
Monroe (MI) Democrat. "The First Public Recognition of the River Raisin Heroes." January 22, 1904.
———. "Mrs. C. W. Beck: Reminiscences of Old Monroe." 1935.
———. "Obituary for Christian F. Beck." June 9, 1887.
———. "Obituary for Joseph Steiner." 1952.
———. July 31, 1884.
———. November 4, 1904.
Monroe (MI) Evening News. "Bones Found in City Identified as Human." July 7, 1966.
———. "Bones May Be Remnant of Massacre." July 8, 1966.
———. "George Kronbach to Close Store, Old Building Occupies Burial Ground Used for Soldiers of the Massacre." September 1930.
———. "Feds Rule Monroe Plane Crash Resulted in High-Speed Maneuver." December 8, 2012.
———. "Looking Back: Newport Michigan." November 18, 2015.
———. "Massacre at the River Raisin Last in State." January 23, 1948.
———. "Old Tavern and Stage Coach Stop," February 19, 1947. Accessed via the Monroe County Library System. https://library.biblioboard.com/content/ebc48194-d0da-41fd-ab4f-f71be14f72ef.
———. February 1920.
———. June 25, 1964.
Observer (Monroe, MI). "Deserved Tributes." November 11, 1939.
———. Untitled article, May 1942.
Record Commercial (Monroe, MI). "Old Home of Pioneer Physician and Poet Opened as New Library Next Week." March 2, 1916.
Reindl, JC. "Did We Really 'Almost Lose Detroit' in Fermi 1 Mishap 50 Years Ago? Before Fukushima, Chernobyl and Three Mile Island, There Was Fermi 1." *Detroit Free Press*, October 9, 2016.
Toledo (OH) Blade. "2011 Monroe Plane Crash Caused by Pilot Error." December 10, 2012.
Tucker, Patrick M. "Saint Anthony's Parish on the River Raisin, 1788–1845: The Recovery of Monroe's Lost Pioneer Cemetery." *Catholic Cemetery* 56, no. 8 (2017): 21–25.

Wisler, Suzanne Nolan. "Monroe County's Location Made It a Prohibition Hot Spot." *Monroe (MI) Evening News*, May 28, 2018.

———. "News Reports Show Monroe Fared Well After Spanish Flu." *Monroe (MI) News*, May 13, 2020.

Websites

American Battlefield Trust. "The Sultana Disaster." https://www.battlefields.org/learn/articles/sultana-disaster.

Eschner, Kat. "This Civil War Boat Explosion Killed More People Than the 'Titanic.'" *Smithsonian Magazine*, April 27, 2017. https://www.smithsonianmag.com/smithsonianmag/civil-war-boat-explosion-killed-more-people-titanic-180963008/.

Find a Grave. "Col Norman Jonathan Hall." https://www.findagrave.com/memorial/14259335/norman-jonathan-hall.

———. "Ezra Younglove." https://www.findagrave.com/memorial/8619268/ezra-younglove.

First Presbyterian Church of Monroe. http://monroefirst.org/.

Garcia, John. "Cannon." Email to the author, 2011.

Harrison, Dan. "Monroe Courthouse Cannon." Email to the author, 2022.

Library of Congress. "Map of Monroe County, Michigan." https://www.loc.gov/item/2012593018/.

MacKay, Janice. "Bruce Museum Gets Ownership of HMS General Hunter Shipwreck Project." CKNX NewsToday.ca, May 26, 2020. https://blackburnnews.com/midwestern-ontario/midwestern-ontario-news/2020/05/26/bruce-museum-gets-ownership-hms-general-hunter-shipwreck-project/.

Michigan Family History Network. "Michigan Men on the Sultana by Michigan County." http://www.mifamilyhistory.org/civilwar/sultana/countyresults.aspx?County=Monroe.

Milan Area Historical Society. "The Milan Area." http://www.historicmilan.com.

Monroe County Labor History Museum. "The Eyes of the World Were Watching: The Newton Steel Strike." http://www.monroelabor.org/eyes-world-were-watching-newton-steel-strike.

Monroe County Library System. "Havre—Lost Town Built in 1836." Digital collections, local stories. https://monroe.biblioboard.com/anthology-collection/e78a3b78-ffa6-48c7-a725-2eedbacc93c3/7e749960-f5d1-4936-9db6-841e7b3d4865.

———. "History of the Dorsch Memorial Library." https://mymcls.com/branch/dorsch-memorial-branch-library/.

National Archives. "War of 1812 Pension and Bounty Land Warrant Application Files." https://www.fold3.com/image/307842470.

River Raisin National Battlefield Park. "History & Culture." https://www.nps.gov/rira/learn/historyculture/index.htm.

Strachan, John. "John Strachan to Thomas Jefferson, 30 January 1815." https://founders.archives.gov/documents/Jefferson/03-08-02-0184.

Trollope, Charles. "Cannon." Email to the author, 2011.

Wikipedia. "Steiner, Michigan." https://en.wikipedia.org/wiki/Steiner,_Michigan.

———. "Turtle Island (Lake Erie)." https://en.wikipedia.org/wiki/Turtle_Island_(Lake_Erie).

Wyckoff, Larry. "Michigan's Indian Reservations, 1807–1855." 2019. https://www.academia.edu/38816617/Michigans_Indian_Reservations_1807_1855?msclkid=bb8feb6aa65c11ec9d7e496424f8bf17.

About the Author

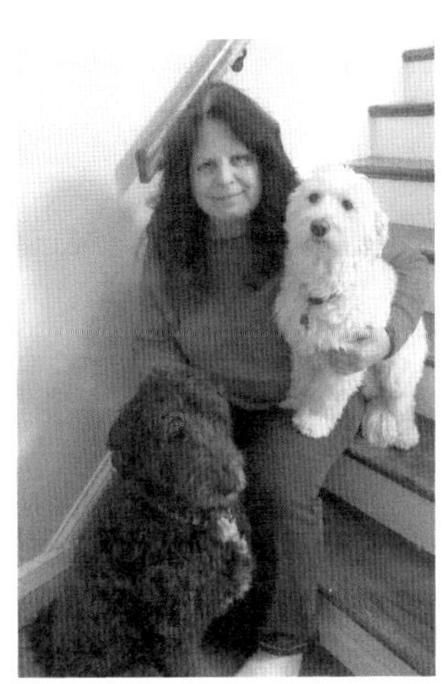

Shawna Lynn Mazur was born and has lived in Monroe all her life. In fact, she grew up on the battlefield. Like many residents, she did not know about the battles until her son Tyler, at that time twelve years old, asked her to take him to the visitor center, which was run by the Monroe County Historical Museums at the time.

It was only a matter of weeks before they both signed up to be volunteers in 2006. In 2007, Shawna was hired by the Monroe County Historical Museums. Having a bachelor's degree in history and literature, she was thrilled to be employed in her field. Shawna's love of history, research and writing led her to write numerous articles for the museum's newsletter. She also had an article published in *Michigan History Magazine* and the Little Big Horn Associates newsletter, as well as the local newspaper. She also researched and ran the museum's popular Lantern Tours program for four years. She has edited a number of other authors' books as well.

When the National Park Service took over the battlefield, she was fortunate enough to be hired and became an interpretive ranger. She contributed to growing the park and developing some of the park's interpretive programs, publications and curriculums. Having worked for the River Raisin National

Battlefield Park for eleven years, she is currently the administrative assistant and retains the position of ranger. She recently researched and wrote a book for the park about tracing the remains of the Kentucky volunteer militia soldiers who did not survive the River Raisin battles. She is currently a member of the Monroe County Historical Society. Shawna lives in Carleton, Michigan, with her husband, Joseph Mazur, and their two dogs, Callie and Cassie.